NEIL

CN00701185

HITCHuLUGY

MR. HITCHCOCK

A FILM-BY-FILM GUIDE TO THE STYLE AND THEMES OF **ALFRED HITCHCOCK**

Neil Alcock has been watching, reading, thinking and banging on about Alfred Hitchcock since first studying his films at college over 30 years ago. Since 2011 he has been a freelance film writer for Empire magazine, Film4.com, Virgin Movies and more. He has appeared on national and local BBC radio programmes, and on podcasts including Radio 1's Screen Time, the Empire podcast and the 90 Minutes Or Less Film Fest, to talk about Alfred Hitchcock, Stanley Kubrick, James Bond and film in general. He lives in north London with his wife and chickens.

To see some of Neil's work, visit **neilalcock.com**.

HITCHOLOGY

A FILM-BY-FILM GUIDE TO THE STYLE AND THEMES OF **ALFRED HITCHCOCK**

BY
NEIL ALCOCK

DANEBANK

CONTENTS

"Hitchcock's work is the best for learning and teaching what film can be, and what it can do."

- Dr Catherine Wheatley, Senior Lecturer in Film Studies, King's College London

INTRODUCTION

Welcome to **Hitchology!** You hold in your hand the only book in the world dedicated to Alfred Hitchcock and the films he directed. OK, fine, that's not true. There are other Hitchcock books. Lots of others. So why is there another one?

Hitchology is not your average Hitchbook, for three reasons. Firstly, this is not a dry, academic tome. There are plenty of those already, and while most of them are excellent resources for further investigation (in fact **Hitchology** wouldn't exist without many of them), some can be a bit hard going. The plan here is not to dumb down, but to provide an accessible introduction to Hitchcock for curious newcomers to his world, and an entertaining companion for established fans.

Secondly, every Hitchcock film is equal in the eyes of **Hitchology**. OK, fine, that's also not true. *Rear Window* is quite a lot better than *Juno And The Paycock*. But every film is given equal attention: no skimming over the British period, or casually dismissing the silents, or spending an inordinate amount of time on *Vertigo* here. In order to give a reasonably fair overview of what we'll call the Hitchcanon, each of his films gets the same amount of space (except *The Mountain Eagle*, but given it's been lost since the late 1920s, there's not much that can be done about that).

Finally, **Hitchology** hopes to open your eyes and ears to the style and themes of Hitchcock's work: the formal flourishes and narrative tropes often referred to as 'the Hitchcock touch'. These are the elements that make a Hitchcock film 'Hitchcockian', and in these pages you'll find out how, when and why the director used them to create such a unique body of work.

So what you're getting here are 52 (one for each film) and a half (again, *The Mountain Eagle*) easily digestible chapters looking at some of the most remarkable movies ever made, as well as - to be perfectly honest - a few largely unremarkable ones. To be even more honest there are also a couple of pretty rubbish ones, but even the worst Hitchcock film is worthy of investigation in the context of his extraordinary output. You're also getting a few bonus chapters, scattered casually throughout the book, intended to give a bit more background to the films and their director.

But wait! Who is this director, this 'Alfred Hitchcock' you've vaguely heard of, assuming you fall into the category of 'curious newcomer' rather than 'established fan'? In a nutshell, he was a British chap from London who made over 50 films between 1925 and 1976. The first nine of those were silent; the tenth, *Blackmail*, exists in silent and sound versions. His career can broadly be split between the early 'British' period (which includes a couple of films made in Germany) and the post-1939 'American' period (which includes a couple of films made in

Britain). He is famous for his suspense thrillers, but he made just as many dramas, the odd comedy, and a little film called *Psycho*, which is generally (though somewhat inaccurately) labelled as a horror. You've probably heard of it. Although usually uncredited as such, he had a major hand in the writing of almost every script he shot. He also directed 20 television episodes, mostly for his series *Alfred Hitchcock Presents*.

But these are mere facts, and facts are boring. What's not boring are the bits we can discuss and argue about forever: the good, bad and in-between bits that make Hitchcock one of a kind. The immeasurable impact he had on cinema, his boundless quest for technical innovation, his canny self-publicity, his complex and problematic representations of women and minorities, his phenomenal ability to tell a story visually, his mastery of all the nuts and bolts of filmmaking to create purely cinematic experiences. **Hitchology** hopes to touch on all these and then some, but more fondly hopes to encourage you to find out more yourself, maybe from those dry, academic tomes there seem to be so many of. With any luck the curious newcomers among you will become established fans, and the established fans might just become committed obsessives. Whatever your level of Hitchcockery, **Hitchology** is your guide, like a battered old *Lonely Planet* but with fewer accommodation recommendations. Although here's one: steer clear of Bates Motel.

HOW TO READ THIS BOOK

Hitchology is not *Psycho*. Nobody is going to insist you start at the very beginning and remain in your seat until it's over. That said, if you do decide to be all chronological about it, you'll get some idea of how Hitchcock developed his style and themes over time, when they made their first appearances, and how they were tweaked and modulated to achieve certain ends.

But maybe you've just watched a Hitchcock film and are in the mood for a little light analysis? Then head straight to that film's chapter, where you'll be made welcome. Or perhaps there's a film you haven't seen, and you're wondering what all the fuss about it is? Again, the individual chapters await you, but in this case beware, for spoilers lurk within. **Every** chapter will give away some of the plot by necessity, but some will divulge major twists and surprises with reckless abandon. These chapters are clearly marked like this:

so please don't write in and complain that **Hitchology** ruined the surprise of *[redacted character]* being violently *[redacted fate of character]* in the *[redacted location of said fate]* half way through *[redacted incredibly famous film released over half a century ago]*.

THE ESSENTIAL TEN

If you're new to the world of Alfred Hitchcock, you have so much to look forward to. Improbable and fantastic tales of drama, suspense, spies, trains, showers, birds, windows, obscure compass directions and more, told with impeccable visual storytelling and a wicked sense of humour, are anxiously waiting for you to discover them. But where to begin? The 52 available Hitchcock-directed feature films out there would take you a whole year to watch if you made them a weekly treat. And in an ideal world that's exactly what you'd do, but - as any Hitchcock character knows - life is short, and frankly some of those 52 films are not very good.

So here, **Hitchology** recommends the ten essential Hitchcock films you should definitely watch in order to get a broad overview of the director's style and themes. These aren't necessarily his best films (although that list, however subjective, would be quite similar), but they do fairly represent the Hitch-canon as a whole: British and American films, silent and sound, black-and-white and colour, thrillers and dramas. These films are clearly marked in their individual chapters; watch them in any order you like, but for a good idea of Hitch's directorial progression, approach them chronologically.

1. THE LODGER: A STORY OF THE LONDON FOG (1926)

2. BLACKMAIL (1929)

3. THE 39 STEPS (1935)

4. REBECCA (1940)

5. NOTORIOUS (1946)

6. ROPE (1948)

7. REAR WINDOW (1954)

8. VERTIGO (1958)

9. NORTH BY NORTHWEST (1959)

10. PSYCHO (1960)

FAMILIAR PLOT: THE STYLE
AND THEMES OF HITCHCOCK'S FILMS

"Everyone really only makes one film in his life, and then he breaks it up into fragments and makes it again, with just a few little variations each time."

- Jean Renoir

The Hitchcanon is heaving under the weight of common *thematic* and *stylistic* elements that unify it and identify its films as 'Hitchcockian'. For instance, you can hardly swing a cat in a Hitchcock picture without hitting a dead body, a fair-haired woman or an ambiguous concept of moral culpability and the destabilising effects of its relocation from one person to another, to name but a few.

While murder, blondes (either dangerous or in danger) and a peculiarly Catholic notion of transference of guilt are certainly among the most common themes, Hitch is also famous for telling stories about wrongly-accused men on the run, overbearing mothers, and - more often than you might think - the fundamental incompatibility of men and women. Fun fact: there are around five times as many unhappy marriages in Hitchcock's films as there are smothering matriarchs.

Other recurring elements Hitch had trouble keeping out of his films include love triangles (in, for example, *The Lodger*; *Rebecca*; *Notorious*), useless or ineffectual police *(Young And Innocent*; *The Third Man*; *Psycho)*, charming villains *(The 39 Steps*; *Foreign Correspondent*; *Dial M For Murder)*, sets of doubles *(The Lady Vanishes*; *Strangers On A Train*; *Vertigo)*, dramatic scenes set on staircases *(Suspicion*; *Shadow Of A Doubt*; *The Man Who Knew Too Much)* or in trains and stations *(Number Seventeen*; *Secret Agent*; *Spellbound)*, and thrilling climaxes at famous landmarks *(The Ring*; *Blackmail*; *Saboteur)*. Voyeurism is a key recurring Hitchcockian concept, and a narrative device known as a 'MacGuffin' - usually an object that drives the plot forwards but is largely irrelevant to that plot - pops up with amusing frequency (the microfilm in *North By Northwest* is a cracking MacGuffin). There are more, and we'll come to them later and talk about why some of them might appear so often.

Arguably it's quite lazy of Hitchcock to keep banging on about the same things for 53 films, and this is a perfectly valid criticism. But many great directors tend to lock on to a handful of recurrent ideas (hubris, absurdity and man's cosmic insignificance in Kubrick; religion, violence and excess in Scorsese; heroism, spectacle and absent fathers in Spielberg), and their variations on - and the evolution of - those themes are what keep us coming back for more.

These familiar aspects have also provided fuel for decades of critical analysis, particularly in how the artist is connected to their art. What does it say about Hitchcock's own marriage that there are so many difficult relationships in his films? What was his own mother like if he felt the need to create so many Mrs Bateses? Why does *everyone* drink brandy? Clues are out there for the curious, but Hitch never really gave a straight answer in his lifetime, and we're even less likely to get any from him now.

Perhaps one of the most intriguing aspects of Hitchcock's themes is how they energised his filmmaking. It's clearly reductive to claim that the more Hitchcockian elements there are in any given Hitchcock film then the better it is, and that theory certainly doesn't stand up to rigorous scrutiny. But with repeat viewings, it does become clear that Hitch is far more invested in his storytelling when he's dealing with his favourite preoccupations. It's a generalisation, but one that's hard to deny.

Aside from their narrative *themes*, Hitchcock films are also often recognisable from repeated *stylistic* ingredients. Occasionally the two are inextricably linked: the theme of voyeurism is usually realised via the stylistic choice to show a close up of a character looking at something (usually something they might be better off not looking at), followed by a shot of what they see, followed by a shot of them reacting. *Rear Window* is basically two hours of this. Another key feature of Hitchcockian style is that, having learned his trade in the silent period, Hitch loved to tell a story by purely visual means. As a result, we're absolutely spoiled for striking images throughout his filmography, and dialogue-free sequences regularly pop up in his sound films: watch Jimmy Stewart's perplexed detective tail Kim Novak in *Vertigo* for ten minutes without a single word spoken. The scene was originally envisaged with a rambling voiceover, but Hitchcock found it more effective to rely on his images, their juxtaposition with each other, and Bernard Herrmann's music to generate emotion and understanding in his audience.

You'll also find cutting-edge technical innovation in Hitchcock's films that might appear quaint today but would have popped the eyeballs out of the film industry's sockets at the time. Simple and complex effects alike are deployed throughout the Hitchcanon to tell his stories: from optical processes (like *The Lodger*'s glass ceiling) and experiments with sound (*Blackmail*'s famous 'knife' sequence), through inventive solutions to challenges Hitchcock set himself (*Rope*'s ostensible 'single-shot' approach) to wild, physics-defying camera trickery (*Vertigo*'s disorientating 'contrazoom' shots). It's in these moments that you don't just see or hear the films, you can actually *feel* them.

An exhaustive knowledge of all these fundamentally Hitchcockian motifs is by no means essential to enjoying the individual films, but there's a certain amount of additional appreciation to be had from approaching Hitchcock's work with a cursory awareness of his preoccupations. How those disparate components bump up against (or seamlessly blend with) each other in order to signify what we recognise as 'An Alfred Hitchcock Film' is a foundational part of understanding his filmmaking. Feel free to make your own list of them as you watch, and you'll be an expert in Hitchcock Bingo before you know it.

ALFRED HITCHCOCK: THE FIRST 25 YEARS

It's easy to assume that Alfred Hitchcock was born to direct films; that he somehow emerged from the womb in a suit and tie, landed gracefully in a folding canvas chair and called "Action!" to a studio full of people before the midwife even had chance to wipe him down. Sadly - and, frankly, obviously - that wasn't the case. From drawing his first breath on August 13th, 1899, it would be over a quarter of a century before cameras rolled on Hitchcock's debut feature film. So what was he up to while cinema waited patiently for him to change it forever?

Well, for the first few years, not much. Born to William and Emma Hitchcock in the rooms above their greengrocer's shop in Leytonstone, east London, young Alfred was a quiet, unassuming boy. He wasn't particularly close to his brother and sister, who were both older, and didn't mix much with other children either. He preferred to observe people, rather than interact with them. It is entirely likely that he didn't even own a folding canvas chair.

The Hitchcocks were Catholics, and 'Fred', as his parents called him (schoolmates called him 'Cocky', he – understandably – pushed for 'Hitch'), had what he described as "a strict religious upbringing." How far this would influence him in later years is a matter of much debate, but Hitchcock films uninterested in notions of sin and guilt are very much in the minority. A clearer influence, at least according to the director himself, is a childhood incident he would dine out on in numerous future interviews. Legend has it (and it has become *the* significant formative Hitchcock legend, thanks to him telling it to anyone within earshot) that aged around five - the age changes from one recounting of the story to another - Alfred was sent by his father to the local police station with a note. An officer read the note, then promptly locked the child in a cell for five minutes, telling him "This is what we do to naughty boys".

Hitchcock scholars have learned to take this story with artery-threatening amounts of salt, but its veracity is largely irrelevant. If true, the tale conveniently provides the source of some of his films' major thematic preoccupations (a wrongly accused man; a distrust of the police). If false, well, it's another tall tale from a master of manipulative storytelling, to be added to the rest with a wink and an enigmatic smile. Either way it enhances the Alfred Hitchcock mythology, and that was fine with him.

Any fear of authority born during Hitchcock's brief stint in the slammer was exacerbated by his attendance at St Ignatius' College between the ages of 11 and 14. Discipline was strict, corporal punishment was common and sermons on morality were tediously frequent. But this was also a time when Hitch began to develop significant interests in literature and true crime. He read Dickens and Shakespeare, and later favoured the fantastical tales of Edgar Allan Poe and the detective stories and literary criticism of GK Chesterton, creator of Roman Catholic priest / amateur detective Father Brown. And, like any normal, healthy boy, he spent hours at the Old Bailey making notes on murder trials, or at the Black Museum, Scotland Yard's treasure trove of criminal memorabilia. The casual observer may have been less surprised to see young Alfred embark on a career as a serial killer than a film director.

Needless to say, Hitchcock also spent a great deal of his teenage years at the cinema. He regularly devoured new shorts by Buster Keaton, Charlie Chaplin, Douglas Fairbanks and Mary Pickford, and was fascinated by the innovative methods of DW Griffith in epic features like *Birth Of A Nation* (1915) and *Intolerance* (1916).

In early 1915 Hitchcock got his first job, as a clerk at the Henley Telegraph and Cable Company, which manufactured electrical cables. War had broken out shortly before, but he managed to avoid conscription (partly due to a lack of fitness, partly because Henley's was doing vital work for the war effort) and attended night school to develop his artistic leanings. This led to a transfer to Henley's advertising department, where he used his flourishing creative skills to design inventive ads that relied on imagery over words.

And then, just after the First World War ended, cinema began to get the first whiff that Alfred Hitchcock was on his way to change it. American film company Famous Players-Lasky (who would later become Paramount Pictures) built a studio in Islington, and Hitch popped over with a portfolio of artwork to see if they might take him on. They bought what he was selling, and hired him part-time to design intertitles: the dialogue slides that appeared in silent films, which also featured elaborate decoration or illustrations to complement the action. The first films Hitch worked on were the first that Famous Players-Lasky made in Islington, *The Great Day* (1920) and *The Call Of Youth* (1921), and were so successful that he was hired full time.

A hard worker and a voracious learner, Hitchcock designed all the studio's title cards and began making inroads into set design. He watched the directors carefully, and spent time with them discussing their craft. Such was his enthusiasm that in 1923 he was asked to supervise the completion of *Always Tell Your Wife*, a comedy short whose original director fell out with its star (or, in studio PR terms, 'became ill') and left the project. The film didn't set the world on fire, but soon after, Hitchcock was given his own project: another comedy short, variously known as *Number Thirteen* or *Mrs. Peabody*.

Unfortunately, British films of the early 1920s weren't busting blocks like those being made across the Atlantic, and a nervous Famous Players-Lasky pulled its funding from the studio and its projects, including *Number Thirteen*. The film was never finished. But independent producers rented the studio space, and one of them was Victory Films' Michael Balcon. In 1923 Balcon, with director Graham Cutts, made a feature-length film at Islington called *Woman To Woman*, for which Hitchcock was hired as assistant director, writer and art director. Hitch took it upon himself to hire an experienced and well-respected freelance editor he knew of, but had never spoken to before: a young woman by the name of Alma Reville.

An optimistic Michael Balcon bought the Islington studios from Famous Players-Lasky, making them the home of his newly-formed Gainsborough Pictures. Gainsborough's first film was *The Passionate Adventure* (1924), again directed by

Cutts but with Hitchcock sticking his fingers into as many pies as he could. Ostensibly assistant director, he got involved in writing (about which he'd been learning from the in-house team of scriptwriters), art direction, set and costume design, and production management.

With the British film industry's decline deepening, Balcon had to look to contacts in Germany to fund his next project, *The Blackguard* (1925). Cutts and Hitchcock headed to Berlin to make the film at the studios of the Universum-Film Aktiengesellschaft production company, popularly known as Ufa. Hitch was in his element. Filmmakers working at Ufa included Ernst Lubitsch, Fritz Lang and FW Murnau, and Hitchcock adored them all. He watched Murnau making *The Last Laugh* (1924), a silent film told without any intertitles, and soaked up everything he could learn about this thrilling way of telling stories entirely visually.

Cutts and Hitchcock made one more film together: 1925's *The Prude's Fall*, which was a troubled experience. The production's problems were apparently due to Cutts's unreliability and unpredictability, which were increasing in direct proportion to Hitchcock's chirpy eagerness and burgeoning talent. It was only a matter of time before the young, ambitious upstart could no longer play second fiddle to his older colleague.

While the trip to Germany must have pumped Hitchcock with even more ambitious ideas than he knew what to do with, he always claimed he had no intention to become a full time director. But Balcon saw his potential, and set to work on a feature-length project for Hitch to helm. British financiers weren't keen on new names though, so Balcon had to turn to Germany again. And so, in 1925, Hitchcock - with his assistant director Alma Reville, the backing of Gainsborough Pictures and a great big bag of ideas - headed to Munich's Emelka Studios to make *The Pleasure Garden*: the first Alfred Hitchcock film.

For cinema, the wait was finally over.

THE PLEASURE GARDEN

1926, b/w, silent

Based on the novel by Oliver Sandys

Gainsborough Pictures

UK/Germany

Hitchcock's first completed feature already contains many of the themes with which the fledgling director would become synonymous: adultery, betrayal, love, lust, madness, marriage, melodrama, misogyny and murder, to alphabetise but a few.

The opening scene of Alfred Hitchcock's 53-film canon has his mucky fingerprints all over it. The chorus line of a West End theatre descends a spiral staircase, their long legs spinning by like a saucy zoetrope, before taking the stage and high-kicking their way into movie history. Hitch's camera tracks across the front row of the audience, where the girls are grotesquely mirrored by a parade of wealthy-looking old men struggling to contain their saliva and, no doubt, considering the judicious placement of their top hats in order to conceal any trouser arousal.

One of the old codgers, his eyes already out on stalks, makes use of a pair of opera glasses to get a better look at the girls' gams. As he lifts them to his face, Hitchcock does something very mischievous: he thrusts us into the leering lecher's point of view, and we get to ogle those legs with him as they gradually come into focus. This is the birthplace of Hitch's interest in point of view, in placing the audience behind a character's eyes to elicit a specific emotional response. It's a tool he would use to manipulate viewers for the rest of his career.

But it's also the point where Hitchcock shows us that his women aren't going to take this nonsense lying down. Patsy (Virginia Valli), the object of that grubby male gaze, gives her admirer a stern stare in return, and when he later tries a terrible pick-up line on her, she sends him packing with good-natured sass.

Within minutes of *The Pleasure Garden*'s opening, we've been introduced to two decent women, as Patsy is joined by Jill (Carmelita Geraghty), another dancer who turns up at the theatre penniless and looking for work. But we're also handed an assortment of pitiful excuses for men: the aforementioned front-row droolers, a pair of dastardly pickpockets (they're the ones responsible for Jill's lack of funds) and a couple of sleazy geezers eyeing up our heroines as potential bedpost notches. It's a damning view of masculinity; one Hitchcock would return to time and again, but one that would be reflected in episodes of misogyny of which he himself would later be guilty. Here, though, it neatly positions Patsy and Jill as the kind hearts of the story. From now on, the film suggests, it's sisters versus misters.

Except it isn't, because it turns out that Jill is an ambitious gold-digger who throws Patsy over in a heartbeat when fame comes calling, despite the charity Patsy's shown her. Jill also ditches her fiancé Hugh (John Stuart), who's stationed overseas trying to earn enough money to marry her, in favour of wealthy suitor Prince Ivan, even though he wears way too much guyliner and looks like he sleeps in a coffin. Distraught by Jill's betrayal, Patsy sleepwalks into marriage with Hugh's colleague Mr. Levet (Miles Mander), despite being acquainted with him for such a short time that she doesn't even know his first name.

In further bad news for Patsy, Levet undergoes a swift post-wedding transformation from charming smoothie to selfish prick, and Hitchcock gets to introduce another of his future preoccupations - his deeply cynical view of marriage. The true nature of Levet's cold-heartedness is revealed in a scene of masterful editing: as he abandons his bride mid-honeymoon, heading for Africa on a cruise liner, Hitch cuts between the ship's point of view of Patsy tearfully waving goodbye (even long after Levet's stopped looking) and shots of him clocking a female passenger from behind his newspaper. The bitter icing on the sour cake of this scene is a cruel dissolve from Patsy's hand waving goodbye to the hand of another woman waving hello to Levet as he arrives in Africa. The rotter's got a girl in every port.

From here on in the melodrama ramps up exponentially. Hitchcock commits his first screen murder (not literally, you understand) and throws in a surprising special effect - a double exposure brings the murder victim back in ghostly form - before neatly wrapping up his first feature with some predictable but deserved romance and a spot of canine comedy. The most widely available version of *The Pleasure Garden* clocks in at almost exactly an hour (although a BFI restoration carried out in 2012 runs for 92 minutes), and it's a whirlwind of efficient storytelling via accomplished filmmaking.

Hitchcock scholars have long pointed to the young director's preternatural use of cross-cutting to evoke dramatic irony as an early sign of greatness, and it's true that the scenes of Levet in Africa add an extra layer of emotion to those of Patsy's naive longing for him back in London. To knit the drama together, Hitch also employs visual motifs (flowers play a significant role in the storytelling) and foreshadowing (Patsy literally falls for Jill's fiancé Hugh in an early scene, before figuratively doing so later on), and does so with remarkable skill for a first-timer.

The location shoot was not without its problems: 10,000 feet of film were confiscated by Italian customs, and Hitchcock's hotel room was burgled. For someone who much preferred their drama on the screen rather than in real life, these events may well have contributed to his future preference to remain studio-bound. So the film's proficiency is a testament to its director's unruffled demeanour, as well as his self-confidence, the confidence placed in him by producer Michael Balcon, and his voracious intake of contemporary narrative techniques. The cross-cutting came from the Hollywood epics of DW Griffith, while that first shot of the chorus girls on the staircase is presented in an unusual pillarbox aspect ratio, inspired by the German films Hitchcock had worked on. Ironically, the unconventional visual techniques put *The Pleasure Garden*'s distributors off, and they would withhold its release until Hitch had made a sure-fire hit with his third picture, *The Lodger*. But at just 26 years old, Alfred Hitchcock had taken his first steps to immortality.

THE MOUNTAIN EAGLE

1926, b/w, silent

Based on an idea by Charles Lapworth

Gainsborough Pictures

UK/Germany

This long-lost curio is the only Hitchcock feature that remains missing. Little is known about it beyond the plot, so its full significance within the Hitchcanon is a matter of frustrating conjecture. If you've got a copy knocking about, do call the BFI.

Nobody since the 1920s has seen *The Mountain Eagle*, which makes it a tricky proposition to discuss in a book that claims to examine all of Hitchcock's films. Sorry about that. Presumed lost in a dusty archive or down the back of a sofa somewhere just waiting to be discovered by a diligent cine-archaeologist, it's arguably the most fascinating film mentioned in this book, simply because it's the one about which we know the least.

If Hitch is to be believed (and he often isn't), that state of affairs is no great tragedy. He described it to François Truffaut as "a very bad movie", and the most interesting thing he could recall about its production was his disbelief at the length of his lead actress's nails. Contemporary critics shared his absence of enthusiasm, describing the Kentucky-set melodrama (shot in Austria and Germany) as "slow" and with "unconvincing twists".

Although at the time of writing the Hitchcock canon is one Mountain Eagle short of a full menagerie, the picture deserves a mention. We know from contemporary sources and tireless research by dedicated Hitchologists that it existed, and that it saw the inside of cinemas in England and Germany. We even know the plot, thanks to silent-era trade journal *The Bioscope*, and it goes a little something like this:

Pettigrew (Bernard Goetzke), a shopkeeper and Justice of the Peace in a Kentucky village, is irked by a teacher called Beatrice (Nita Naldi) because he believes she's tempting his disabled son, Edward (John Hamilton). Despite this, Pettigrew falls for Beatrice, but she's not interested. His obvious and natural response to her rejection is to banish her from their village, and in exile she shacks up with a loner called Fearogod (Malcolm Keen). Meanwhile Edward has gone AWOL, so out of spite Pettigrew has Fearogod arrested for Edward's murder despite a total absence of evidence.

After a year in prison, Fearogod escapes to find Beatrice with their baby, and they run away to live in the mountains. When the baby becomes ill, Fearogod takes it to the village where he runs into Pettigrew. Pettigrew gets shot in the shoulder for reasons lost in the mists of time, Edward returns alive and well, Pettigrew befriends Fearogod and everyone lives happily ever after.

You have to hope it worked better on screen than on paper.

There's little to grab hold of here to see how comfortably *The Mountain Eagle* sits with the rest of Hitchcock's films, but at the very least it may be significant for introducing his first wrongly accused man on the run. It also appears we can tick off murder and a love triangle as themes carried over from *The Pleasure Garden*, and which would frequently pop up in the rest of the Hitchcanon. Much more than that remains Hitchcock's greatest mystery.

THE LODGER: A STORY OF THE LONDON FOG

1926, b/w, silent

Based on the novel by Marie Belloc Lowndes

Gainsborough Pictures

UK

ESSENTIAL HITCHCOCK

SPOILER WARNING

Hitch's first masterpiece is a mesmerising combination of German Expressionism, Hollywood stylings and British humour. His first two films were shelved by distributors, but this one forced them to sit up and take notice. Alfred Hitchcock had arrived.

The Pleasure Garden had introduced a handful of eventual Hitchcock tropes, but it was *The Lodger* that would set the template for the type of filmmaking for which the director would become most famous. The Alfred Hitchcock murder-mystery crime thriller subgenre began life here, its birth heralded by a silent scream that would echo throughout every decade of Hitch's filmography.

A killer calling himself 'The Avenger' is on the loose in London, and *The Lodger* opens with the murder of his seventh victim: a blonde girl, just like the previous six. Her face is shown in alarming close-up; we can only imagine how she's meeting her horrific doom. Over the next few minutes, Hitchcock unleashes a barrage of super-efficient exposition and jet-black comedy, setting up his film and the bulk of his future career with dazzling economy.

While murder is very much on the menu, *The Lodger*'s first act is less interested in the act of killing than in its psychological effect on the public. We see news of the murder spread like wildfire from on-the-ground reporters, via phone and telegraph networks to radios, billboards and newspapers across the city. The people can't get enough of it. They listen, rapt, to the wireless, and overwhelm paperboys with demand for the gory details. And, inevitably, they relieve the awfulness by making jokes about it. It's a sly dig at our insatiable thirst for the worst and how we react to - and process - horror; behaviours that Hitchcock would ruthlessly exploit to appeal to the darkest recesses of cinema audiences' desires for years to come.

Our introduction to the nuclear family at the heart of the drama is also a first glimpse at a few of Hitchcock's recurring motifs. Daisy (June Tripp), our heroine, is an independent blonde who may or may not be in danger, and her boyfriend Joe (Malcolm Keen) is a policeman trying to track down The Avenger, but he's literally not much cop ("A lot of use you police are," jokes Daisy's father, signalling a general distrust of the law Hitch would frequently rely on to give his everyman characters more agency). There's a love triangle too, the third point of which arrives in the almost comically sinister shape of the nameless, eponymous lodger (Ivor Novello), who rocks up at Daisy's house looking exactly as The Avenger has been described and acting with all the subtlety of a pantomime villain. Is he responsible for the brutal slayings of seven innocent women? Oh, yes he is! Oh, no he isn't!

The lodger's guilt or innocence forms the basis of the rest of the film's tension, although it all boils down to a cheap trick played by Hitchcock and his partners in crime, Novello and screenwriter Eliot Stannard. The lodger's behaviour is so overwhelmingly suspicious that it's impossible not to assume he's a cold-blooded maniac and that Daisy will inevitably become a target of The Avenger. Our suspicions are backed up by those of Daisy's mother and of Joe, who increasingly allows his jealousy of Daisy and the lodger's blossoming friendship to cloud his professional judgement.

It's only at the film's climax, when the real Avenger is conveniently caught and arrested offscreen, that we realise we've been played. Hitchcock's manipulation of the audience is rather crude here, amounting to little more than a series of narrative fake-outs and over-the-top gestures on Novello's part, but it's a technique Hitch would refine and develop to historically significant levels in the future. On this occasion he was hamstrung by his casting: in the book upon which the film is based, the lodger *does* turn out to be the killer, but Novello's matinee idol status meant contemporary audiences would never accept him as the bad guy.

What makes *The Lodger* an essential entry in the Hitchcanon, apart from being the formative film in a series of peerless Hitchcock-directed crime thrillers, is the way the director enhances the drama in entirely visual terms. "It was the first time I exercised my style," he later told François Truffaut, and it's plain to see where that style was employed to circumvent the restrictions of silent cinema. Take the extraordinary scene where Joe, Daisy and her mother look up at the ceiling because they can hear something from the room above, which the audience can't. Hitch shows us the ceiling, then dissolves to a shot of the lodger pacing back and forth as seen from below, as if the ceiling has melted away. In a single transition we understand more about all the characters, while our own doubts about the lodger are discreetly exacerbated.

Perhaps more subtle is the triangle motif, which occurs visually on the calling cards The Avenger leaves pinned to his victims' clothes and on the map of the killings' locations, as well as in the design of the film's angular title sequence and intertitles. But it's also there in the love triangle between Joe, Daisy and the lodger, shifting subtly throughout the film as the ostensible 'hero' and 'villain' gradually switch places.

The further you dig, the more of Hitchcock's long-term preoccupations you uncover in *The Lodger*. Is The Avenger Hitchcock's first MacGuffin? He drives the plot and yet we only see him once in a fleeting glimpse from behind, his fate casually tossed off in a brief line of dialogue towards the end. And in the absence of a surviving print of *The Mountain Eagle*, *The Lodger* also contains the earliest available iteration of Hitchcock's falsely accused man, on the run from a misguided police force. Later films would ensure the audience knew our man was innocent from the off, strengthening the bond between viewer and character, but the seed of that idea is sown here: one of an arsenal of narrative devices that would eventually come to define an Alfred Hitchcock film.

DOWNHILL

1927, b/w, silent

Based on the play *Down Hill* by 'David L'Estrange' (Ivor Novello & Constance Collier)

Gainsborough Pictures

UK

SPOILER WARNING

Still honing his directorial superpowers, Hitchcock embarks on a forgettable melodrama with a protagonist who practically invites antipathy. Roddy's journey from the heights of privilege to the depths of misery is almost as unpleasant an experience for him as it is for us.

Assigned to Hitchcock by Michael Balcon as the penultimate film required to fulfil his contract with Gainsborough, *Down-hill* is an adaptation of *The Lodger* star Ivor Novello's stage play *Down Hill*. Having co-written and starred in the play, Novello reprised his role for the film, and while his reteaming with

Hitch (and screenwriter Eliot Stannard) might have looked good on paper, the result is no *The Lodger 2: Lodge Harder*.

Novello plays Roddy, a star pupil at a swanky Oxbridge feeder school. His best pal is Tim (Robin Irvine), and Tim's girlfriend Mabel (Annette Benson) is a waitress at the quaintly named Ye Olde Bunne Shoppe, a bakery near the school. Roddy's idyllic existence is shattered by an unexpected revelation, and it's not that this fresh-faced schoolboy is being played by a grown man in his mid-thirties. Unexpectedly, Mabel announces she's got a bunne in ye olde ovenne, and it's quite the scandal – especially as she fingers Roddy as the father. We know he's not her babydaddy, but with DNA tests and tabloid talk shows decades away, Mabel's word is enough to get Roddy expelled and subsequently booted out of the family home by his outraged and embarrassed father.

Mabel's deceitful tale of illegitimate paternity generates a couple of *Downhill*'s early highlights. When the headmaster summons Roddy and Tim to his office to hear Mabel unfold her lies, Hitchcock employs threatening forward tracking shots to ramp up the tension. It's a device he'd used before (the push in to Daisy's front door in *The Lodger*), and would return to on numerous future occasions. And in overlaying a close-up of Mabel's face with multiple exposures showing scenes we've already seen, but subtly altered to suit her version of events, Hitch again overcomes his medium's constraints with innovative formal trickery.

With Roddy shunned, cut off and alone, he heads to big, bad London and into an uncertain future. But Hitchcock has great fun wrong-footing us over Roddy's fate in *Downhill*'s best gag. We see a close-up of Roddy smiling in a dinner suit, so he must be doing fine, surely? The camera pulls out to reveal that he's actually a waiter in a cafe; he's not doing as well as we thought, and we chuckle at the misdirection. And then Roddy surreptitiously pockets a diner's purse, and now we understand that he's desperate. But Hitch hasn't finished his joke. His camera widens further and pans to reveal the entire scene has been taking place on a theatre stage, and Roddy is a background extra in a musical. It's a beautifully constructed series of rug-pulls; a purely visual joke with a setup, a surprise and a punchline, all contained in a single shot designed entirely (and, arguably, unnecessarily) to fool the audience. And in his implication that acting is an even more shameful and degrading fate than being a waiter or a thief, Hitchcock signposts an apparent attitude toward actors that would one day find its ultimate expression in his infamous comparison of them with cattle.

Roddy's misery really kicks in when he marries Julia (Isabel Jeans), the musical's lead actress. "That was the worst mess of all," he later tells another character - a line which the recently-hitched Hitchcock must have found irresistible. In one of the film's several negative representations of women, the actress is a gold-digger, only interested in Roddy when he conveniently inherits £30,000 from a deceased godmother. Having said "I do," she proceeds to bleed him dry while carrying on with her ex, and Roddy's natural reaction is to run off to Paris to become a gigolo at the Moulin Rouge. Selling dances to lonely women at 50 francs a waltz, Roddy is exploited by his female boss and - in a powerful exercise in film lighting - made to realise just how low he's sunk.

Roddy's odyssey - his Roddyssey, if you will - forms the constant downward trajectory of the film's title, and is signified throughout the film with shots of him trudging dejectedly down stairs or taking escalators and lifts down to subterranean levels of misery. It's the kind of on-the-nose imagery that would embarrass the older Hitchcock, and is symptomatic of the fledgling director's inconsistency. *Downhill* is overlong and suffers from an uneven tone, but Hitchcock isn't entirely to blame. Ivor Novello's story expects us to sympathise with an entitled, privileged man whose tragic fate includes inheriting a fortune, marrying a beautiful actress and living in Paris, and his biggest concern seems to be the spine-chilling prospect that expulsion means he won't get to play for his school's Old Boys' rugby team.

It doesn't help that the story wraps itself up with the neatest of bows, as Roddy eventually returns home of his own accord to find himself welcomed back into a family who long ago discovered the truth about Mabel's indiscretions. The reward for Roddy's ordeal is his dream come true: he finally gets to play for the Old Boys.

History hasn't been kind to *Downhill*, and modern audiences rightly struggle with its most problematic section, in which - at the absolute nadir of his woes - Roddy is forced to hang out with "the rats of a Marseilles dockside", as an intertitle tells us. These include the first two (of very few) Black characters in the Hitchcock canon, and it's telling that the director uses them as signifiers of society's underbelly. Most uncomfortably, one of them is an horrendous stereotype clearly played by a white woman in black make-up. They're kind-hearted souls who eventually help Roddy back on his feet, but there's no escaping the fact that Hitchcock very rarely employed actors of colour, and his films' attitude to them was never anywhere near as progressive as his filmmaking.

EASY VIRTUE

1927, b/w, silent
Based on the play by Noël Coward
Gainsborough Pictures
UK

Venturing into the moral maze faced by independent women in a post-war Britain, Hitchcock presents a clash of attitudes between 1920s youth and a society founded on Victorian values. And forget Samuel L Jackson: Easy Virtue *contains the original bad mother.*

Hitch's final film for Gainsborough is hard going, feeling even more like a contract-fulfiller (which it was) than *Downhill*. It's an adaptation of a Noël Coward play which had found success in New York and London, but Hitchcock failed to transfer any of its zip and zing to the screen - unsurprising, given that Coward's way with words was unlikely to make a successful transition to a silent medium. That said, *Easy Virtue* isn't entirely without merit, and does at least introduce one of the most significant exhibits in the Hitchcock chamber of horrors.

Things begin promisingly with a visual gag reminiscent of *The Pleasure Garden*'s opening. A myopic judge in a divorce case lifts his monocle to more clearly see the lawyer before him, and Hitchcock gives us the judge's point-of-view: through the monocle the lawyer is magnified and sharpened. To achieve the effect, the monocle was actually a large mirror, the judge's hand an oversized model and the actor playing the lawyer stood just next to the camera, reflected rather than refracted. It's a fun moment, achieved with the complexity of a Georges Méliès stunt, but adds nothing to our understanding of the scene. It's hard to shake the impression that Hitch took more interest in this single flourish than in the rest of the film.

That moment is soon forgotten, as the court case - a prologue which doesn't feature in Coward's play - drags on for nearly 20 minutes; long enough to make you wonder if the director is the same Alfred Hitchcock who displayed such economy and efficiency in his earlier movies. Apparent socialite Larita Filton (Isabel Jeans, looking like she may have been the inspiration for Jack Lemmon's disguise in *Some Like It Hot*) is being divorced by her husband, who suspects her of having it away with an artist who painted her portrait. In flashbacks, which are neatly woven into the present via a series of close-ups that blur the transitions in time, we see that Larita is innocent of adultery and her husband is an abusive alcoholic.

Nevertheless, the jury finds her guilty of 'misconduct' (Hitchcock's 'wrong man' undergoing a brief gender swap), and Larita escapes her woes - and a ravenous paparazzi - by hiding away at a Mediterranean resort. It's here, in an early example of the rom-com meet-cute, that she's whacked in the face by an errant tennis ball thanks to cack-handed David Bowie lookalike John Whittaker (Robin Irvine). Romance develops, although

Larita is reluctant to get involved with another man due to her shocking and salacious past, of which John is blissfully unaware.

After mixing Larita one of cinema's sloppiest martinis (too much vermouth, not enough ice, shaken rather than stirred), John proposes marriage. Rather than insisting he undertake basic mixology lessons before she can even consider marriage, Larita promises to give him her answer by telephone later that night. It seems a weird way of doing things, until you realise it's a setup for another of Hitchcock's little games. He chooses to show the phone conversation entirely through the reactions of the snooping exchange operator who puts the call through, and we understand exactly what's being said from her expressions. It's a delightful bit of theatre, especially when Larita finally says yes, and as a bonus would've saved an expensive afternoon's shooting with the film's stars.

John ships Larita back to his family pile in rural England: a bizarre stately home known as The Moat House, which is appropriate given its isolation, the insular attitudes of its occupants and their general hostility toward strangers. It's here that we meet John's mother (Violet Farebrother), the prototype for countless domineering matriarchs who would antagonise a series of pathetic sons - and the women they bring home - throughout Hitchcock's filmography. *Rebecca*'s Mrs Danvers, *Notorious*'s Madame Sebastian, *Psycho*'s Mrs Bates, *The Birds*' Lydia Brenner and more all owe a debt to the smothering overprotectiveness and venomous animosity of Mrs Whittaker; it's no coincidence that she's the most fun of *Easy Virtue*'s otherwise dull, thinly drawn characters.

Life at The Moat House is a barrel of misery for Larita, a blonde outsider amongst a trio of brunettes who include John's sisters and his ex, Sarah, who seems to be a permanent visitor. Mrs Whittaker the elder, who's clearly Team Sarah, makes no secret of her contempt for Mrs Whittaker the younger. Family meals are gloomy affairs conducted in an oppressively sepulchral dining room evidently decorated by a religious maniac: gigantic murals of saints loom over the diners like manifestations of old Mrs W's puritanical disapproval. Before long John admits that his mother has made him see he was wrong to marry Larita, and shortly afterwards her "vile secret" - that she's an adulterous divorcée - is exposed, much to Mrs Whittaker's disgusted delight.

A party is held at The Moat House for no particular reason, and Larita is warned to stay in her room by her overbearing in-law. The stage should be set for some last-act fireworks, but the film has been such a slog thus far that hopes of a thrilling face-off are low. Sure enough, Larita's vengeance consists of turning up at the party in an excessively fancy frock, Mrs Whittaker is unimpressed, and that's that. *Easy Virtue* ends as it began, with another divorce case. A final clanger is dropped when Larita, facing photographers after her second divorce, melodramatically cries "Shoot! There's nothing left to kill." Hitchcock would later describe that line as "the worst I've ever written," and nobody is arguing.

Presented largely in frontal wide shots with few reaction cutaways, *Easy Virtue* displays uncharacteristically unimaginative direction from Hitchcock. Ideas around outdated attitudes towards feminine sexual independence hover in the shadows, but Larita's refusal to ever stand up to her antagonists make it tough to get behind her cause. As a result, the film is only really interesting as a marker of Hitchcock's formative years and a commentary on his developing preoccupations as a storyteller. The pessimistic view of marriage, the tyrannical mother and the dangerously independent blonde are beginning to coalesce as thematic motifs, but it would be some time before they achieved their full impact.

THE RING

1927, b/w, silent
Story by Alfred Hitchcock
British International Pictures
UK

This stunningly shot and edited boxing-based melodrama is a genuine knockout. Thematically and visually rich, with a perfect balance of humour and emotional tension, it's one of the standout works of Hitch's silent era. It also features some cracking knitwear.

The Ring is everything Hitchcock's previous film, *Easy Virtue*, isn't. It's an original story for a new studio (British International Pictures in Elstree), it's brimming with energy and invention, characters are sympathetic and well-realised, there's humour and pathos, and nobody mixes a bad martini (although they do let the champagne go flat). Yet it's one of the least 'Hitchcockian' films Hitchcock ever made, and the themes for which he would become famous are pretty much absent. The most familiar element carried over from his previous pictures is his obsession with unhappy marriage; *The Ring* is the fifth of his six films so far to dwell on marital misery. At a pinch you could argue that the final boxing match at the Royal Albert Hall is an early example of the climactic showdowns at famous landmarks that would cap later thrillers (we'll be back at the Albert Hall twice more by the end of this book), but it's not quite the same.

"One-Round" Jack Sander (Carl Brisson, with eyes like Daniel Craig and a deep affinity for cardigans) is an amateur boxer; a fairground scrapper who claims he can beat any opponent in a single round. But when he's defeated by Bob Corby (Ian Hunter), a podgy bloke who keeps his bow tie on during the bout, Jack finds that his job, and his engagement to fickle flirt Mabel (Lillian Hall Davis), are under threat. Can he rise up to the challenge of his rival and rescue his rocky relationship? Or is his marriage on the ropes before it's begun?

It's that tension that keeps *The Ring* as taut as the canvas floor of its titular arena. Our sympathies lie squarely with Jack: a decent, working class fella whose fiancée has relaxed ideas about fidelity, and who's been hustled by a bounder who turns out to be none other than the heavyweight boxing champion of Australia. Hitchcock, teaming up again with writing partner Eliot Stannard, filters his story through Jack's increasing paranoia, convincing us that Bob and Mabel are enjoying below-the-belt action every time his back is turned.

In fact, whether or not an affair is going on is quite open to interpretation. Apart from an early smooch between Bob and Mabel that could be written off as an isolated incident, there's no evidence that Jack's being cuckolded. Bob certainly has eyes for Mabel, and she does very little to discourage him, but we never see them *in flagrante delicto*. Of course that could simply be a by-product of what passed for 1920s film censorship, but Hitch plays on it in much the same way that he convinced us

Ivor Novello's lodger was a serial murderer, before revealing otherwise. Even the silent nature of the medium helps Hitch's diabolical cause: in the absence of much dialogue, we're left to interpret events through actions and expressions, leaving us at the mercy of a master manipulator.

While the soap opera of this hot-blooded threesome plays out, Hitchcock repeatedly jabs and hooks us with his signature visual flair. In the scene where Jack first fights Bob, the worn-out old sign indicating Round One is replaced by a shiny new number two, implying this is the first of Jack's fights to reach that milestone. Jack's progress through the boxing ranks is expressed by a montage of billboards, showing him steadily climbing from the bottom of the bill to the top. Champagne, poured in excited anticipation of Mabel's arrival, goes from fizzy to flat in a single dissolve to indicate the passage of time and the souring of Jack's mood as she fails to show up. And the fight sequences, often shot from within the ring and punchily edited, are arguably the 1920s equivalent of *Raging Bull*'s ferociously executed bouts.

But perhaps the most significant motif is the ring itself, which can be applied not just to the boxing ring, but also the wedding ring Jack gives to Mabel and its ostentatious counterpart, the snake bracelet she receives from Bob (the latter object, a heavily loaded signifier of sin and forbidden love, is repeatedly employed in deliciously dark vignettes that protract the drama). The ring motif is also there in the film's opening shots: a drum; various fairground rides that describe a circle in whole or in part; mouths open wide in excitement or yelling about attractions. And to extend the title's meaning beyond mere visuals, there's the circle of love and jealousy formed by the three protagonists, which recalls the triangle formed by the lead characters in *The Lodger*. The metaphorical geometry has changed but the emotional turmoil stays the same.

Bookended by two contrasting fights between Jack and Bob (the first in a spit-and-sawdust sideshow tent, the last in the prestigious surroundings of the Albert Hall - or at least in front of a semi-convincing painted backdrop of it), *The Ring* foreshadows the structural elegance of Hitchcock's later masterpieces. It's also the most beautifully shot and lit of his films so far: this would be the first of 11 collaborations with Jack Cox, a cheerfully experimental cinematographer who, like countless Hitchcock associates, would rarely receive the recognition he deserved for his contribution to the director's stylistic development.

Modern discussion of *The Ring* can't allow its less savoury moments to pass by unacknowledged. A Black man at the fairground is a literal sideshow attraction, with gleeful punters lobbing objects at a target to knock him off his perch and mischievous brats chucking eggs in his face, much to the amusement of the (all-white) crowd. Later, a Black boxer is casually referred to in terms offensive to present-day eyes and ears. The existence of these scenes stands as a record of outdated attitudes which, regrettably, have not yet been consigned to history. If they're uncomfortable to watch today, they should be. That Hitchcock was a product of his time doesn't excuse his complicity in perpetuating harmful stereotypes, and every negative representation or total absence of people of colour in his films is an unpleasant reminder of it.

THE FARMER'S WIFE

1928, b/w, silent
Based on the play by Eden Philpotts
British International Pictures
UK

A brutal skewering of upper-class toxic masculinity, or a slapstick comedy about the perils of oversized trousers? Hitchcock has it both ways with this delightful romp through rural English society and the pitfalls of middle-aged courtship.

The Farmer's Wife is that rare thing: an Alfred Hitchcock comedy. A seam of pitch-black humour runs through most of Hitch's films, but very few sell themselves as outright chucklefests - and when they do, they're not entirely successful. His first crack at the genre suffers a little from indecision over what kind of comedy it wants to be: slapstick and farce butt up against a gentle comedy of manners and an almost *Carry On*-esque dollop of bawdy humour. What's more, the film is bookended by two dramatic scenes that don't play for laughs at all, contributing to a somewhat uneven tone. Once it gets going though, *The Farmer's Wife* is a charming and amusing outlier in the Hitchcanon.

After making five films prodding the sanctity of marriage with a sharply cynical stick, Hitch changes his approach to the subject. Whether he's temporarily softening his stance nearly a year into his own marriage to Alma Reville, or just satirising a different aspect - the courtship process that leads to marriage - is open to debate. The film's ambiguous viewpoint on the matter is characterised by the back-and-forth between two spectacularly-monikered characters: housemaid Araminta Dench ('Minta' for short, played by Lilian Hall-Davis) and handyman Churdles Ash (Gordon Harker). "There's something magical in the married state," Minta wistfully remarks. "It have a beautiful side." "Holy Matrimony be a proper steam roller for flattening the hope out of a man and the joy out of a woman," comes Churdles' retort. The absence of a Mrs Churdles Ash anywhere in the vicinity speaks quiet volumes.

Minta and Churdles both work for Samuel Sweetland (Jameson Thomas), a farmer who undertakes absolutely no actual farming during the course of the story, concentrating instead on sourcing a new bride after his wife's death in the film's melancholy prologue. It doesn't sound like the setup for the most uproarious comedy, and indeed the first giggles are almost certainly unintentional. The dying Mrs Sweetland's somewhat undignified last words, delivered to Minta, are "Don't forget to air your master's pants", immediately followed by an unexpected and lengthy montage of pants-airing shots. The intention is to indicate the passage of time, but as a by-product audiences are left with a baffling familiarity with the leading man's undercrackers.

With Minta's help, Sweetland draws up a shortlist of four potential new Mrs Sweetlands, none of whom seem ideal: widow

Louisa ("Her back view's not a day over thirty!"); the prim and mousey Thirza (about whom Sweetland can think of literally nothing to say); postmistress Mary ("I don't mind they pillowy women"), and pub landlady Mercy ("for luck"). In a purely cinematic device absent from the play on which the film is based, Sweetland imagines each of the women in his wife's fireside chair, and at the end of the shortlisting scene Minta sits in the chair herself before a fade to black. It's a slightly heavy-handed foreshadowing of events that most audiences will have already seen coming a mile away, but it does demonstrate Hitchcock's skill at conjuring up entirely visual methods of telling his story.

Sweetland's courting game is, it must be said, less than stellar. His arrogance and vanity - watch him checking out his own luxurious moustache in a mirror - lead him to assume that any woman would be delighted to experience that face fuzz at close quarters. Pleasingly, the women reject him one by one, evoking an infantile rage in Sweetland which unexpectedly fuels the comedy. Thirza is rendered a nervous wreck, causing calamity at a party she's trying to host, while a distressed Mary's reaction to Sweetland's fury is to ask "Is this a nightmare?". His response - "Your hat is" - is surely one of cinema's sickest burns.

Hidden beneath all this is Sweetland's arc, which is his journey from pompous chauvinist to humbled, appreciative gentleman. He needs to experience the pain of rejection to bring himself down to earth and realise his soulmate has been alongside him the whole time. Tragically it's not Churdles (their neanderthal views on women would have made them a perfect match), but loyal maid Minta. The thorny question of whether she ends up doing just as much pants-airing, only now without pay, remains sadly unaddressed at the film's close.

The union of country squire and housekeeper breaches a class divide which is a crucial background for - but rarely a tool for social commentary in - *The Farmer's Wife*. Hitchcock, the son of an east end greengrocer, shows a great affection for the working class, and while they often appear as stereotypes in his films he imbues them with an abundance of character. Chief among them here is Churdles, the cantankerous labourer whose strained efforts at politeness while acting as doorman at a fancy party are hindered by his equally desperate attempts to avoid dropping his baggy trousers in front of the parson's mother. In a less comic moment, watch carefully when Minta welcomes Sweetland's new son-in-law to the house with a handshake before taking his hat: the young man subtly but decisively wipes his hand with his handkerchief immediately afterwards, as if he's afraid of catching something from the help.

Hitchologist Charles Barr notes an interesting development with *The Farmer's Wife*, and it's worth mentioning here. Hitch mobilises his camera much more than he has up to this point - Barr calculates around ten percent of shots are on the move, compared to one or two percent in his previous films. It was a time of cinematic leaps and bounds, with Buster Keaton's *The General*, Abel Gance's *Napoléon* and Fritz Lang's *Metropolis* ushering in increased production values and technical know-how that vastly outweighed what Hitchcock could achieve within the budgetary confines of British cinema. His ideas were easily equal to those of his foreign counterparts, but he would have to wait for the right circumstances to arise before he could realise them.

MR. HITCHCOCK

THE HITCHCOCK FILMS THAT AREN'T

If you've ever looked up Hitchcock's films on the internet, you've probably come across a bunch of titles that don't crop up on the official Hitch filmographies published by the likes of the British Film Institute. Sadly those anomalies aren't hidden gems: they're generally a mixture of unfinished or half-lost projects, short films, promotional material and other Hitchish allsorts. Because they're not identifiably feature films directed by Alfred Hitchcock, you won't find them in the individual chapters of **Hitchology**, but it's worth clearing up exactly what they are and what - if any - Hitchcock's involvement with them was.

NUMBER 13 (AKA MRS PEABODY)

Intended as the first film Hitchcock would direct, *Number 13* was to be a comedy about a cleaner who dreams of winning the lottery. Her fantasy involves having all her friends round to her mansion, where her enemies are forced to become her servants. Sadly the money ran out with only two reels of footage shot (and subsequently lost), and although producer Michael Balcon looked into resurrecting it in 1925 after Hitch had made *The Pleasure Garden*, that doesn't seem to have panned out. Surviving production stills show the plump charlady staring forlornly into a mug, and a sinister-looking chap with a top hat and villainously twirlable moustache, but much more than this is a mystery.

ALWAYS TELL YOUR WIFE (1923)

Hitch directed half of this two-reel farce after original director Hugh Croise left under a cloud of indeterminate nature. Sadly the second reel - the bit that Hitch probably oversaw - is lost, although what remains doesn't suggest we're missing out on much. A stagey farce about a husband's past catching up with him via a vindictive old flame and a comedy parrot, *Always Tell Your Wife* features the kind of fragile marriage that would become a Hitchcockian trope.

AN ELASTIC AFFAIR (1930)

A single reel comedy made solely to give acting gigs to the two winners of a talent contest held by *Film Weekly* magazine. Hitchcock probably directed it, but the film remains lost.

ELSTREE CALLING (1930)

This peculiar compendium of comedy and music sketches, which is frankly pretty hard going for anyone who enjoys comedy or music, is often listed as an Alfred Hitchcock film. In fact he's only credited as having contributed "sketches and other interpolated items", and his exact input remains a matter of conjecture to this day. Hitch totally dismissed it in conversation with François Truffaut, describing it as "of no interest whatever". Film historians might disagree, but if you've seen it you might be tempted to reach the same conclusion as Hitchcock.

MARY (1930)

A German-language version of Hitchcock's *Murder!*. As was not uncommon at the time, both films were shot simultaneously: once with an English cast and once with a German cast, but both by Hitchcock. By all accounts the German take is less amusing than the English, a fact which Hitch ascribed to his own ignorance of the German sense of humour.

LORD CAMBER'S LADIES (1932)

Off the back of a run of increasingly unsuccessful movies, Hitch took a break from directing to produce three films for British International Pictures. In the end only one was made: *Lord Camber's Ladies*, a drama which, with its deadly love triangle and theatrical setting, would have been right up Hitchcock's street. It was directed by Benn Levy, who had written dialogue for the sound version of *Blackmail*. Hitch and Levy's relationship on set underwent a dramatic spat that went unresolved for three decades, until - weirdly - Levy helped Hitch develop *Kaleidoscope* (see below).

THE FIGHTING GENERATION (1944)

A nurse turns to camera after tending a wounded soldier, and delivers a two-minute plea to the American public to buy War Bonds. The promo was directed by Hitchcock, shot by *Citizen*

Kane cinematographer Gregg Toland and produced by David O Selznick. The nurse was played by Jennifer Jones, Selznick's current squeeze; Hitch noted with some amusement that the project seemed more interested in advertising Miss Jones's talents than the War Bonds.

WATCHTOWER OVER TOMORROW (1945)

A short film promoting the as-yet-unformed United Nations to the great unwashed. According to author Sidney Gottlieb, it seems likely that Hitchcock (along with *Notorious* and *Spellbound* screenwriter Ben Hecht) had some input into the film's concept, but exactly how much of it (if any) he directed remains unknown.

MEMORY OF THE CAMPS (AKA GERMAN CONCENTRATION CAMPS FACTUAL SURVEY) (1945)

Sidney Bernstein, with whom Hitchcock founded short-lived production company Transatlantic Pictures, tried in 1945 to put together a documentary about Nazi concentration camps. He gathered footage from international news crews but struggled to piece it together in a way that would fully convey the reality of its horror. Hitchcock was brought on board to offer editing advice, and what resulted was an incomplete film which, overseen by the Imperial War Museum, credits Hitch as 'treatment adviser'.

KALEIDOSCOPE

In the late 1960s Hitchcock began to develop *Kaleidoscope* (also known, confusingly, as *Frenzy*): a daring new kind of serial killer film which would use techniques influenced by European directors like Michelangelo Antonioni. It would also push the boundaries for accepted nudity and violence in mainstream Hollywood cinema, as existing test footage and stills suggest. Universal Studios baulked at the idea though, and Hitch was forced to abandon the project.

THE SHORT NIGHT

Bothered by *Family Plot*'s lukewarm reception, Hitch insisted on going out with a bang, beginning work on what would have been his 54th feature in 1977 despite his crushingly obvious ill health. It was to be a spy thriller about a double agent who busts out of Wormwood Scrubs to find his family and take them to the Soviet Union. Unfortunately for him, his wife has fallen for a man who wants the double agent dead, and Hitch-cockian complications ensue. *The Short Night* is the most fully realised of several unmade Hitchprojects - a complete script is freely available to read today - but Hitchcock was in no shape, physically or mentally, to finish it. With regret he cancelled the project at the end of 1979, just months before he died.

CHAMPAGNE

1928, b/w, silent
Story by Walter Mycroft
British International Pictures
UK

Hitchcock gets experimental with his camera for this gender-reversed retread of Downhill: *a frothy comedy about an entitled woman whose fortunes and independence are at the mercy of the men in her life. Contains Hitch's two best insults: "cake hound" and "boulevard sheik".*

Dreamed up by Hitchcock as a melodramatic sermon on moral decay when he must have been in an epic self-righteous grump, *Champagne* was retooled by scenarist Water Mycroft into a breezy, more appealing comedy at the understandable insistence of British International Pictures. Hitch and his faithful writing companion Eliot Stannard found themselves improvising the script during the shoot, and the end result must have contributed heavily to Hitchcock's insistence on being 100% prepared before committing a single frame to film in the future. In 1962 he described *Champagne* to François Truffaut as "probably the lowest ebb in my output", and while that's up for some debate, it's fair to say there's precious little fizz in this vintage.

Betty Balfour, one of British silent cinema's brightest comedy stars, plays Betty, the socialite daughter of a Wall Street tycoon (Gordon Harker, unrecognisable from his working-class, turnip-faced roles in *The Ring* and *The Farmer's Wife*). Dad disapproves of Betty's carefree gallivanting and her intention to marry her lover (Jean Bradin, credited only as 'The Boy'), so he cooks up a thunderously inept and convoluted plot to split them up. At the film's climax, having inadvertently driven his own daughter to the verge of destitution and prostitution, he reveals his plan to her with all the pride of a schoolboy showing off a sports trophy. Rather than take the obvious step of reporting her father for sustained psychological torture, Betty simply has a jolly good laugh and everyone lives happily ever after.

Betty is one of Hitchcock's headstrong, independent blondes, but she's also a selfish, arrogant brat who spends most of the film running away from her first world problems, making her tough to root for. The men in her life are all dicks too, either manipulating or trying to control her, and when a film is populated entirely with characters you'd go to great lengths to avoid if they were real people, it's hard to give a hoot about any of their problems.

Hitch clearly shares this lack of interest, so spends the film conjuring up visual distractions at every opportunity. A couple of moments of exposition are conveyed via newspaper headlines, which is efficient storytelling, but does make you wonder how slow a news day it is when the details of a trivial family squabble make the front pages. Those shot transitions he's so fond of also help pass the time - literally, in the case of one elliptical mix from a bedsheet to a tablecloth, and a dissolve from a wretched home-cooked meal to a succulent gourmet feast is, in context, a fun gag that also teases a plot mystery.

Perhaps the most obvious failed experiment occurs during the first act, when Betty and The Boy are on a transatlantic passenger ship bound for France. In a subtle moment of metaphorical signposting, the liner hits stormy weather just before the couple have an engagement-ending bust-up. Hitchcock cants his camera from side to side to imply the swaying of the ship, while the cast act as if they're under attack on the Starship Enterprise. Unfortunately Hitch forgets to tilt the camera for some shots, and nobody has told the actors when or which way to lean, so they just take their own cues. The unintentional effect is that everyone working on the film appears to be completely wasted.

But you can't fault Hitchcock for trying. If *The Farmer's Wife* saw him go further than dipping a toe in the waters of camera movement than he had before, *Champagne* is where he pretty much strips off and dive-bombs the deep end. Any excuse for an elaborate pan or tracking shot to spice up proceedings is fine by Hitch and, frankly, welcome for an audience who might have otherwise nodded off.

Most of this kineticism is employed to show off the set of a hotel restaurant where an unexpectedly insolvent Betty has found work. Individual camera setups are numerous, although the technical bravado sometimes comes at the expense of common sense: one long pan follows Betty halfway around the perimeter of the restaurant when she could just as easily have strolled through the middle of the room. There are some impressive tracking shots though, bringing us along with Betty through the restaurant, and the camera at one point races through a packed dance floor to reveal the unexpected presence of a mysterious and sinister character.

Perhaps of more interest is the shedload of subjective shots Hitchcock uses to draw us into his characters' states of mind: multiple exposures are used effectively to denote woozy seasickness and whimsical daydreams, although characters appearing to kiss the camera when greeting each other just make you want to push yourself slightly further back in your seat. The most virtuosic point-of-view shot appears twice, bookending the film - a view through the bottom of a champagne glass from the perspective of the drinker. Again, it adds little to the story, but it's worth noting that *Champagne* is the third of Hitchcock's first seven surviving films to deploy a man's PoV shot through some kind of magnifier in its opening moments. The male gaze is settling in for the long haul.

Ironically, the most compelling example of the audience being pulled into a character's psyche uses no special effects at all. An encounter between Betty and the mysterious stranger turns unpleasant when he lures her to a secluded corner and forces himself on her. But then, in a simple dissolve, Hitchcock yanks us a few minutes back in time, and we realise Betty was merely imagining the worst. For once in the film Hitch makes us sympathise with his heroine, and the relief we feel for her - a palpable emotion brought on by nothing more technically complex than a single edit - is representative of Hitchcock's belief in the power of pure cinema.

THE MANXMAN

1929, b/w, silent
Based on the novel by Hall Caine
British International Pictures
UK

After the technical flamboyance and lacklustre plot of Champagne, *Hitch brings everything back into balance for his kind-of-final silent film. This steamy melodrama about passion and betrayal in a Manx fishing village puts the 'love' into the Isle Of Man.*

Hitchcock often illustrated his method of creating suspense by proposing a movie scene in which two people sit at a table, chatting. Suddenly a bomb goes off, and the audience jump, gasp and laugh at themselves. Now, teased Hitch, what if the audience knew there was a bomb under the table, set to explode in five minutes? The tension is ratcheted up exponentially. We're helpless to do anything and infuriated by the characters' small talk. That, he argued, is true suspense: the essential ingredient of a Hitchcock thriller.

The Manxman is not a Hitchcock thriller. Quite the opposite, in fact. It's another melodrama, this time set on the Isle Of Man, about another woman romantically entangled with two men. But because the men are best pals, and one is blissfully unaware of his mate's relationship with his missus, the affair becomes the ticking time bomb. We don't know when it'll go off, but we know it must, and devastation will be wrought. Consequently, and unexpectedly, this gentle love story becomes Hitchcock's most suspenseful film so far.

Rugged fisherman Pete Quilliam (Carl Brisson) and slick lawyer Philip Christian (Malcolm Keen) are lifelong friends, and they're introduced in a scene in which Pete, bringing the day's catch into harbour, is met by Philip with a petition he intends to present to the island's governor. The petition aims, on behalf of the fishermen, "to protest against the encroachment of the steam trawlers on their fishing grounds". Hitchcock sows subtle seeds of disquiet in the scene: Hitchologist Charles Barr notes the two boys play-fighting in the background and suggests a symbolic connection to the lead characters' past and future. Even the wording of the petition, describing a sophisticated rival force muscling in on the underdog's territory, anticipates the forthcoming feud.

These clues are only apparent with hindsight though, because we're yet to meet the lady-shaped wedge that will be driven between the men. Anny Ondra plays Kate Cregeen, barmaid (and landlord's daughter) at local boozer The Manx Fairy. As soon as Pete and Philip clap eyes on Kate, it's clear they're both smitten. Hitchcock has his male leads deliver their performances directly into camera for this first meeting, then places his camera between them for the reverse shots of Kate - until it's clear she's more impressed with Philip. Now Kate moons into the camera as she thanks Philip for all he's done, and Pete may as well be invisible. These point-of-view shots, and the reactions within them, are all that's required to set up the imbalance in this typically Hitchcockian love triangle.

Hitchcock continues the technique of characters looking straight into camera for much of the film, letting it play out like a 1920s *Peep Show*. It's a little disconcerting, but it brings a unique quality to the film that's perhaps most succinctly described by Gloria Swanson's faded silent movie star Norma Desmond in *Sunset Boulevard* (1950): "We didn't need dialogue... we had *faces*." Hitch adores his leads' faces in *The Manxman*, especially that of Anny Ondra, the most lovingly-captured Hitchcock blonde so far.

It's Pete who stakes his claim on Kate first, regardless of whether or not she's actually more interested in him than Philip, or how his best friend very obviously feels (Pete isn't the brightest button, spelling his own name wrong when signing the petition, despite concentrating so hard his tongue pops out). But Kate is metaphorically untouchable to Pete in these early scenes, variously placed by Hitchcock behind some kind of obstruction: the bar, a window, the banister of the pub's stairs. And before long she's literally off limits, as her father forbids Pete - a "penniless lout" in his words - from seeing his daughter, inadvertently setting in motion the forthcoming turmoil.

In a night-time sequence deliberately punctuated by the flashes of a nearby lighthouse, Pete wins Kate's heart in a *Romeo And Juliet*-esque window scene, rashly declares he's off to Africa to make his fortune and asks Philip to "look after her" for him while he's gone. Philip agrees, but nobody heeds the lighthouse's constant warning signal. This bromance is headed straight for the rocks, an inevitability borne out by a montage of classic Hitchcockian exposition: in close up, we see Kate flick through her diary (try to ignore how comically tiny it is and how inappropriately massive her handwriting), in which 'Mr Christian' becomes 'Philip' over time, then eventually 'Phil'. Hitch cuts away before Kate goes as far as referring to him as 'Snuggles', but having compressed around six weeks into 30 seconds, his work here is done.

Philip and Kate consummate their relationship in a scene loaded with metaphorical steam. Wandering into a deserted water mill, Kate sets the millstones turning; the two kiss, and Hitchcock cuts to a close up of the two stones grinding away. His first visual analogy for sex is only slightly more subtle than the one with which he would famously end *North By Northwest* 30 years later.

From this point on the melodrama ramps up - about a year's worth of the average soap opera's events are crammed into the film's second half - but Hitchcock takes his foot off the gas with the flourishes, allowing solid but unshowy direction to carry the drama to its surprisingly downbeat conclusion. As has become a mini tradition, he caps the story with another ending that references the film's opening (see also *The Lodger*, *Downhill*, *Easy Virtue*, *The Ring* and *Champagne*), this time watching Pete glumly sail out of the harbour he cheerfully entered so long ago.

The Manxman had its first Trade Show (a preview screening for cast, crew, exhibitors, press and other industry types) in January 1929. Four months earlier, *The Jazz Singer* - the first 'talkie' - had opened in London, and the face of cinema changed virtually overnight. The race was on to make Britain's first talking picture, and Hitchcock was determined to be the one to win it.

In his dust he left a remarkable body of silent movies: nine films in which he learned - and arguably perfected - the art of what he called "the purest form of cinema", consistently pushing the boundaries of visual storytelling with unrivalled skill and wit. But the coming of sound represented perilous, uncharted territory for every filmmaker, and like his contemporaries, Alfred Hitchcock's future was balanced on a knife edge.

A BLACKMAIL NOTE

The advent of synchronised sound in films (actually being able to *hear* what characters were saying to each other, if you can believe such a thing) was nothing short of revolutionary. If you weren't there in the late 1920s and early '30s, and it's increasingly likely you weren't, it's hard to appreciate the mind-boggling transformation to the film industry that 'the talkies' represented. Actors who looked good but hadn't nailed the whole 'speaking' thing feared it, while studio executives reluctant to splash out on the necessary technology laughed it off as a passing gimmick.

More thoughtful were the directors who wondered how the logistical restrictions presented by the cumbersome new sound kit would affect their storytelling abilities. While many of them underwent mild panic at the prospect, Alfred Hitchcock did what he always did: he kept calm and carried on. Hitch was "bitterly disappointed" when the head of British International

Pictures, John Maxwell (one of those aforementioned nervous execs), told him his tenth feature would be silent. But with one eye on the present and both ears on the future, Hitchcock planned ahead. *Blackmail* was filmed in such a way that, in the event that Maxwell changed his mind, Hitch could turn around a sound version with minimal reshoots.

Sure enough, towards the end of *Blackmail*'s production, Maxwell changed his mind. So Hitchcock reassembled his cast, filmed a handful of scenes again with recorded dialogue, and cut together the UK's first talking picture. And, as a bonus, he had a silent version in the bank for the cinemas unequipped to show talkies. A largely irrelevant debate continues to this day over which version is superior (for what it's worth, if you can catch the silent version accompanied by the score composed by Neil Brand for the BFI's 2012 restoration, you really, really should), but as the sound version is more widely available and culturally significant, that's the one we'll look at more closely over the page.

BLACKMAIL

1929, b/w, silent and sound versions

Based on the play by Charles Bennett

British International Pictures

UK

SPOILER WARNING

ESSENTIAL HITCHCOCK

Hitchcock kickstarts the 'talking pictures' phenomenon in Britain with a return to the thriller stylings of The Lodger. *Exploring the potential of synchronised sound while still busting out his trademark visual flourishes, Hitch casually reinvents cinema as we know it.*

Blackmail launches out of the gate in breathtaking style. In one of Hitchcock's typically efficient montages, a Flying Squad van races to a dingy London bedsit where detectives apprehend a criminal before convicting and imprisoning him. Audiences barely had time to take their hats off before the prologue was over. There's no dialogue throughout this sequence, but somewhere beneath the score we hear diegetic sound for the first time in the Hitchcanon: van doors opening, boots on the ground, glass breaking. And then, around eight minutes in, British sound cinema explodes into life as a detective's plummy voice utters those immortal, unforgettable words: "Well, we've finished earlier tonight than I expected." OK, so it's not quite *The Jazz Singer*'s "Wait a minute: you ain't heard nothin' yet!", but this is Britain, we're not show-offs.

Back at the police station Detective Frank Webber (John Longden) meets his girlfriend Alice (Anny Ondra), and they have *an actual conversation we can hear*. It's a technological marvel, but their chat does sound a little stilted. It's partly due to the unusual way in which Alice's voice is captured: Ondra was a Czech actress, and Hitchcock didn't think her eastern European accent quite suited the daughter of a Chelsea shopkeeper. So she mouthed her lines, while English actress Joan Barry spoke them into a microphone just off camera. The convoluted technique just about works, but at the expense of free-flowing dialogue. And Barry's cut-glass, upper-class accent ("Ay say, Frenk") is arguably no more suitable than Ondra's.

Frank and Alice embark on a disastrous dinner date, concluding with him watching her leave with another man: an artist called Crewe (Cyril Ritchard). Back at Crewe's apartment, Hitchcock unleashes hell on his female protagonist, as he would in the future with more headstrong blondes who dare to transgress accepted moral boundaries. Forcing himself on Alice, Crewe drags her to his bed and attempts to rape her. She reaches out for the nearest thing she can find to defend herself, which happens to be a bread knife on the bedside table, and kills him.

It's a brutal scene, but crucial to both the film and Hitchcock's career. It's the first time he inextricably links sex and death - not with the rape attempt, which can hardly be classed as sex, but with Alice's sexual availability, her undressing for the camera (we're the voyeurs here; Crewe isn't even looking) and the lingering shot of her, post-killing, in her underwear, clutching the knife in a daze. It's an iconic Hitchcockian image, and as well as birthing an obsession that would fuel some of his greatest films, it also caps another famous trope: the imaginatively-shot killing.

The struggle between Alice and Crewe is initially shown only in shadow before moving to his bed, where all we see are the movements of the bed-curtain as the horror unfolds behind it. Hitchcock's camera pushes menacingly towards the knife, and Alice's hand reaching out for it is shortly replaced by Crewe's dead hand falling into the same position. Hitch uses both the knife and the hand as powerful visual motifs for the next sequence: wandering London in a stupor, Alice sees the stabbing in an innocent animated gin advert, and the protruding limb is mirrored in the outstretched hands of a policeman and a tramp. The latter also gifts us Hitchcock's first sound gag: as Alice encounters the vagrant, a scream we assume is hers bridges a cut to a shot of Crewe's landlady, discovering his body with the same alarmed howl. British sound cinema isn't even 45 minutes old before Alfred Hitchcock is having fun with his new toy. But wait a minute: you ain't heard nothin' yet.

The centrepiece of *Blackmail* is its entire middle act: a lengthy scene at Alice's father's shop, and the dining room behind it, on the morning after the night before. It's a study in the shifting of power between Frank, the detective boyfriend who's conveniently been assigned to the homicide and knows Alice is the killer, and 'Mr Tracy', a nefarious low-life who has proof she's guilty and blackmails the couple with this knowledge. To be truthful, the sequence is more successful in the silent version; the sound version drags a little due to a series of stodgy pauses. But it's also a showcase for the new technology, with which Hitch has enormous fun in the film's most remarkable scene.

Sitting at the breakfast table, Alice and her family endure the witterings of a visiting gossip who's morbidly delighted at having a juicy murder to yap about. Her prattle makes frequent reference to the knife used in the killing, and as Hitchcock's camera isolates Alice, the gossip's voice fades into the background - except for the word 'knife', which repeatedly slices through the soundtrack until it reaches a crescendo that almost gives Alice a heart attack. Hitchcock makes the new-fangled sound tech his own in precocious style, in order to put his audience firmly in a character's headspace. It's the aural equivalent of all those subjective point-of-view shots he used in his silents, and you can almost see (and hear) him rubbing his hands with glee at having a new tool with which to manipulate viewers.

Blackmail's final act is short but satisfying, employing another of Hitchcock's enduring tropes to apparently tie up the plot. The climactic chase at a famous landmark gets its first proper outing here after Tracy is identified by the cops as a known criminal, and his extortion plan collapses. In a thrilling pursuit, determined bobbies follow him to, through and over the British Museum, where his fate is tragically sealed. But the epilogue, *Blackmail*'s more subtle climax, cooks up an indigestible moral stew. Alice is in the clear after Tracy literally takes the fall for her, the police assuming *he* killed Crewe. But she and Frank know Tracy was only guilty of blackmail, making them morally responsible for his death. In the end they choose to live with that secret, carrying a burden of guilt they'll presumably bear forever. That concept of guilt, and its transference between characters, would become another defining theme in Hitchcock's films. And as the stories got more complex, so would the explorations of guilt.

JUNO AND THE PAYCOCK

1930, b/w
Based on the play by Seán O'Casey
British International Pictures
UK

Hitchcock faithfully adapts Irish dramatist Seán O'Casey's popular play. Its universal themes include economic hardship, unwanted pregnancy, post traumatic stress disorder and being unable to locate one's braces because one is already wearing them.

Hitchcock's first film entirely envisaged as a talking picture is everything naysayers feared cinema would become immediately after the coming of sound: static, stagey and catatonically dull. If Hitch had dropped British jaws with his groundbreaking use of the new technology in *Blackmail*, his next film clamped them firmly back in place. It's almost impossible to believe the two movies were made by the same director.

Juno And The Paycock is a long, slow look at the trials and tribulations of the Dublin-based, working class Boyle family during the Irish Civil War of 1922-23. Juno Boyle (Sara Allgood) is the family matriarch, working hard to support feckless husband Jack (Edward Chapman), troubled son Johnny (John Laurie) and flighty daughter Mary (Kathleen O'Regan). A slick city lawyer tells the impoverished Boyles they've come into a substantial inheritance, but the money never transpires. This is unfortunate, because by the time it becomes clear the cash isn't forthcoming, they've already spent most of it on garish furniture, fancy duds and a swish new gramophone. To compound their problems, the lawyer has knocked up Mary and fled the scene of the crime, and Johnny is arrested for informing on - and thereby signing the death warrant of - his republican pal.

If the Boyles are having a tough time of it, the audience isn't far behind in the misery stakes. Consciousness-challenging scenes of characters rambling on for what feels like days are unimaginatively staged and filmed almost entirely in flat, static shots. It's unclear what the story is actually about for much of it: is it a treatise on religious sectarianism and a lament for Ireland's lost sons, or a comedy about a workshy layabout? The first inkling of a plot development - the news of the inheritance - is in no rush to make an appearance, half-heartedly nudging the film out of its torpor a good third into the 90-minute running time. And Juno, the only truly sympathetic character, is relegated to the background while her useless husband witters on endlessly with his colossally annoying chum Joxer, about whom the only interesting thing is his name.

Each act unfolds in real time, and the action - such as it is - takes place almost entirely in the Boyles' living room, reinforcing the sensation of watching a filmed play. Hitchcock would later wring bucketfuls of entertainment out of single-setting films like *Lifeboat*, *Rope*, *Dial M For Murder* and *Rear Window*, but here the location stymies rather than stimulates the drama. In fairness, contemporary critics praised the film for these very reasons: it brought a reasonably faithful adaptation of the play to a wider audience, and was a showcase for the starring troupe of actors. Uncharacteristically, Hitchcock rejected this praise, believing it reflected more on the quality of the source material than his presentation of it.

While *Juno And The Paycock* would be a mediocre picture by any filmmaker's standards, it's borderline baffling how Alfred Hitchcock came to direct such a stagnant experience. It's not that he was infallible, least of all at this early stage in his career, but most of his previous films had been adaptations of plays and novels and all were strikingly cinematic. Only *Easy Virtue* betrays its stage roots, and even that featured sparks of Hitchcockian ingenuity. Subjective point-of-view shots and witty editing are conspicuous by their absence here; Hitch pans his camera between characters rather than cutting, and occasionally edits two jarringly similar wide shots together. And while his favourite themes are no guarantees of an enjoyable film, *Juno* suffers more without them than, say, *The Farmer's Wife* does.

The film's failings could easily be ascribed to the restrictions of the new sound technology, if only Hitchcock hadn't made Britain's first talkie, *Blackmail*, with such consummate skill and style just a few months earlier. It doesn't help that where *Blackmail* relied heavily on visual information with which Hitch could weave his magic, *Juno And The Paycock* is weighed down with pages of dialogue. It's significant that Johnny is the most interesting character simply because he says the least, leaving you to wonder what's going on in his obviously troubled noggin. It's hard not to come to the conclusion that the play was simply a poor choice of source material in the first place.

Although Hitchcock bemoaned the film in later years, he was keen to point out a particular effect that audiences may have taken for granted. As the Boyles and assorted hangers-on sit listening to the gramophone, a funeral procession outside catches Johnny's ear. We don't know it yet - although we may guess - but Johnny is harbouring a dark secret concerning the deceased. Hitchcock conveys his anguish with a push in from a wide shot to a close up of Johnny (no mean feat considering the bulky, noisy camera equipment) which excludes the rest of the family, emphasising his isolation. Meanwhile the song on the record fades away while the sounds of the funeral, which we don't see, become clearer. It might be the only subjective moment in the film, and it took some ingenuity to pull off: while a group of people shuffled about and mumbled in one corner of the studio to imply the mourners outside, the sound of the record was achieved by a prop man singing in another corner, through a megaphone and with a clothes peg on his nose to replicate the tinny sound of the gramophone. You can't help but wonder if the behind-the-scenes mechanics of Hitch's filmmaking would have been far more fun to watch than the finished product.

Juno And The Paycock finally wraps up with one of Hitchcock's most depressing endings, which perhaps befits the viewing experience. Juno's final speech could have been heart-wrenching under different circumstances, but here it's like forcing down the last of an inadvisably large number of bottles of stout. Talking to François Truffaut about the film, Hitch later recalled that "from a creative viewpoint, it was not a pleasant experience." If he thought making the film was a downer, he should try watching it.

MURDER!

1930, b/w

Based on the novel *Enter Sir John* by Clemence Dane

British International Pictures

UK

Hitch tries hard to reboot his mojo after the disappointing Juno And The Paycock, *adapting a murder mystery novel where the victim, suspects and detective are all actors. The stage is set for a killer show, but by and large it's an agonising performance.*

If the exclamation mark in the title points to anything, it's the overwhelming sense of the theatrical that pervades *Murder!*. Opening with the stirring strings of Beethoven's Fifth, which give way to a blood-curdling scream, Hitchcock's twelfth gets its title from the fate of Edna Druce, an actress in a troupe of second-rate players who's bludgeoned to death by one of her fellow board-treaders. The alleged killer, Diana Baring (Norah Baring), is found guilty in court, but one of the jurors - Olivier-esque thespian Sir John Menier (Herbert Marshall), whom Diana idolises - takes it upon himself to clear her name using his Holmesian aspirations, his unrivalled acting skills and a trick borrowed from *Hamlet*. Also one of the suspects is a cross-dressing actor and acrobat. Is all that theatrical enough for you?

If not, consider this: while Diana awaits trial, the play she and her colleagues are touring goes on without her. Hitchcock shows the stage curtain rising on their production, then slips in a cheeky match cut to the viewing window of Diana's prison cell door being lifted. She imagines herself being called on stage to rapturous applause. Now skip forward to the final scene - a shot of her returning home to a lover, which pulls back to reveal a proscenium arch as the curtain lowers. Has Diana's whole story been a play within a film? Or a pre-execution wish-fulfilment fantasy? That might explain some of the more ludicrous developments, like Diana's skin being saved by a juror she privately adores, who comes to her rescue with the kind of entry-level detecting that even the greenest rookie bobby should have undertaken.

That's one interpretation, but what's more realistic is that such improbabilities are simply down to bad writing. *Murder!* is a frequently rushed and garbled film, requiring repeat viewings and regular rewinding to fully understand the plot. One crucial speech is delivered by an actress at high speed, in ear-piercingly shrill tones, while holding a howling infant, making you yearn for the silent days. And the mystery is conveniently wrapped up by an over-explanatory suicide note, which also underlines Hitchcock's own misgivings about the 'whodunnit' subgenre.

It's perhaps surprising, given all the murder and mystery in Hitchcock's films, that this is the only true whodunnit, but he simply didn't get on with the rules of the game. Whodunnits depend on a detective piecing together clues in a way that's withheld from the audience until the big reveal, but Hitch much preferred to let his viewers in on the plot before his characters in order to create suspense.

Yet the film redeems itself with a certain charm (mostly courtesy of Herbert Marshall, the smoothest Hitchcock lead who isn't Cary Grant) and the kind of technical proficiency we've come to expect. Jack Cox's photography is evocatively expressionistic, as is the functional set design: note that most of the exposition from the trial is given to us in the jury room scene, presumably because that set was cheaper to construct than an entire replica courtroom. Look out, too, for the scene of Sir John pondering his situation in the bathroom mirror while listening to Wagner. His thoughts, heard in voiceover (an unusual narrative device at the time), are being played through an offscreen speaker, while an unseen 30-piece orchestra on the other side of the bathroom wall provides the music.

Perhaps of most interest is a sequence wherein we *hear* a suspect being tracked down in voiceover, while Hitchcock cuts between alternating shots of Diana pacing her cell, a weather vane shifting in the wind and the shadow of a noose creeping slowly up the cell wall. Those three shots are cycled through several times, each shorter than the last, building up to a visual crescendo which - sadly - doesn't arrive. Never one to underuse a good idea though, Hitchcock filed the sequence away in his mind and successfully reworked it over 30 years later for the petrol station scene in *The Birds*. And in a brief but wild moment of expressionism, watch the carpet turn to a quivering sea of jelly for the nervous stage manager as he enters the legendary Sir John's office.

Although we're into crime and punishment territory here, *Murder!* isn't replete with what would become Hitchcockian themes. He toys again with the idea of transference of guilt, whereby Diana assumes responsibility for someone else's crime, and Sir John struggles with his own conscience after declaring her guilty despite his doubts. There's some potentially interesting debate about justice and society in the jury scene, but it's brushed aside in favour of a pointed speech about "the modern trend of psychological investigations" and "dual personality," based on Diana's defence that she must have killed Edna in a trance. This is the first timid outing in the Hitchcanon for psychoanalysis, a relatively new idea at the time which would eventually be more fully realised in films like *Spellbound* and *Psycho*.

What does seem to interest Hitchcock in *Murder!* is the notion of societal barriers, some of which are less surmountable than others. Sir John, for example, is a thoroughly upper-crust toff; a man of wealth and taste who's surrounded by middle- and lower-class characters throughout the story. While the am-dram entertainers who find themselves thrust into a murder plot are in awe of Sir John, he mixes affably with them, never patronises them and does what he can to help them. It could be argued that his regret at sending Diana away to act in "the provinces" in the past, inadvertently leading to her murder accusation, drives him to attempt to break down those potentially devastating class barriers.

But the crux of the story lies in the anguish of a character who's of mixed race, and therefore forbidden by contemporary society to conduct a relationship with a Caucasian. This social impediment is the true cause of all the plot's misery. Sadly Hitchcock rarely used his films to push any kind of agenda, and that - combined with the times he lived in - meant this particular issue remained nothing more than a handy plot device.

THE SKIN GAME

1931, b/w
Based on the play by John Galsworthy
British International Pictures
UK

The 'skin game' of the title is a rigged or dishonest scheme. But if your film is about a conniving married couple planning to blackmail a neighbour after a quarrel over ownership of land near their inherited estate, why wouldn't you call it Family Plot?

The early years of cinema saw one groundbreaking development after another, and 1931 was no different. Universal launched their iconic series of monster movies with *Dracula* and *Frankenstein*, while Warner Brothers kickstarted the gangster genre with *Little Caesar* and *The Public Enemy*. Fritz Lang directed the daring child-killer thriller *M*, and Charlie Chaplin proved silent movies weren't dead yet with *City Lights*, the year's second-highest grossing film. Meanwhile, back in Blighty, Alfred

Hitchcock - the man destined to become one of the greatest directors of all time - gave us *The Skin Game*: a film almost nobody alive today has heard of, about two toffs arguing over a pile of dirt.

You have to sympathise with Hitch at this point. He was the highest paid and best-known director in his country, but that country was the United Kingdom, and British cinema simply didn't have the funds or the technology to match its international rivals. What's more, Hitchcock's boss, head of British International Pictures John Maxwell, kept shoving plays at Hitch to adapt into films. While the director had forged movie gold from the stage version of *Blackmail*, his alchemy was less powerful on other theatrical properties, realising more cinematic potential from novels. It's not that his stage adaptations weren't successful at the time - contemporary audiences lapped them up - but Hitchcock's creativity was being crippled by industrial circumstances.

The Skin Game's plot concerns a feud between two wealthy families in the bucolic Oxfordshire village of Deepwater. The Hillcrists are landed gentry who cherish the natural surroundings of their country pile, and are ostensibly led by local squire Jack (CV France) - although matriarch Ivy (Helen Haye) is a more propulsive force. The Hornblowers, meanwhile, are nouveau riche: a family of industrialists headed by a ruthless, self-made businessman (Edmund Gwenn, whose Yorkshire-via-Wandsworth accent says everything about his character's attempt at class migration). Hornblower buys the Centry Estate, a chunk of land at the end of the Hillcrists' garden, at auction. His plan to stick a factory on it does not go down well with the Hillcrists, mainly because it would ruin the view from one of their many, many windows. So they blackmail Hornblower into giving up the land by threatening to go public with the shameful truth about his daughter-in-law Chloe (Phyllis Konstam): that she used to 'visit hotels' with married men who needed a good excuse to get divorced.

If nothing else, the film at least educates modern audiences in the social mores of '30s Britain. Who knew the most legally efficient way for fed-up husbands to leave their wives was to sleep with a prostitute? Or that an entire family could be hounded out of a county if word got out that one of their number had once - whisper it - *slept with men for money?* Sadly that's pretty much the extent of *The Skin Game*'s worth. As entertainment, it's sorely lacking: an uneventful plot is driven by unlikeable characters behaving unpleasantly to each other. Sure, Mr Hornblower - an avaricious morality vacuum who's spawned two equally awful sons - is the *de facto* villain, but the Hillcrists are unconscionable snobs. Jack's daughter Jill complains she doesn't like his associate Dawker because "he's so common", to which Jack replies: "My dear, we can't *all* be uncommon." Furthermore, the Hillcrists' main objections to Hornblower's development plans are entirely selfish and rooted in the fear of a threat to the status quo, out of which they've done very nicely for the last several generations thank you very much.

Of course the point is that nobody is so refined that they wouldn't use the silver spoons they were born with to scoop out a rival's eyeballs. The Hillcrists' shaming of Chloe to get at Hornblower is so low a blow that it drives home the film's pessimistic message: no amount of money can buy you humanity. But even at under 80 minutes, *The Skin Game* is a lengthy sermon to sit through for little reward, and it's mostly due to Hitchcock's ongoing problems translating dialogue-heavy plays to the big screen. Like *Juno And The Paycock*, most scenes play out in long, flatly-composed shots without cutaways or close ups. Some

Hitchologists point to this positively as formal experimentation, but it's hard to argue that the experiment succeeds.

Unlike *Juno*, however, and like almost all of Hitchcock's lesser works, there are moments of visual ingenuity. The difference between the rural Hillcrists and the industrially-minded Hornblowers is illustrated in a neat early shot of the Hillcrist daughter riding her horse away from the camera down a tree-lined track, which dissolves into a shot of one of the Hornblowers driving his car in the same screen direction towards their stately home. And there's some technical ingenuity going on in the auction scene, which makes heavy use of the auctioneer's point-of-view: Hitch's camera swings wildly across the crowd, pausing to pick out each bidder before darting across the room to find another. That shot is followed up by some machine-gun editing between the two rival bidders which gives the film a much-needed jolt of vitality. Watch out too for the quaintly ambitious tracking shot outside the auction house, which clearly reveals the tracks on the ground left by the wheels of the camera dolly.

Perhaps unsurprisingly, Hitchcock seems most interested in Chloe and her sordid shame, and her scenes are constructed and executed with more thought and attention than most. Hitch certainly relishes the chance to employ Phyllis Konstam's décolletage to signify Chloe's promiscuous past. Troublingly, that fascination turned a little sinister during filming, when Konstam was unceremoniously dunked in a pond ten times before Hitch was satisfied with one shot - which he never used. It would be an early instance of Hitchcock mistreating his actresses, and a disturbing sign of things to come.

Ultimately it seems there just wasn't enough in *The Skin Game* to tickle the Hitchcock pickle. The class distinctions seen in *The Farmer's Wife*, *Champagne* and *Murder!* are present but less acutely observed here, and there's a near-total absence of the themes that most engaged the director's attention. "I didn't make it by choice," Hitch later said, "and there isn't much to be said about it." In which case, let's move on.

RICH AND STRANGE

1931, b/w
Based on the novel by Dale Collins
British International Pictures
UK

A husband, a wife and a cat experience a series of unfortunate events in this technically ambitious, globe-trotting comedy-drama. But whatever fate throws at them, Hitchcock firmly believes nothing he could come up with is as absurd as the idea of marriage.

If the moral of Hitchcock's *The Skin Game* was that money can't buy you common decency, then his next film wants you to know that it's equally unlikely to buy you happiness. In fact, according to *Rich And Strange*, all money can really buy you is a calamitous holiday, the chance to drown in an exotic, distant ocean, and a steaming bowl of stir-fried cat. Sadly history does not record whether Hitch did most of these musings on the dreadful effects of vast wealth from his four-storey Kensington pad or his weekend retreat in leafy Surrey.

White-collar nine-to-fiver Fred Hill (Henry Kendall) and housewife Emily (Joan Barry) are happily married, which in an Alfred Hitchcock film is as sure a sign as any of impending disaster. While Emily seems quite content sewing dresses and having her husband's steak and kidney pudding on the table every night, Fred is bored witless of the daily grind and dreams of adventure on the high seas. Mere seconds after expressing his frustration one evening, Fred receives the conveniently-timed news that he's inherited a fortune. The Hills immediately pack their bags and set off on an odyssey that will TEAR THEIR LIVES APART. And then put them back together again.

What follows is a darkly cynical romcom that's equal parts frothy travelogue, adultery drama and survival movie, and is as tonally unbalanced as that sounds. A jaunty prologue plays out like a carefully choreographed musical number, with Hitch-cock's flair for visual comedy enhancing a sequence showing Fred's evening commute to be a regular kerfuffle of miserable English weather and public-transport-based awkwardness. The laughs continue through the early part of the Hills' round-the-world trip, but when they board a cruise ship and get involved in a four-cornered love triangle - a love quadrilateral, if you will - things get a bit less chucklesome. In fact, the final half hour is virtual flat-out despair, as the couple's extramarital dalliances dissolve and they're forced to reconcile while facing certain doom on a sinking ship / gigantic metaphor. Ethnic stereotyp-ing compounds the last act's despair: when they're rescued by Chinese pirates who impassively watch one of their own crew die horribly, before proudly displaying the skin of a cute kitty they've just cooked and served to the unsuspecting couple, it's not just the Hills who are left with a bad taste in their mouths.

The uncertainty over exactly what the film wants to be even stretches to the bizarre inclusion of intertitles, as if nobody's told it it's not a silent movie. Those captions aren't entirely intrusive, but arguably we don't need one that says "Fred" before the character we know full well to be Fred appears; much less do we need it twice.

Despite the film's awkward mood swings, it executes each of those moods perfectly well. The comedy is deft but not broad, the melodrama is affecting (we want the Hills' marriage to succeed, even though Fred is an ungrateful berk and Emily's affair seems to bring her genuine happiness) and the desperation of their climactic situation is palpably grim. And, of course, the Hitchcock touch is sprinkled throughout. The jump cuts of the boggle-eyed pair taking in the sights of Paris are refreshingly expressionistic, and the optically treated point-of-view shots Hitch loves to use are rife: watch the words on the ship's restaurant menu queasily float out towards a seasick Fred, or the note from Emily's admirer disappear in a blur as her eyes fill up with tears.

There's an underlying sense in the film that Fred and Emily are at the mercy of some malevolent (or perhaps benevolent) force; a supernatural agent determined to make them appreciate what they've got by putting their marriage through a series of tests. The timing of Fred's inheritance is nothing short of uncanny given that he's only just finished bitching about his terrible life; fate conveniently places sexual temptation before both of them on the love boat, and we never see exactly what sinks the ship on which they make their return journey. A potential metatextual resolution may have existed in a scene Hitchcock described to director Peter Bogdanovich, though if it was ever filmed it wasn't included in the finished film. In the scene, after their ordeal is over, the Hills relate their adventures to a chubby, balding stranger. "No," he tells them in familiar east London tones, "I don't think it'll make a movie."

That depiction of a troubled marriage, a theme mined more extensively here than in any of the six previous Hitchcock films to have dealt with wedded woes, is arguably the most fascinating aspect of *Rich And Strange*. When the Hills get squiffy after a night of Euro-sauciness at the Folies Bergère, and Fred presents Emily with a slinky negligee, she remarks "I can't wear this, people will think we aren't married," to which Fred responds: "Doesn't feel a bit as if we are". Imagine two people having so much fun that it's like they're not married! Later, Emily pours out her thoughts on love to a stranger she's falling for. "It makes everything difficult and dangerous," she ruminates. "It makes people frightened when they're happy and sadder when they're sad."

This is gloomy stuff from a director who had been married less than five years, but it takes on new levels of bleakness when you take into account that his wife Alma has been at his story-telling side the whole time. She even co-wrote *Rich And Strange*, adapting it from a novel rumoured to have been inspired by the Hitchcocks' own honeymoon and recent Atlantic cruise. What makes a husband and wife so intent on portraying marriage as a ludicrous, unworkable concept; a doomed experiment willingly undertaken by misery-loving masochists? Alfred and Alma would stay married, through thick and thin, until his death in 1980, so they must have discovered some way to survive the torment. Whatever went on between them, one thing is certain: if you were to describe their relationship in two words, you'd struggle to find more appropriate adjectives than 'rich' and 'strange'.

ALMA

Alma Reville was one of the most important and influential women in film history. That's a cold, hard fact, and if you didn't know it already then **Hitchology**'s work here is done (although please keep reading, **Hitchology**'s work here is not quite done). There's no doubt Alfred Hitchcock was a creative genius, but every single film he directed was, in some way, a partnership with his wife, Alma. His legacy is also hers: the Hitchcanon would not be what it is without the work, support, advice and saint-shaming patience she gifted him for his entire career.

Born in Nottingham on August 14th, 1899, mere hours after Hitchcock's own entrance into the world, Alma later moved to Middlesex with her family. Her dad worked for the London Film Company's costume department at Twickenham studios, and after leaving school she got a job there too, in the 'cutting' department - a good four years before Hitchcock started his first job in film. Before long Alma established herself as a proficient editor and, like her future husband, was talented and multi-skilled enough to quickly climb the ranks. Across her short careers at the London Film Company and Famous Players-Lasky in Islington, where she moved to in 1921, she graduated to continuity girl, script editor and assistant director. She even did a little acting, playing the daughter of David Lloyd George in a biopic of the wartime Prime Minister.

It was at Islington Studios that Alma first clapped eyes on Alfred Hitchcock, who was then designing title cards for *Appearances* (1922), a film she was cutting. It would be two years before they spoke, though, during which time Famous Players-Lasky packed up their London operation and Alma was made redundant. But her reputation was well-known across the industry, and in 1923 Hitchcock - who had by then risen to the level of assistant director - asked her to work with him on Graham Cutts's *Woman To Woman* as editor. Alfred and Alma became closer professionally and personally, and on December 2nd, 1926, they were married.

Alma would work on other projects during the 1920s and '30s, and in the infancy of Hitchcock's directorial career she was by far the better-known of the pair, earning industry plaudits and magazine articles long before anyone showed much interest in Hitch. Eventually though, she devoted herself exclusively to her husband's pictures and their only child (Patricia, born in 1928), and quietly melted into the background. For Hitchcock's entire career she would collaborate with him at all levels, from searching for suitable properties to adapt into films, through writing, casting and shooting to editing. Her notes were invaluable to him; her approval essential.

Other collaborators came and went, but the Hitchcocks remained a team through thick and thin. It soon became tradition for the scripts of a Hitchcock film to be bashed into shape at their family homes - first in London, then in LA's Bel Air - where a succession of writers joined Alfred and Alma for lengthy brainstorming sessions. Husband and wife rarely gave themselves screen credit for their writing, but they were both knee-deep in the process. After becoming a grandmother Alma took her foot off the writing gas (her last official credit was 1950's *Stage Fright*), and it may not be a coincidence that the further towards the end of Hitchcock's filmography you get, the less believable and sympathetic the female characters become.

And yet Alma remained an invaluable asset to Hitch. Biographer Patrick McGilligan notes that she devised the car chase in *To Catch A Thief*, based entirely on her memories of the French Riviera roads, and that filming it with a helicopter - an uncommon practice at the time - was her idea. According to *Psycho* historian Stephen Rebello, it was Alma who convinced Hitchcock to give Bernard Herrmann's music for the shower scene a listen; the director was originally set on the idea of leaving the scene unscored. And legend has it that it was Alma who first spotted Tippi Hedren in a commercial and recommended her to Hitch for *The Birds*, although if many of the behind-the-scenes stories of that film are to be believed, she may have wished she'd just changed the channel and kept her mouth shut.

But therein lies another of Alma's formidable strengths: the ability to put up with her husband's bullshit. Their marriage was certainly tested, even beyond the extraordinary circumstances of their living and working together for 50 years, and almost exclusively by him. (McGilligan is reasonably certain Alma let off some extramarital steam with her *Stage Fright* and *Strangers On A Train* co-writer Whitfield Cook.) It's impossible to know what went on behind closed doors, and it's clear that Alma and Alfred loved each other deeply, but it's also clear there are times when he didn't deserve her loyalty and devotion.

Troubled relationships - usually marriages - crop up in around two-thirds of Hitchcock's films, and there must have been a reason for that. But given Alma's level of involvement (not least with 1931's quasi-autobiographical *Rich And Strange*, one of her credited co-writing gigs and one of the most sceptical views of marriage in the Hitchcanon), it may be safe to assume that the view of men and women as fundamentally incompatible is, ironically, one that both Hitchcocks agreed on. And if that's the case, maybe Alfred and Alma worked out their issues on the page and screen, rather than in private? If so, all those couples' botheration - from *The Pleasure Garden*'s Mr and Mrs Levet to *Frenzy*'s Mr and (ex-) Mrs Blaney, via *Mr & Mrs Smith*'s Mr and Mrs Smith - might just have been a by-product of saving their creators' marriage.

A full and detailed record of Alma's contributions to Hitchcock's films - and therefore to western cinema as an art form - is likely to remain a mystery, thanks to her modesty and reticence regarding her work. That may have been her decision, or it may have been the result of the film industry's ongoing problem with recognising the talents of its women. It may even have been down to her husband, who was much happier in the limelight than she was - although Hitch at least let it be known that she was a valued collaborator, which is more than he did for most of those who contributed to his pictures. But notes and diaries are still surfacing, and dogged researchers continue the hunt for further evidence of her skills. It's worth repeating: Alma Reville was one of the most important and influential women in film history. This is one lady who mustn't be allowed to vanish.

NUMBER SEVENTEEN

1932, b/w

Based on the play by J Jefferson Farjeon

British International Pictures

UK

Hitchcock's shortest feature film is a madcap mystery that packs a lot into its running time – a spooky house, a dead body that isn't, and a rollicking finale on a train. It even finds time to tackle the big questions: just how effective a murder weapon is a sausage?

Hitchcock's time under John Maxwell at British International Pictures had not been quite the blockbusting success either man had hoped for. Despite finessing his skills as a director of silent films and triumphantly introducing talking pictures to Britain with *Blackmail*, Hitch had spent most of the past five years struggling with stage adaptations and cumbersome new sound technology. In 1931 he'd been planning a film called *London Wall* when Maxwell inexplicably took the project off him, handed it to another director, Thomas Bentley, and gave Hitchcock yet another play to shoot: *Number Seventeen*, which Bentley had wanted to direct. Hitch's contract at BIP was coming to an end anyway, but nobody was about to shed any tears over it.

Hitch and *Number Seventeen*'s co-writer Rodney Ackland would later go on record to say that in revenge against Maxwell, they turned the original play - one of many 'spooky house' mysteries popular at the time - into a grotesque parody of spooky house mysteries. They also admitted they didn't do a very good job of it. But Hitchologist Charles Barr argues that the play was already a parody, and with around a century's distance, it's tough for modern eyes to work out which bits of the film are meant to be satire and what's just cheesy, outdated filmmaking. So while you'd be forgiven for assuming it's too weird to be any good, bear in mind that it works better if you don't take it too seriously. Surrender yourself to its freewheeling plot and zippy energy and you might just have fun with it, as Hitch himself seems to have done by accident.

The spooky house in question is, of course, No. 17, and the mysteries it contains number at least that many. Whose is the body at the top of the stairs? How did it get there? Why would you wander into such a house in the middle of the night just because you saw some strange lights inside? And what's a homeless man with a sausage in his pocket got to do with any of it? These and many, many more baffling oddities are posed during the film's sprightly running time, and most of them are eventually answered, providing you can pay attention and surf the comically relentless waves of plot twists. An immediate second viewing is not just recommended but essential, because *a)* everything makes slightly more sense, and *b)* it's only an hour long.

At any rate, *Number Seventeen* is notable for its inclusion of much that would become recognisable Hitchcockian tropes.

There's murder (or is there?*), a charming villain, extensive use of a staircase, the debut occurrence of dangers on a train, and - if you don't count *The Lodger*'s enigmatic killer, which most Hitch scholars don't - there's the first real MacGuffin: a stolen necklace which drives the plot but is essentially irrelevant. And we're dragged through the madness by an apparently ordinary bloke, Fordyce (John Stuart), the kind of everyman who'll act as an audience surrogate in dozens of future Hitchcock classics.

Themes familiar from previous films are also present and correct, not least the amusing lower-class comic relief, who this time takes the shape of Ben (Leon M. Lion), the sausage-wielding vagrant who can't stop saying things like "Lumme!" and "Gawd, luv a duck!". The recurring visual motif is back too: down your drink every time a disembodied hand menacingly pokes into frame and you'll be sozzled before the halfway mark.

Technically, Hitchcock pulls out as many stops here as John Maxwell would pay for. Jack Cox's lighting is innovative and evocative, contributing enormously to the shadowy, creepy atmosphere of the house. There's a lengthy fight sequence, the relative brutality of which we haven't seen before in Hitchcock. And we also see his first big stunt: a literally suspenseful scene in which Fordyce and plucky companion Rose Ackroyd (Ann Casson) crash through a top-floor banister and find themselves dangling over a two-storey drop. Yes, you can see the safety wire holding them up. It's 1932, give 'em a break.

But the most spectacular element of *Number Seventeen* is easily the raucously shot and edited climactic train chase, which doesn't feature in the play - Hitchcock was never too demure to take vast liberties with his source material if he thought he'd had a better idea. For reasons far too convoluted to go into here,

---

*While the apparent corpse on the landing turns out to be less dead than is initially assumed, a luckless train engineer is callously offed during the finale. So let's say yes, there is a murder.

Fordyce finds himself using a bus packed with passengers (despite the fact that it's the early hours of the morning) to pursue a gang of crooks on a train heading for a cross-channel ferry. Much of the chase employs painfully obvious miniatures, as if Hitch has taken a camera into his attic and filmed his Hornby collection, but he deftly cuts them together with footage of a full size, moving train that looks like it was hair-raisingly perilous to shoot. And what cutting: the train sequence is a blizzard of shots, far more ambitiously edited than anything Hitchcock had done up to this point, and it remains one of his most thrilling sequences.

But don't be fooled; Hitchcock is still learning on the job. The early scenes of *Number Seventeen* are dangerously off-putting thanks to some rattled-through dialogue and a confusing sense of geography (it takes far too long to realise there are *two* sets of stairs in the house, which is why one ascending character doesn't bump into another who's descending). And this is a primitive time for Hitch in terms of a musical score: Adolph Hallis' soundtrack cues are perfectly appropriate but pop up at entirely random moments, none of which are the right ones.

With its tongue rammed firmly into its cheek, *Number Seventeen*'s effortless blend of murder, mystery and mirth makes it a worthy companion to *Blackmail* in the director's formative works. Hitchcock unfairly referred to it as "a disaster", but there's a strong sense he was thinking more of the circumstances in which he made it than the finished product. After all, any film whose final minutes include two enormous reveals - one of a secret identity, one of disgusting underwear - can't be all bad.

WALTZES FROM VIENNA

1934, b/w

Based on the stage musical by Heinz Reichart, Dr AM Willner & Ernest Marischka

Gaumont British Picture Corporation / A Tom Arnold Production

UK

It's Vienna, 1866, and one man is about to make history. Well, actually it's Shepherd's Bush, 1933, and one man is about to make a film that history has virtually forgotten. If you're a Johann Strauss fan looking for a historically accurate, reverent biopic of your hero, look away now.

Finally liberated from his contract with British International Pictures, Hitchcock found himself a free agent in 1933. But with a child, two houses and a crippling steak habit to support, he couldn't afford to sit around waiting for the perfect opportunity. So when theatre impresario Tom Arnold approached him with the idea to adapt a musical romance about Austrian composer Johann Strauss II, Hitch agreed, despite having made precisely no musicals before. He had a foolproof plan to overcome that hurdle, though: simply ditch all the songs and turn it into a comedy.

As was customary, Hitch filleted his source material for the elements that suited his purpose (in this case a fractious bond between Strauss and his father, Johann Strauss I, and an entirely fictional love story) and binned the rest. With Alma and co-writer Guy Bolton, he used those relationships to construct a solid - if flawed - romcom around the conception of Strauss's best-loved banger, *The Blue Danube*. In Hitchcock's flippantly revisionist take, the famous waltz would be the result of an awkward love triangle, filial rivalry and - most improbably - a brief tour of a bakery.

Struggling composer Johann "Schani" Strauss Jr (Esmond Knight) is in love with Rasi (Jessie Matthews), who works at her father's bakery. While trying to come up with a chart-topping waltz, Strauss finds matters complicated by the wealthy Countess Helga von Stahl (Fay Compton), who offers to get his work published and played in return for certain favours. Standard romantic comedy tropes - deception, jealousy, misunderstandings - are deployed with varying degrees of success: Rasi's baffling insistence that Strauss chooses between his music and a life with her as a baker's assistant loses audience sympathy, which is antithetical to the casting of lovable musical starlet Jessie Matthews. But the script is beautifully structured, especially in the way it manoeuvres its characters towards a rousing climactic showdown.

Hitch mines an unexpected amount of laughs from this potentially bone-dry scenario, beginning with a sequence so packed with slapstick that you wouldn't be surprised if Charlie Chaplin appeared, kicked Strauss up the bum and waddled off into the distance. The comedy works surprisingly well, but the film's most notable achievement is the effectiveness of its soundtrack. Hitch had been keen on the idea of marrying music to film since the introduction of synchronised sound; the total lack of control over what music was played over his silent films must have driven him potty. Like *Blackmail*'s innovative use of dialogue, *Waltzes From Vienna* takes a primitive film-making concept and immediately starts to subvert it, blurring the boundaries between diegetic and non-diegetic music, and using the score to elicit audience emotions previously achieved through editing.

We also see Hitchcock playing with music in the way he gradually introduces *The Blue Danube*, as Strauss develops it from a simple idea to a full-blown masterpiece. Part of that development sees Strauss in the bakery kitchen watching pastries being chucked about, and the rhythm of them landing inspires the staccato 'da-da, da-da' that's such a familiar part of the waltz. It's devilishly mischievous of Hitch to suggest such a humdrum genesis for a timeless, iconic work of art, but perfectly reflects his own attitude to creativity. "Some films are slices of life," he famously claimed, "mine are slices of cake." And after all, what is *The Blue Danube* waltz but the ultimate Viennese Whirl?

There's probably more self-reflexivity in *Waltzes From Vienna* than Hitchcock might have admitted. Like Hitch, Strauss is a frustrated artist struggling against external forces, seemingly unable to realise his full potential. And while the film's protagonist is desperate to move music out of the rut of tradition represented by his father, its director was equally hungry to further the possibilities of his medium and leave his predecessors (and, perhaps, the father figure of his former boss John Maxwell) behind.

Indeed, every successive Hitchcock film at this time was technically superior to the last (politely overlooking *Juno And*

The Paycock), and *Waltzes From Vienna* is no exception. It's a hugely cinematic adaptation of a stage show, with elaborate set designs, innovative shooting angles and deep compositions that draw the eye to exactly where it needs to be. Hitch even goes subtle with his camera moves, describing a long, slow arc around a piano that cuts beautifully with a gentle push-in to an image of Rasi singing that exists only in Strauss's head. There are lovely match cuts and wipes dotted about too, including a slightly ostentatious 'clock wipe' from a close up of a pocket watch.

Sadly, Hitchcock didn't care for the film. Though it doesn't show, he reportedly felt out of his depth making it, and took it out on his cast, frequently interrupting rehearsals and takes with outbursts of sarcasm and rudeness. According to Hitchcock biographer Donald Spoto, Jessie Matthews was singled out for ill treatment because Hitchcock thought she was overpaid and overrated. His tendency to direct his frustrations at his actresses was becoming, it seemed, a more common occurrence.

But everything was about to change for Hitchcock, whose prospects at this time were gloomy at best. While *Waltzes From Vienna* was in production at Gaumont-British studios in Shepherd's Bush, his former producer at Gainsborough, Michael Balcon, visited him and asked him what he'd like to do next. Hitchcock said he and screenwriter Charles Bennett had an idea for an original story based on the popular literary character Bulldog Drummond, but John Maxwell held the rights to the character. Balcon convinced Hitchcock to buy the rights from Maxwell, then promptly bought them off Hitchcock for twice what he'd paid and signed the director for a five-picture deal. The two friends were back in business. Hitchcock, the man who knew too much about filmmaking to carry on churning out mediocre movies, was about to find his true calling.

THE MAN WHO KNEW TOO MUCH

1934, b/w

Story by Charles Bennett and D.B. Wyndham Lewis

Gaumont-British Picture Corporation

UK

Paving the way for dozens of modern thrillers about kidnapped daughters, The Man Who Knew Too Much *features a heroic Dad with no particular set of skills besides furniture–hurling. Fortunately Mum is on hand with a deadly shotgun and one of Hitchcock's most iconic screams.*

The Alfred Hitchcock you know begins here. That doesn't mean you can dismiss everything that came before; that was merely the Alfred Hitchcock you maybe don't know as well. But from this point, Hitch brought all he'd learned over 16 films into focus: his abilities to tell a story visually, to arrange the elements of *mise en scène*, editing and sound to create mood and suspense, to come up with innovative and unusual ways to make a point, and to master rapidly evolving technical processes. That focus was the suspense thriller, and the first unqualified success in that field was *The Man Who Knew Too Much*, the film so good he made it twice.

Hitchcock's grand plan to create an original story based on the literary character Bulldog Drummond slowly mutated into a story that didn't require Drummond at all. In the intrepid adventurer's place came the unassuming Bob Lawrence (Leslie Banks), a classic Hitchcock everyman who goes on a winter sports holiday to St Moritz with wife Jill (Edna Best) and daughter Betty (Nova Pilbeam), only to become embroiled in unlikely shenanigans involving a British spy, a diabolical mastermind and an assassination plot. Inspired in part by the simmering European tensions following Hitler's rise to power in 1933, Hitch and his co-writers made breezy, breathless entertainment out of global political discord. It would be a recurring approach for nine of the 16 features he made between this point and the end of World War II.

The key players are introduced in a beautifully efficient five-minute opening sequence. Bob may be unexceptional, but we learn that Jill - in a glaringly literal example of the Chekhov's Gun principle of storytelling - is a crack shot with a rifle. Three more characters are each assigned a small motif which Hitch would subsequently use as narrative shorthand: Betty is given a brooch by her mother which takes on a dark significance when it's returned to Jill later, minus its wearer; Jill's shooting opponent Ramon is disliked by Betty because he overuses hair cream, and a close up of his slicked-back barnet at a key moment proves she was right; meanwhile Peter Lorre's suspicious-looking Abbott shows off a chiming pocket watch that will give him away twice before the credits roll. Finally there's the Lawrences' new friend Louis Bernard, a ski-jumper with a dark secret hinted at in a single wordless exchange with Abbott.

For now though, these scenes are light-hearted and fun. Bob's practical joke with a length of wool and a room full of dancers is exactly the kind of thing Hitch would love to have pulled himself. But out of nowhere comes a gunshot, and Louis just has time to give Jill a key and a cryptic message before he breathes his last. In the blink of an eye everything changes, and the Lawrences are plunged into intrigue and adventure. Hitchcock loved to take ordinary characters and put them through far-fetched, life-threatening botheration - after all, there's no better audience surrogate than the average Joe (or Bob, or Richard, or Roger). The Lawrences represent the first full realisation of this dastardly trope, as their daughter is kidnapped to stop them telling the police what Louis Bernard, now revealed as a ski-jumping spy, knew.

There's a brief lull in the excitement for a government wonk to explain the film's MacGuffin - the plot to assassinate a foreign dignitary - but from there the film barrels off into a sequence of increasingly dramatic events, barely pausing for breath. Most memorable is the Albert Hall concert, a six-minute montage of shots and reverse shots cutting between an anxious Jill and what she sees: the assassin, his target, and an orchestra preparing for a crescendo we know (but she doesn't) is the cue for murder. That privileged knowledge the audience has over the characters is Hitchcock's primary tool for suspense, and here it's backed up by progressively rapid editing and a merciless ramping up of tension from the music. And apart from a brief cutaway to the villain's hideout, in which just three words are spoken, the scene contains no dialogue. Hitchcock, ever the visual storyteller, simply didn't need it.

We're also gifted the first great Hitchcock villain in Peter Lorre's charming, scarred and bizarrely-coiffed Abbott, a prototype Bond baddie if ever there was one (it's no coincidence that 20 years later Lorre would play Le Chiffre, 007's original nemesis, in an American TV adaptation of *Casino Royale*). Hitch liked his antagonists cultured and erudite: all the better for enabling wittily sinister dialogue with his heroes, as we'll see with Claude Rains in *Notorious*, John Dall in *Rope* and James Mason in *North By Northwest*.

The Man Who Knew Too Much contains a couple of other small but effective moments of Hitchcockian wryness that crop up in many of his films. First, the abstract, theatrically staged insert shot: here, when the dancers spot the hole in the window left by the bullet that kills Louis Bernard, seven pointing fingers come into shot one by one to indicate it. It's an arresting image, over and done with before you have chance to wonder why six extra people felt the need to point at the hole, or what peculiar tableau their bodies must have formed for their arms to appear in that arrangement. Second, look out for the moments during the climactic siege where Hitch humanises the (mostly working class) supporting characters. A copper grumbles about long hours, a postman refuses to let a deadly shootout stop him doing his rounds, a bachelor is congratulated by a policeman on being unmarried (a quintessential Hitchcock grace note) and an officer holed up in a confectioner's shop helps himself to a mid-siege snack, 54 years before one of *Die Hard*'s terrorists succumbed to the same temptation.

Hitchcock had finally found an ideal working environment at the Gaumont-British studios in Shepherd's Bush, working for his old friend Michael Balcon, who gave Hitch the creative freedom he'd longed for. With his new writing partner Charles Bennett, he would go on to craft a handful of the finest thrillers produced in Britain. But as good as *The Man Who Knew Too*

Much is, it was merely a taster for what was to come next. Alfred Hitchcock was ready to take the British thriller a step further. Several steps further, in fact.

THE 39 STEPS

1935, b/w

Based on the novel by John Buchan

Gaumont-British Picture Corporation

UK

"Beautiful, mysterious woman pursued by gunmen? Sounds like a spy story!" "That's exactly what it is." Hitchcock seals his rep as Britain's most exciting director by adapting (and improving) John Buchan's famous novel about the trouble with Hannay.

The Man Who Knew Too Much had marked the beginning of what critic Raymond Durgnat coined Hitchcock's 'classic thriller sextet': six successive comedy-infused thrillers which mark an extraordinary purple patch in the director's career. The sextet boasts two masterpieces, and the first of those is *The 39 Steps*. Like its predecessor, the film picks up thematic and stylistic elements from previous films in the Hitchcanon, polishes them to perfection and drops them neatly into a new adventure: a ripping cross-country yarn that sets the template for much of Hitch's future work.

In this high-scoring game of Hitchcock bingo, an unremarkable man (Richard Hannay, played by Robert Donat) is wrongly accused of a crime and becomes entangled in an improbable spy plot. Determined to uncover the true culprits and prove his innocence, he's hunted across the country by ineffectual police and a criminal network led by a charming, deadly villain. He forms a frosty alliance with a beautiful blonde (Madeleine Carroll's Pamela), and in a series of suspenseful episodes including an eventful train journey, they race against time to foil the villains' plot in a thrilling climax at a famous location. The script tosses off casual cynical references to marriage, and at one point a familiar portly chap wanders into frame to maintain his own brand recognition. House!

Everything described above - barring the character names - can be applied to at least two subsequent Hitchcock films (*Saboteur* and *North By Northwest*), and most of it to several more, which is some indication of how pleased Hitch was with *The 39 Steps*. After almost a decade experimenting with different genres, techniques and working practices, he'd found his happy place. He wasn't ashamed to repeat himself if something worked, and parts of *The 39 Steps* almost feel like a tribute to earlier films. The lit-up 'MUSIC HALL' sign at the beginning echoes the 'TO-NIGHT GOLDEN CURLS' advert from *The Lodger*, *Blackmail*'s infamous bread knife finds its way into another unfortunate torso, and the symmetry of opening and closing scenes so often employed in Hitchcock's silents also returns. Like *The Ring*, *The 39 Steps*' climax replays its beginning (a show of popular working-class entertainment: boxing in *The Ring*, vaudeville here) but on a grander scale and with increased stakes.

There's little in the way of ostentatious visual trickery here, suggesting Hitchcock is more at ease with his storytelling skills. The most famous gag is the charlady's scream that mutates into a train whistle, but watch out too for shots like the one that snakes its way out of a clearly studio-bound car to show a vista of the Scottish Highlands via a hidden edit. In place of abundant bravura camerawork, *The 39 Steps'* technical excellence is found mainly in the script's construction. Working again with Charles Bennett - as well as Alma, dialogue writer Ian Hay and a number of uncredited contributors - Hitchcock crafts a ruthlessly streamlined odyssey for the hapless Hannay. Each scene ("a little film in itself," as Hitch described them) bowls along with the dexterity of a close-up magic trick, distracting you with a restless pace so you don't have time to query the myriad improbabilities and convenient twists of fate.

While its hero is bounced from one adventure to the next like an immaculately-moustachioed pinball, the script swings from comedy to danger to tragedy and back again with breathless economy. This is a film which balances something as daft as a variety show starring a preposterously knowledgeable performer called Mr Memory (basically a 1930s Google) with a heartbreaking vignette about a young woman trapped in an abusive marriage, without either scene seeming out of place. The latter also includes one of Hitchcock's ingenious silent sequences, wherein plot and characters are developed through glances, reactions and nifty editing.

Marriage is alluded to, explicitly and implicitly, throughout *The 39 Steps*, and as is so often the case, Hitchcock presents it as life's ultimate torture before cheerily packing his leading couple off towards it when the credits roll. Consider the bickering pair in the music hall with the problematic poultry, the unhappily married milkman who won't help Hannay when he says he's evading armed killers (which is true) but is happy to assist when he claims he's really having an affair (which is not), and the aforementioned abusive marriage. In a trial run for their own potential future, Hannay and Pamela end up handcuffed together and squabble relentlessly. Hitch seems of the opinion they're only a few diseased chickens away from becoming that music hall couple, until the shackled pair encounter the film's only positive representation of marriage: the Scottish innkeeper and his wife, who knows a blossoming love story when she sees it. Her observations mellow Pamela towards Hannay, leading to their eventual union through choice.

A crucial development in the sextet which actually began in the film that precedes it, *Waltzes From Vienna*, is Hitchcock's sophisticated use of music; not necessarily to tell the audience how to feel - he was confident enough in his other cinematic tools to do that - but to drive the narrative from within the film's world. Hitch commissioned the *Storm Clouds* cantata from composer Arthur Benjamin specifically for *The Man Who Knew Too Much*, and the piece plays a vital part in that story. In *The 39 Steps* Mr Memory's theme tune becomes a leitmotif: a recurring musical phrase associated with specific characters or ideas. After Hannay hears it in the first scene it becomes an unshiftable earworm, and he absent-mindedly whistles it throughout the film until it reappears in the finale. The tune is threaded through the entire plot, connecting the bookend scenes and discreetly signposting the resolution to Hannay's predicament - so discreetly, in fact, that he can't spot it even though it's literally under his nose whenever he purses his lips.

The 39 Steps was Hitchcock's first film to make a dent in overseas box office, and American producers who'd been watching the young British director's career with interest began to make overtures regarding a transatlantic move. Some of these were deflected by Hitch's producer Michael Balcon, who didn't want to lose his star director, but the fact was that Hitchcock -

who was still under contract at Gaumont-British anyway - was quite happy where he was for now, as the rest of the sextet would thrillingly demonstrate.

SECRET AGENT

1936, b/w

From the play by Campbell Dixon, based on the book
Ashenden **by W Somerset Maugham**

Gaumont-British Picture Corporation

UK

A British spy, licenced to kill, is given a mission by a superior known only by a single initial. In exotic locations and glamorous casinos he encounters beautiful women, friendly agents and a deadly villain. The name's Brodie. Edgar Brodie. You were expecting someone else?

Rumour has it that in the late 1950s, Alfred Hitchcock was approached to direct the first James Bond film. Whether or not that's correct, the disappointing truth is that a Hitch-helmed 007 adventure never came to pass, and one possible reason for that might be that he'd virtually made one already. *Secret Agent*, based on the character of Ashenden - a World War I spy created by author W Somerset Maugham - bears many of the hallmarks of the Bond books and movies long before any of them were written, suggesting a likely influence of both Maugham and Hitchcock on Ian Fleming's famous creation.

The obvious reason *Secret Agent* shares so many tropes with the Bond universe is that they both belong to the spy movie genre, whose essential ingredients are limited and frequently recycled. Those elements work because they appeal to escapism-craving audiences, and Hitchcock recognised that just as Bond's producers would. Hitch was delighted by the narrative possibilities afforded by the nuts and bolts of tradecraft, but *Secret Agent* also hints at a by-product of espionage that Hitchcock would explore again ten years later in *Notorious*: the psychological impact on an individual of constant exposure to duplicity, betrayal and death.

It's 1916, and Edgar Brodie (John Gielgud) is a British soldier on the front line in France. Recalled from action, his death is faked by the government and he's given a false identity - 'Ashenden' - and a special assignment: to head to Switzerland to stop a German agent reaching the Arabian Peninsula and furthering the enemy's progress in the Middle East. Less than thrilled with his mission but left with no choice but to undertake it, Brodie is teamed with two assistants: Elsa (Madeleine Carroll), with whom he must pose as husband and wife (a scenario which naturally allows for the odd jab at the institution of marriage), and a morally bankrupt agent known as The General (Peter Lorre). Matters are complicated, as they inevitably must be, by double agents, deadly mountain hikes and detached jacket buttons.

Despite being another spy thriller that employs many of the same themes as *The Man Who Knew Too Much* and *The 39 Steps*, *Secret Agent* enjoys nothing like the reputation of its predecessors in the classic thriller sextet. It's partly because, with the idea of 'the Hitchcock thriller' still in its infancy, those themes are experimentally - arguably unsuccessfully - tweaked here. There's the hero thrust into an extraordinary situation, except he's not an everyman, he's a trained soldier. There's the 'wrong man' pursued by the authorities for a crime he didn't commit, but he's not the hero, he's a secondary character. There's the goal that drives the plot, but it's not a MacGuffin - its every detail is clearly explained throughout the film. And there's the key scene featuring a murder, but it's committed by the good guys, and they royally bugger it up. It's like a Hitchcock film from an alternate universe where everything is almost imperceptibly, but unsettlingly, different from reality.

It also doesn't help that little effort seems to have gone into characterisation. Brodie is already by some distance the film's dullest character, but he's played with a crushing absence of charisma by John Gielgud. His reluctance to kill an enemy of the state in cold blood, despite having been a soldier in France, vaguely suggests a commentary on the morality of killing for one's country, but Hitchcock is more interested in getting to the next set piece than engineering a debate about wartime ethics. Meanwhile, Elsa is a woman who's worked hard to earn her place in the service and demands not to be patronised until the script demands that she is, with Brodie frequently ordering her to stay behind whenever he's got some exciting spy business to get on with. Then there's Robert Marvin (Robert Young), an attractive rogue with absolutely no backstory, leading any semi-intelligent viewer to question his motives from the off. But all of them are thrown into the shade by Peter Lorre's wild-eyed portrayal of the General, a loose cannon with a porn-star moustache and the sexual politics to match. Depending on your point of view, the General is either the film's MVP or just a crazy-haired sex pest. At the very least, Lorre injects a shot of vitality into the film's arm, in much the same way that he was allegedly using morphine during filming.

The set pieces are still fun though, and we're beginning to see how much Hitchcock clearly enjoys their construction and execution more than all those dreary talky bits. A macabre meeting with a double agent in a church, a suspenseful assassination viewed through a telescope, and a climactic train wreck are all genuinely exciting pieces of cinema, even if the latter is capped by a disappointingly flubbed denouement. There's also an almost entirely dialogue-free investigation of (and subsequent chase through) a chocolate factory, which unfolds with Hitchcock's trademark visual inventiveness.

One curious element of *Secret Agent* is a recurring sonic motif: a loud, monotonous sound sustained for an uncomfortably long time, as if Hitchcock was deliberately trying to give his audience tinnitus. It crops up several times throughout the film: as a chord played on a church organ - by a dead man, no less - for over two minutes; a clanging church bell (nearly 40 seconds); a Swiss folk band swirling coins in a bowl (over two minutes); the incessant hammering of machinery in the chocolate factory (around five minutes, split over two scenes), and a fire alarm (30 seconds). These droning effects, often exaggerated for subjectivity's sake, are remarkably experimental given the relative youth of the sound age, and they create a unique, peculiar soundscape. Discussing *Secret Agent* in her book *The Silent Scream*, Elisabeth Weis refers to them as "discord overwhelming apparent harmony": a sonic representation of the familiar Hitchcockian theme of chaos intruding on order.

Hitchcock wraps up his film with a rousing montage of allied troops and patriotic newspaper headlines, which seem to push the message that while all this cloak and dagger stuff might be unseemly and morally dubious, it does help to win wars. Meanwhile Brodie and Elsa resign from the spy trade; unlike James Bond, 'Ashenden' will not return. That's fine, Hitch didn't need him. He had plenty more heroes and villains in his pocket.

SABOTAGE

1936, b/w

Based on the book *The Secret Agent* by Joseph Conrad

Gaumont-British Picture Corporation

UK

War is on the horizon. Devious foreigners are everywhere. You can't even trust your nearest and dearest. But it's not all doom and gloom; here's a film with a young Charles Hawtrey mansplaining the fertility rate of oysters to a baffled girlfriend.

Hitchcock's run of jaunty British suspense thrillers took a sinister turn with *Sabotage*, a film whose title translates as 'Terrorism' in modern terms, and which uncomfortably predicts acts of terror perpetrated in the real world decades after its release. Its most notorious scene culminates in the killing of a schoolboy, to whom Hitch has spent the best part of an hour endearing his audience, in an attack which also claims 50 or so other innocent lives - including, most egregiously, a cute puppy. The dark side of Hitchcock, so far only hinted at, was finally beginning to show its face.

In *Sabotage*, that face belongs to Karl Verloc (Oscar Homolka), perhaps Hitch's most monstrous and fully-realised villain to date. Verloc runs a cinema in southeast London, in the back rooms of which he lives with his considerably younger wife (Sylvia Sidney) and her teenage brother Stevie (Desmond Tester). Verloc is also a saboteur, as we discover immediately: a power cut temporarily cripples the city, and four engineers at Battersea Power Station trace the fault to sand dumped in a generator (in one of Hitchcock's weirdly abstract moments of exposition, each man sombrely utters a single word: "Sand!" "Sabotage!" "Wrecking!" "Deliberate!"). Menacing music accompanies a shot of Verloc walking away from Battersea, and if you were still in any doubt of his guilt, once he gets home we see him wash sand from his hands.

Hitchcock wants us to know Verloc's a wrong 'un as soon as possible, because Mrs Verloc and Stevie clearly don't, and so the suspense is already underway. Will they find out? When? How? The answers to those questions are, respectively: of course, when it's too late, and horribly. Stevie will become the victim of another, far deadlier deed of sabotage after Verloc's masters demand a more effective demonstration than the laughably feeble act of turning London's lights off for a few minutes. On the plus side for Stevie, he's killed in Hitchcock's most nail-biting exercise in mounting tension so far - one which caused controversy in 1936 and continues to do so today.

Sent by Verloc to take a mysterious package to Piccadilly Circus, Stevie is the mule who unwittingly carries a bomb from Camberwell to the West End. It's Verloc's intention that Stevie will have dropped off the package by 1.30pm and be long gone when it explodes at 1.45 - after all, he's not a total monster (just kidding, he very much is). So begins an excruciating sequence in which Stevie's journey is repeatedly delayed, either by chance or by his own infuriating absent-mindedness. Hitchcock frequently reminds us of the 1.45 deadline while cutting between close-ups of the package, shots of clocks mercilessly ticking away the minutes and Stevie blissfully bimbling through London on a bus as if he's got all day. But he hasn't got all day, and just when your nerves can't take any more, the bus explodes and the controversy begins.

Critics immediately turned on Hitchcock for killing Stevie, and Hitch took it to heart, later claiming he'd made a terrible mistake in denying the audience the appropriate relief from the tension. But Stevie's death illustrates the terrible human cost of sabotage / terrorism, and sets up the rest of the story in a way that would have been impossible had he survived. Because now we desperately want revenge on Verloc, and we want his wife to take it. To paraphrase the Beastie Boys in the film's musical namesake, she can't stand it, she knows he planned it and she will set it straight. And that's just what happens in the second of the film's editing masterclasses: the turning of an emotional tide and the deliverance of justice, presented in a series of silent shots that perfectly demonstrate Hitchcock's ability to tell a story through the simple assembly of pieces of film.

Hitch continued to develop his key themes with *Sabotage*, which is another piece of entertainment about entertainment. Just as *Murder!* revolved around the theatre, *The Man Who Knew Too Much* featured a live concert and *The 39 Steps* hinged on a vaudeville act, *Sabotage* has at its heart the Verlocs' cinema. Hitchcock's audiences would be regular consumers of all these activities, and any of them - he suggested - could easily be a backdrop for treason, betrayal and murder. In Hitchcock's world there's no innocent situation that couldn't erupt in danger at a moment's notice, sweeping any innocent bystander - i.e. you, the viewer - off into a world of life-threatening fantasy.

Hitch's bungling policemen are back too, although this one was by accident rather than design. The role of Sergeant Ted Spencer, who's already investigating Verloc when the film starts, was earmarked for *The 39 Steps'* Robert Donat. When Donat pulled out due to ill health he was replaced with John Loder, about whom Hitchcock was characteristically blunt in later interviews; Hitch claimed Loder's unsuitability for the role necessitated rewrites which damaged his character. Unintentionally, then, Spencer is a quite useless copper, getting rumbled by the villains on his first attempt at eavesdropping, failing to stop the bomb despite being warned about a second attack by his boss, and then hitting on Mrs Verloc minutes after she's murdered her husband after learning that he killed her brother. Read the room, Ted.

Finally, those complex ideas around guilt resurface. Verloc shrugs his guilt over Stevie's death off and onto Spencer for interfering, but Mrs Verloc is already collapsing under the weight of that guilt for failing to protect her brother. After killing Verloc, her assumed guilt over one murder becomes genuine over another, but in a twist reminiscent of *Blackmail*, the evidence of her crime conveniently disappears. Spencer convinces her to skip the country with him rather than confess, and the implications of the couple's combined guilt are left hanging. Hitchcock's dark side rarely let anyone live happily ever after.

YOUNG AND INNOCENT

1937, b/w

Based on *A Shilling For Candles* by Josephine Tey

Gainsborough Pictures (Distributed by
Gaumont-British Picture Corporation)

UK

She's young. He's innocent. If this were an ITV drama their names would probably be Karen Young and Dave Innocent. But it isn't, so they're not. Together they set out to catch a killer by attending a child's birthday party, harassing a vagrant and driving into a large hole in the ground.

Hitchcock loved to open his films with attention-grabbing moments of high drama, and *Young And Innocent* is no exception. An argument rages between a husband and wife (obviously; this is Hitchcock, after all), and the man is forced to leave home. Outside, a storm is gathering. Conflict, upheaval and turbulence: the perfect setup to another thriller, and not a million miles away from the chaotic industrial circumstances under which Hitch had begun work on his latest film.

Cutbacks at Gaumont-British led to the company's production arm being shut down and Hitchcock's trusted producer Michael Balcon being fired. His writing partner Charles Bennett - who'd helped shape the identity of 'the Hitchcock thriller' since *The Man Who Knew Too Much* - packed his bags for Hollywood mid-script. And after just a few days' filming on *Young And Innocent*, the entire production was turfed out of its Shepherd's Bush studios and relocated to the newly-opened Pinewood. Gaumont survived as a distributor, but Hitch's contract was transferred to Gainsborough and a new producer, Ted Black. Conflict, upheaval and turbulence: Hitch took it all in his stride, and even managed to turn it to his advantage.

Young And Innocent betrays none of its behind-the-scenes turmoil. In fact Hitchcock rarely made anything as cheerfully breezy; it's so light and fluffy that its portentous prologue is about the only thing keeping it from floating away. The plot is a frothy retread of *The 39 Steps*: Robert Tisdall (Derrick De Marney) is wrongly accused of the murder of film star Christine Clay, the woman in the prologue. Robert teams up with Erica Burgoyne (Nova Pilbeam), daughter of the local police chief, to find the real killer and clear his own name. The events surrounding Christine's death are entirely irrelevant to the story: all that matters here is the catalogue of capers young Erica and innocent Robert go through to locate the murderer. The villain's name is never spoken, but for all intents and purposes it may as well be Mr MacGuffin.

As befits a film aimed at younger audiences than Hitchcock had previously catered for, the threat to life is minimal, espionage and politics are nowhere to be found, and sexual innuendo is off the table. Erica and Robert's relationship is refreshingly equal, with each coming to the other's rescue at various points in the story, and Erica is one of Hitchcock's better female representations: she's smart, capable and compassionate - much more so than the policemen who work for her father, who are frequently lampooned as bumbling twits. In one wicked moment of Hitchcockian unsubtlety, a pair of bobbies are forced to share a cart with a family of squealing pigs.

It's another slick adventure that tumbles along like an excitable puppy, but *Young And Innocent* didn't particularly stretch the writing skills of Hitchcock and his team. It was, however, a huge opportunity for him to show what he could put before a camera, and the unexpected move to Pinewood allowed Hitch to make use of better facilities than anything he'd been able to get his hands on before. Finally, the technology available to him was beginning to catch up with his ideas, and *Young And Innocent* boasts two particular scenes that stand out as defining moments of Hitchcock's late British period.

The first is a wildly pointless but fantastic-looking set-piece. Looking for a hiding place, Erica and Robert drive into an abandoned mine which promptly and spectacularly collapses, sucking their car into the bowels of the earth and threatening to take Erica with it. Very aware that movers and shakers from across the Atlantic were by now watching his every move, Hitchcock crafts a perilous, full-scale, lavish action sequence to match anything coming out of Hollywood. In fact it's possible the sequence was a little *too* lavish, because other scenes in the film are rendered with painfully obvious model trains, buses and people that aren't fooling anyone.

But the most remarkable moment of *Young And Innocent* is the kind of breathtakingly audacious camera move that Hitch had been working towards for years. By the film's final scene, our protagonists - thanks to a convoluted series of events involving a missing coat, a tramp and a box of matches - know only one thing about the killer's identity: that he has an uncontrollable eye twitch. They've traced him to a swanky hotel where the music is provided by a minstrel band, but have reached a dead end in their investigation.

Just as all seems lost, Hitchcock cuts to a wide overhead shot of the hotel lobby. Then, over the course of one meticulously-paced minute, he cranes his camera across the ballroom and over the dancers' heads, slowly but deliberately moving towards the band. Gradually we realise he's honing in on the drummer. Could this be the man Erica and Robert are after? If only the killer had a single, identifying character trait by which we could recognise him! The camera continues to creep closer to the drummer, much closer than is comfortable, until it's inches from his face. His eyes fill the frame. If he twitches, we've got him. Hitchcock makes us wait for agonising seconds before confirmation arrives, literally in the blink of an eye.

The whole shot is a technical marvel, choreographed over two days before it was ready to film, but is also a canny piece of audience manipulation on Hitchcock's part. The camera, beckoning us away from the protagonists, gives us information they don't yet have. We've seen how hidden away the killer is, and now we're even more invested in Erica and Robert's task. It's a classic Hitchcock moment: a blatantly foregrounded piece of formal showmanship which, conversely, pulls us deeper into the story. We know we're being played, but the game is too much fun to resist.

Hitch would repeat the extreme-wide-shot-to-extreme-close-up trick in *Notorious* nearly ten years later, but it was the idea of giving his audience privileged information in unexpected ways that he would return to time and again. The body in the chest in *Rope*, crows gathering in the playground in *The Birds* and *Vertigo*'s jaw-dropping flashback sequence all owe a small debt to *Young And Innocent*'s sly, conspiratorial camera.

PARTNERS IN CRIME: THE COLLABORATORS

"Hitchcock was at home when his collaborators were storytellers."

- Guillermo del Toro

As much as this book is about Hitchcock's style, and as much as Hitch has been promoted (not least by himself) as the grand *auteur* of his unique storytelling methods, he simply couldn't have done any of it without the right collaborators. In his early days Hitchcock was lucky to have had the right colleagues handed to him at the right time (although that wasn't always the case); in later years he was able to pick and choose his besties.

Stars are stars for a reason, and some behind-the-camera talent achieved stardom (David O Selznick, Edith Head, Bernard Herrmann, to name but a few). But there are more of Hitchcock's regular collaborators who remain virtually unknown, even to keen movie buffs. All of them brought something to Hitch that helped build his legend, and all of them learned something from him. Sadly he suffered from selective amnesia when it came to crediting many of these artists, despite their indispensable contributions. With the caveat that there are far too many names to whom these pages can give full justice, here's a brief rundown of just some of those key figures, and their undeniable impact on Brand Hitchcock.

THE PRODUCERS

Michael Balcon (*The Pleasure Garden, The Mountain Eagle, The Lodger, Downhill, Easy Virtue, The Man Who Knew Too Much, The 39 Steps, Secret Agent, Sabotage*)

Hitchcock would almost certainly have found his way into directing at some point, but it was Michael Balcon who initially spotted his talent and assigned him his first feature, *The Pleasure Garden*, in 1925. Balcon's confidence in Hitchcock was not misplaced, and generations of cinemagoers owe him a debt for giving Hitch a chance - not once, but twice. More a businessman than a film expert, Balcon recognised Hitchcock's potential and gave his protégé virtual carte blanche. While producing Hitch's first five films, Balcon maintained a respectful distance and supported his director when less foresighted senior studio figures tried to smother his creativity.

In 1927 Hitchcock left Balcon's Gainsborough Pictures for British International, but his output there was a patchy mixture of classics and clunkers. Meanwhile Balcon set up a new studio, Gaumont-British, and in 1934 brought Hitchcock back for the first of his 'classic thriller sextet', *The Man Who Knew Too Much*. After three more films together, Balcon was fired in a cost-cutting exercise and never worked with Hitchcock again. But his encouragement and faith were shots in the arm to Hitchcock's career - and, indeed, to cinema - and Hitch would look back fondly on their time together.

David O Selznick (*Rebecca, Spellbound, The Paradine Case*)

Despite churning out a near-constant supply of terrific British thrillers in the 1930s, Hitchcock struggled to convince a major American studio to give him a chance. A run of failed negotiations with various parties meant his best offer was from David O Selznick, whose independent studio was about to make cinema history with *Gone With The Wind* (1939). Selznick provided the Hollywood gloss Hitchcock yearned for, but their contrasting filmmaking methods and equally stubborn desire for control made their working relationship a turbulent one.

Though they found immediate success with 1940's *Rebecca* they never repeated it, and over seven years they would make just two more films together (*Spellbound* and *The Paradine Case*), each less impressive than its predecessor. In between these projects Selznick loaned Hitchcock out for seven other features, earning a fortune for himself but giving Hitch a taste of life away from his boss that eventually became too good to resist. During the Selznick years Hitchcock learned to blend his German- and Soviet-influenced British stylings with the slick machinery of American moviemaking, but he also learned that being tied to one producer was stifling, and vowed to keep his options open in future.

THE WRITERS

Eliot Stannard (*The Pleasure Garden, The Mountain Eagle, The Lodger, Downhill, Easy Virtue, The Farmer's Wife, Champagne, The Manxman*)

The contribution of Eliot Stannard to Hitchcock's entire career can't be overstated. Already a prolific and talented scenarist while Hitch was still learning one end of a camera from the other, Stannard had amassed around 90 screenwriting credits before working on Hitchcock's debut feature. His mother was a novelist and he'd adapted the likes of Dickens, Shakespeare and Emily Brontë for early cinema. He advanced and promoted British screenwriting when few outside the business understood it at all. Basically, Stannard knew his writing onions.

His vast experience was invaluable to Hitchcock, and Stannard shaped the scenarios of all Hitch's silents - including *The Ring*, for which he went uncredited after a minor spat with the director. Stannard was a master of theme and continuity, ensuring Hitch's boundless visual wheezes had meaningful connective tissue. He worked with Hitch more than any other writer (except Alma), even following him from Gainsborough to British International Pictures. Dialogue was not his strong suit, however, and his unfortunate prediction that the coming of sound would be "a ghastly failure" might explain his absence from Hitchcock's career - and cinema generally - from *Blackmail* onwards.

Charles Bennett (*The Man Who Knew Too Much, The 39 Steps, Secret Agent, Sabotage, Young And Innocent, Foreign Correspondent*)

Charles Bennett was also well-versed in the worlds of stage and screen before his spectacular collision with Hitchcock:

an actor turned writer, he penned *Blackmail* in 1928, the play Hitchcock adapted the following year. Bennett had a pin-sharp understanding of suspense (you might even say he was a master of it), and this he brought to the first five of the classic thriller sextet, as well as the equally exciting *Foreign Correspondent* from the director's early American period. His construction of plot and narrative were vital for the success of these thrillers, and Hitch learned much from Bennett that he carried through the rest of his career.

The Bennett years saved Hitchcock from a post-Stannard creative slump that could have prematurely ended his directorial career, and which proved to some extent that as good as Hitch and Alma were, they would need to rely on writers more skilled than themselves in future. Lesson learned. Sadly Bennett's rocky relationship with Hitchcock ultimately left him sidelined by the director and, to some extent, by history. But he knew his own worth: as Bennett himself modestly proclaimed, "I'm not being conceited, but I was awfully bloody good."

John Michael Hayes (*Rear Window, To Catch A Thief, The Trouble With Harry, The Man Who Knew Too Much*)

The third most prolific of Hitchcock's writers, John Michael Hayes, collaborated with him on four consecutive films. Coinciding with Alma's virtual retirement from script contribution, Hayes's arrival helped redefine Hitch as a purveyor of slick '50s Hollywood product packed with unexpected plot developments and lip-smacking dialogue. Hayes's words were honey in the mouths of James Stewart, Grace Kelly and Cary Grant, not least because Hayes knew in advance who would be playing which roles and wrote for their respective talents. Sexual innuendo and gloriously constructed *double entendres* in Hitchcock reached their peak with the Hayes years, giving Hitch a hell of a job when it came to getting his films past the Production Code.

Hayes's focus on sexual politics was also a key development in Hitchcock's work, beginning with the Jeff/Lisa conundrum of *Rear Window* and culminating in Jo and Ben McKenna's relatively complex relationship in *The Man Who Knew Too Much*. For the latter film, Hitch insisted on a collaboration between Hayes and Hitchcock alumnus Angus MacPhail, which led to a battle of egos from which nobody emerged unscathed. It would be the last time Hayes worked for Hitchcock, but he had left his mark on the canon.

THE ACTORS

Cary Grant (*Suspicion, Notorious, To Catch A Thief, North By Northwest*)

As a fellow Brit who also realised his destiny in Hollywood, Cary Grant understood Hitchcock. And Hitch understood Grant, perhaps like no other director. Grant was usually typecast as a charmer, pursued by women and prone to suffering various clothing-based indignities. But Hitch saw a darkness in Grant, perfect for their first collaboration in *Suspicion*, where Grant's Johnny may or may not be a murderer. That ambiguity of identity was common across all his roles for Hitchcock: in *Notorious*, Devlin buries his feelings for Alicia, assuming an uncaring facade; *To Catch A Thief* sees John Robie trying to convince everyone he's not what they think he is; ditto *North By Northwest*, in which Roger Thornhill is a nobody mistaken for a somebody.

Both men were aware of their mutual beneficence. Hitchcock's ambivalence towards actors didn't stop him using Cary Grant's name to attract bigger audiences; Grant was grateful to find a director who stretched him. They could have collaborated more - Hitch courted Grant for *Rope, I Confess, Torn Curtain* and even a version of *Hamlet*, but it was not to be, a frequently cited stumbling block being Grant's fee. But such talents were lucky to collide as often as they did, and we're lucky to have their films.

Ingrid Bergman (*Spellbound, Notorious, Under Capricorn*)

Hitchcock found another soulmate in Ingrid Bergman. Like Hitch, she was a European signed by David O Selznick for her first American picture (1939's *Intermezzo*), and like Hitch, she spent most of her Selznick contract loaned out to other studios. Sensing the director and actress could make magic together, Selznick paired them up for *Spellbound*. Bergman brought a new, richer representation of femininity to Hitchcock's films: another cool blonde on the surface, but smarter, more independent and more recognisable as a real woman than her predecessors. Hitch used her talents to his advantage by writing his most psychologically complex female character to date for her in *Notorious*.

Biographers concur that it wasn't just Bergman's acting Hitchcock was in love with, and the character of Devlin in *Notorious* - a man forced to hide his desire for Ingrid Bergman for personal and professional reasons - suggests a thinly veiled avatar for the director. Inevitably things went south when Hitch made *Under Capricorn* as some kind of gift to Bergman: the technical logistics frustrated her, the film was a disappointment and she began an affair with another director, Roberto Rossellini. Hitchcock and Bergman never worked together again, but her impact on future portrayals of women echoes throughout the Hitchcanon.

James Stewart (*Rope, Rear Window, The Man Who Knew Too Much, Vertigo*)

Jimmy Stewart's dependable, trustworthy screen persona was the holy grail for Hitchcock: after decades spent casting actors of varying ability as his put-upon protagonists, Hitch was delighted to be able to exploit Stewart's extraordinary ordinariness. But like Cary Grant, Stewart's everymen were tainted by an emotional dark side, which had developed after his experiences as a US Air Force pilot in World War II. The collaboration began uncertainly with *Rope*: audiences were uncomfortable with the folksy Stewart playing a morally ambiguous intellectual who was, frankly, a bit of a dick, but isolating the role from the baggage of Stewart's career allows an incredible performance to shine through.

Stewart introduced the same kind of complexity to representations of masculinity in Hitchcock that Ingrid Bergman did for femininity. The sexually ambiguous power dynamics of *Rope* gave way to the entirely emasculated Jeff of *Rear Window*, the patriarchal hubris of *The Man Who Knew Too Much* and the catastrophic toxicity of *Vertigo*'s dangerously confused Scottie. Despite Stewart's inherent charm and likeability, his Hitchcockian men are far from heroes: they can be arrogant and insensitive, and frequently make terrible choices. It takes a great actor to keep you invested in those characters, and Stewart was one of the greatest.

Grace Kelly (*Dial M For Murder, Rear Window, To Catch A Thief*)

It's not hard to see what attracted Hitchcock to Grace Kelly: like most of Hollywood, he found her beautiful, witty and more than a little saucy. Inevitably Hitch fell under her spell, and their one-sided romance manifested itself through his camera. Kelly's appearances in three consecutive Hitchcock films rank among the most stunning depictions of screen beauty in American cinema. Hitch took it upon himself to craft Kelly as a Hollywood goddess, choosing her wardrobe on *Dial M For Murder*, and then working closely with costume designer Edith Head on the jaw-dropping gowns of *Rear Window* and *To Catch A Thief*.

But Kelly didn't *need* Hitchcock to make her a legend; she was quite capable of doing that herself. Perfectly aware of her own image, she plays up to it in the later two films, wrapping her lips around the sexual innuendo provided by John Michael Hayes's scripts for them. *Dial M For Murder* was a trial by fire for the inexperienced actress (the attempted murder of her character took a week to rehearse and shoot), but her easy chemistry and playful banter with Jimmy Stewart and Cary Grant proved she could hold her own against the big boys.

THE OTHERS

Two directors of photography from different eras were key to helping Hitchcock transfer the unprecedented visual ideas in his head onto film. **Jack Cox** worked with Hitch on ten films from *The Ring* (1927) to *Number Seventeen* (1932), then returned for *The Lady Vanishes* (1938). An accomplished effects cameraman, Cox was one of silent cinema's most adventurous cinematographers and one of few people who could achieve what Hitchcock demanded. His later counterpart was the enormously versatile **Robert Burks**, another master of special effects. Excluding *Psycho*, Burks shot every Hitchcock film from *Strangers On A Train* (1951) to *Marnie* (1964), meeting challenges like making *Dial M For Murder*'s stagey set cinematic (*and* doing it in 3D), lighting the enormous *Rear Window* set, and tackling *The Birds*' 400-plus trick shots.

Joan Harrison became Hitchcock's secretary in 1933, wading through potential projects for him to direct. Beginning with *Jamaica Inn* (1939), she was one of Hitch's most valued writers, credited with five of his scripts in the early 1940s (and Oscar-nominated twice in 1941 for *Rebecca* and *Foreign Correspondent*). She left Hitchcock to become a successful producer in her own right, returning to do the heavy lifting on his TV series *Alfred Hitchcock Presents*. Equally invaluable was **Peggy Robertson**, continuity director on 1949's *Under Capricorn* (where much of her time was spent peacekeeping between Hitch and Ingrid Bergman) and *Stage Fright* (1951), then script supervisor, PA to Hitch and *de facto* associate producer from *Vertigo* (1958) onwards.

During the 1950s Hitchcock assembled his own Avengers: a team of trusted technicians who he repeatedly relied on to complete his vision. As well as cinematographer Robert Burks, these included editor **George Tomasini**, production designer **Henry 'Bummy' Bumstead**, and assistant director and associate producer **Herb Coleman. Edith Head** was his go-to costume designer: like Hitch, she became a star herself, cultivating her own brand and her own unmistakable look. Her costumes tell you all you need to know about the characters before they've spoken a word, and her designs for Grace Kelly are as iconic as the films they, er, grace. **Saul Bass** designed Hitchcock's most memorable title sequences - *Vertigo*, *North By Northwest* and *Psycho* - and, last but not least, **Bernard Herrmann** composed unforgettable scores for eight films from *The Trouble With Harry* (1955) to *Marnie* (1964). It's impossible to imagine the most famous of Hitchcock's late films without the romance and dread Herrmann's music brings to them.

THE LADY VANISHES

1938, b/w

Based on the book *The Wheel Spins* by Ethel Lina White

Gainsborough Pictures

UK

A tongue-in-cheek love letter and grave political warning to Hitchcock's fellow countrymen, The Lady Vanishes *is a crackling, witty thriller that simultaneously embraces and lampoons the idiosyncrasies of the English like a 1930s Paddington.*

The final film in Hitchcock's classic thriller sextet is its second masterpiece: a hilarious, exhilarating mystery packed with outlandish incidents and memorable characters. While it carries over its predecessors' common themes of international intrigue, ordinary folk scooped up by extraordinary events and antagonistic couples who eventually fall in love, it's perhaps more interesting for the Hitchcockian tropes it *doesn't* exploit. There's no attention-grabbing opening, no dexterously-edited silent sequence, no grandstanding camera moves and no show-stopping set piece. *The Lady Vanishes* is a perfect balance of consistency and experimentation: an approach which would characterise the rest of Hitchcock's career.

Unusually for an Alfred Hitchcock film, *The Lady Vanishes* wasn't written for or by Hitchcock. Whereas he would normally play a major role in shaping an existing property or original idea from the screenplay's inception onwards, this script was by future legendary writing duo Frank Launder and Sidney Gilliat for Gainsborough Pictures, who assigned it to director Roy William Neill. That project fell through, and the script made its way into Hitchcock's lap when his producer Ted Black clocked its obvious appeal to his star director's sensibilities. Hitch made a few customary tweaks before setting to work filming the story of a remarkable train journey in which a group of English strangers, including a sweet old woman, are unexpectedly pitted against dastardly foreign agents when the lady - as you may have guessed - vanishes.

Opening in a small hotel in a fictional European country, the film takes its time introducing its characters. Before now Hitchcock usually preferred to toss off his setups as quickly as possible so he could get on with the fun stuff, but with an ensemble of characters who would each play a vital role in the forthcoming antics, it behoved him to introduce them properly. They're stuck at the hotel for 24 hours after an avalanche scuppers their train journey home, and the accumulated grumbling is the unmistakable and timeless sound of entitled Brits abroad facing the insurmountable despair of a minor alteration to their holiday plans.

Chief among the aggrieved tourists are Launder and Gilliat's career-greatest creations, Charters and Caldicott (Naunton Wayne and Basil Radford), two clueless toffs who can't fathom why the locals don't speak English and who are deeply concerned about England being "on the brink" and "in a time of crisis". Despite the febrile political situation in Europe in 1938, it's not impending war they're worried about but the score in the current Test match between England and Australia. Charters and Caldicott's progression throughout *The Lady Vanishes* from ignorant berks to reluctant allies and eventual heroes is a delight, but also a parody of a stubborn British refusal to acknowledge the very real rise of fascism in Europe: a rare slice of social commentary in a Hitchcock film. So successful were Wayne and Radford's performances that *The Lady Vanishes* inadvertently launched the Charters and Caldicott Cinematic Universe: a dozen or so films (no others directed by Hitchcock, sadly) in which they popped up to add a dash of stiff upper-lipped buffoonery to proceedings.

But the dapper duo are merely second-class passengers in this story. Also introduced in the first act are the major players: the bratty Iris (Margaret Lockwood), a young woman on her way home to get married (a terrible idea, her friends insist, with Hitchcock's encouragement); clarinet-honking twit Gilbert (Michael Redgrave), who immediately butts heads with Iris, thereby sealing their inevitable fate as lovers; and elderly governess and titular dematerialising female Miss Froy (Dame May Whitty). No sooner does everyone board their rescheduled train than Miss Froy unexpectedly evaporates, and Iris seems to be the only passenger who remembers she even existed.

The script gives everyone a good reason for claiming not to have seen Miss Froy when they clearly have, and Hitchcock delights in torturing his audience by stringing out that frustration for as long as possible, aligning us closely with Iris's sense of bewilderment. But he also gets to pull off one of his favourite tricks when Iris is excluded from a scene in which a fake nun reveals the plot. As in *Young And Innocent*, we're now privy to information the lead character doesn't know, and it's simultaneously a relief to know the truth and a gear change into suspense as we wait for Iris to suss what's afoot.

Also aboard this express service to adventure is some first class Hitchcockery. The MacGuffin this time is so marvellously irrelevant that it's revealed in a single line of dialogue just ten minutes before the end, and when it is, it's gloriously absurd. Music plays a crucial role in the story again, with Miss Froy's leitmotif providing more than just a whimsical theme tune. And Hitchcock gets to challenge his prop department once more, ordering two comically massive brandy glasses for a perspective-manipulating scene in which Iris and Gilbert are about to be unwittingly poisoned.

But it's also fun to see Hitch force himself to do things differently, like spend the bulk of a film on a moving train only to grind it to a halt for the big climax, in contrast to previous films like *Number Seventeen* and *Secret Agent* which took the opposite, more obvious approach. It's a small foreshadowing of bigger structural experiments to come, such as *Rope*'s single-shot conceit or *Psycho*'s unexpected bumping off of its leading lady mid-film.

But it's *The Lady Vanishes*' celebration of Englishness and its prophetic call to arms at a momentous point in history that linger longest after viewing. Gathering all the English characters in the dining car for afternoon tea, and then making it an impromptu base of operations for a ragtag resistance force, is a stroke of self-aware genius. And while the script takes a dim view of pacifism in wartime, it's also a sympathetic and sufficiently veiled one. The insistence that the best way out of a jam is to band together, remain polite at all costs and whistle a cheery tune may be hopelessly optimistic, but it certainly makes for gripping entertainment. As far as Hitchcock was concerned, that was always the final destination.

JAMAICA INN

1939, b/w

Based on the book by Daphne Du Maurier

Mayflower Pictures Corporation

UK

SPOILER WARNING

This Cornish melodrama is treated as a lesser Hitchcock, but the director and his leading man ensure a more entertaining watch than its reputation suggests. Hitch romanticises "that lawless corner of England" for a story about a bold heroine, a dim-witted hero and a wildly OTT villain.

The Lady Vanishes sealed Hitchcock's international reputation as a world-class director. After a lengthy courtship, Hitch eventually signed a contract with Hollywood mogul David O Selznick: fed up with critics' refusal to see British films (not least his own) as anything more than disposable entertainment, Hitchcock was finally off to America to make Art. But delays at Selznick's end meant Hitch unexpectedly had time to kill before his big move. So when his friend, actor Charles Laughton, approached him with an adaptation of Daphne Du Maurier's *Jamaica Inn*, Hitch agreed without even reading the script.

As it turned out, agreeing to direct a film for your erratic, egotistical friend without even reading the script is a terrible idea, which Hitchcock discovered when he finally looked it over. He hated it, and immediately tried to wriggle out of the contract. But Laughton, who was producing and starring, refused to budge, and Hitch reluctantly capitulated. Making *Jamaica Inn* was an insufferable experience for Hitchcock, thanks largely to Laughton's methods, and no sooner was it over than he dismissed the film, as did contemporary critics. It remains a generally overlooked entry in the Hitchcanon today, but *Jamaica Inn* is slowly and deservedly gaining traction as a worthy, if atypical, Hitchcock film.

The plot concerns a band of 'wreckers': early 19th century cutthroats who lure ships to destruction on the Cornish coast, plunder their loot and murder their crews. The film opens with one such wrecking scene, which blends obvious miniatures with impressive footage shot in Elstree studios' water tanks. Like *Young And Innocent*'s hair-raising mine collapse, the sequence sees Hitchcock showing off his mad set-piece staging skills.

The gang is run from *Jamaica Inn* by shaggy thug Joss Merlyn (Leslie Banks), who secretly answers to another Mr Big: morally challenged justice of the peace Sir Humphrey Pengallan, played by the mercurial Charles Laughton as a ghastly windbag with a genetic predisposition towards insanity and eyebrows like two trapped and terrified caterpillars trying desperately to escape his face. It's no accident that Laughton is the gas giant around which Jamaica Inn orbits: as producer and star he took virtual control of the film from an exasperated Hitchcock, who found it easier to let Laughton get on with it than to put up a fight over a picture about which he didn't really give a hoot.

Into this world of obscenity and depravity steps Merlyn's niece, the luminous Mary (Maureen O'Hara), who's come to stay with her uncle and aunt at Jamaica Inn. Quite unaware of the inn's reputation as a wretched hive of scum and villainy, Mary is soon apprised of the situation when she witnesses the gang lynching one of their own, Jem Trehearne (Robert Newton), in the room below hers. Saving his life by reaching through the floorboards and cutting his noose with what appears to be the same bread knife from *Blackmail* and *The 39 Steps*, Mary soon discovers that Jem is an undercover government agent, and finds herself torn between the law and family loyalty.

Jamaica Inn's less than stellar reputation is partly due to its position in Hitchcock's filmography. Uncomfortably sandwiched between the classic thriller sextet and the Oscar-winning *Rebecca*, which would ignite Hitch's dazzling career in the US, *Jamaica Inn* feels more at home alongside his melodramatic silents - not least *The Manxman*, with which it shares an isolated, coastal setting. On the surface it bears few of the director's by-now familiar hallmarks, especially its immediate predecessors' espionage thrills. Trehearne may be a spy, but he's an utterly rubbish one: it is he who inexplicably pipes up to say there's a rat in the gang, thereby almost getting himself hanged. Later he totally fails to identify Pengallan as the criminal mastermind, instead attempting to team up with him to smoke out the ringleader. Eventually Pengallan, apparently bored of waiting, voluntarily reveals the truth to the clueless Trehearne.

In actual fact there are a handful of elements from Hitchcock's other work that pop up here. Pengallan is the corrupt authority figure *and* the charming villain (when he's not leering over Mary like a late Georgian Jabba The Hutt); Joss Merlyn and his wife are among Hitchcock's unhappiest married couples; and grace notes like the bread knife, glasses of brandy and a fatal fall from a great height are all present. Rich supporting characters abound too, notably Pengallan's eternally patient butler Chadwick (as quietly infuriated by Pengallan as Hitch was by Laughton) and Dickensian psychopath Harry, who likes to whistle while he wastes people.

It's also true that the film's mechanics are at odds with the style that came to be known as 'Hitchcockian'. The story is told at a distance from the characters, with none of the subjective tools Hitch liked to use to get us into the mindset of his heroes and heroines. Mary's situation here is ripe for that kind of treatment, but Charles Laughton's involvement meant the film was only ever going to have one focal point. That doesn't make the film bad, just less psychologically interesting than it might have been. It's still beautifully shot and lit, especially where O'Hara is concerned, and boasts evocative set design. The inn itself is a winding maze of crooked beams, wonky rooms and stone corridors through which Hitchcock's camera travels carefully enough to give us a sense of its haphazard geography. You can visit the real Jamaica Inn in Cornwall today; it's less deadly than its movie counterpart, but you can stand on a plaque that reads 'On this spot Joss Merlyn was murdered' before enjoying scampi and chips in his memory.

Like *Waltzes From Vienna, Jamaica Inn* is one of Hitchcock's underappreciated period films whose reputation suffers only in comparison to its director's better-known style. It's not as triumphant an end to his British period as *The Lady Vanishes* would have been, but as a postscript to that body of work it's an offbeat and enjoyable example of what he could achieve even when his heart wasn't in it. It also marked the first of his three Daphne Du Maurier adaptations, and while the other two are undeniably better films, neither of them feature a puffed-up Charles Laughton bellowing "MAKE WAAAYY FOR PEN-GALLAN!!" before energetically launching himself from the top of a ship's rigging. More's the pity.

REBECCA

1940, b/w

Based on the book by Daphne du Maurier

Selznick International Pictures

US

ESSENTIAL HITCHCOCK

Daphne Du Maurier's classic Gothic romance provides a new beginning for Hitchcock. His version of the story is a lip-smacking melodrama, whose excellence is made possible by three of his greatest antagonists: a malevolent housekeeper, a dead wife and an overbearing producer.

"It's not a Hitchcock picture," Hitch said of *Rebecca*. In five words he encapsulated an epic struggle to put his fingerprints on his first American feature - a struggle with the very man who'd brought him to Hollywood and given him the opportunity he'd craved for so long: producer David O Selznick. Hitchcock and Selznick's relationship is baked into the very essence of *Rebecca*, to the extent that Hitch wasn't far off the truth with his assessment of the film's authorship. It certainly belongs to its producer more than any other Hitchcock film, but the director's presence - like that of Rebecca herself - is not to be underestimated.

Hollywood's golden age was in full swing when Alfred and Alma Hitchcock rocked up in 1939. It was a time when producers were bigger draws than directors, who tended to be hired guns rather than creative mavens. Hitchcock, along with an expanding group of ambitious contemporaries, would eventually change all that. But for now he had to deal with Selznick, a much more hands-on producer than Hitch was used to. Selznick hated Hitchcock's early drafts of *Rebecca*, ordering him to ditch the irreverent humour and stick to the mood and structure of Daphne du Maurier's novel. He sent innumerable, often ill-tempered memos and made frequent unwelcome set visits, although his simultaneous commitment to *Gone With The Wind* meant Hitch got off more lightly in this department than most of Selznick's directors. And Selznick was used to having final cut: something Hitchcock made very difficult by only shooting the footage he needed to edit the film he had in his head. That's how Hitch had always worked, and it drove Selznick round the bend.

So it's tempting to see a little of Hitchcock in *Rebecca*'s unnamed protagonist (Joan Fontaine), who also finds herself in a strange new environment after hooking up with a domineering man with anger management issues. Hitch's discombobulation at Selznick's ways echoes through the cavernous halls of Manderley, the Gothic mansion in which our naive and awkward heroine struggles to settle after marrying wealthy widower Maxim de Winter (Laurence Olivier). Fortunately, Hitch didn't also have to deal with the legacy of a dead rival. Rebecca - the first, deceased Mrs de Winter - is an oppressive presence at Manderley, never allowing the inconvenience of death to stop her exerting an iron grip on all the characters. The second Mrs de Winter's life becomes a living nightmare in the film's cruel, bleak and increasingly strange mid-section: an orphan, she finds herself with a new father figure for a husband ("Eat up like a good girl" and "stop biting your nails," Maxim chides her) and a terrifying mother figure in Judith Anderson's monstrous housekeeper Mrs Danvers.

Mrs Danvers represents a formative step in Hitchcock's development of the tyrannical mother character. A twisted descendant of *Easy Virtue*'s Mrs Whittaker, Danvers disapproves of the young woman her 'son' has brought home, just as future Hitchcockian mothers would. But more interestingly, she presents an opportunity for an intriguing subtextual reading. Her devotion to Rebecca, and particularly the sensual pleasure she gets from caressing the dead woman's transparent underwear, suggest an affection that goes beyond mere servitude. Queer theory in Hitchcock was kindled by the sexually ambiguous antagonists of *The Lodger* and *Murder!*, but the Rebecca / Danvers relationship sets it ablaze. And once you feel the heat, it's inescapable. Listen closely when Maxim confesses that he hated Rebecca: how he "found out about her, four days after we were married"; how he was disgusted by things she told him; how he "never had a moment's happiness with her." All ostensibly innocent remarks in the eyes of the Production Code, which strictly forbade 'sex perversion' in films, but Hitchcock knew what he was doing.

That confession scene kicks off the final act, and a slightly crunching gear change takes *Rebecca* out of its murky, melodramatic comfort zone and off into murder-mystery procedural territory. It's a twisty, revelation-packed ending, but Mrs Danvers' absence - combined with the second Mrs de Winter suddenly becoming a spare part, after carrying so much of the film on her fragile shoulders - makes you yearn for the exquisite horrors of Manderley. *Rebecca* opens with a dream and presents itself entirely as a memory, inextricably binding Manderley and the heroine's brittle psyche together, and those are the scenes that stay with you.

Rebecca oozes the lavish production values Hitchcock had longed for, from the opulent sets of Manderley and the casting of stage legend Olivier, to Franz Waxman's lush, romantic score. Selznick had provided that, but Hitch believed it had come at the cost of his own directorial identity. Scratch away at the Selznick sheen, though, and you'll find familiar thematic elements lurking just beneath. Note how subjectively Hitch tells the second Mrs de Winter's story (until the final act), placing us not only in her shoes but in her mind as she recounts her ordeal. Look at the simultaneous use of suspense *and* a staircase, as the heroine takes forever to descend those steps in a boo-by-trapped costume, Hitchcock ramping up the unease with that slow point-of-view track towards Maxim. And, of course, there's Maxim and Rebecca's marriage: yet another union heavily weighted towards the back end of 'for better, for worse'.

Rebecca also fascinates as a signpost to grander, darker work in Hitchcock's future. The idea of a dead woman controlling the living would inform the psychological foundations of *Vertigo* and *Psycho* (the latter of which even echoes details from *Rebecca*, such as the heroine's rain-drenched approach to the iconic house of horrors). Tweak the deceased's gender and you could almost make a similar case for *The Trouble With Harry*.

So while Hitchcock bemoaned *Rebecca* as the one that got away, the wider context of his work shows the film as - at least partly - identifiably his. Selznick's contribution was more intrusive than Hitch anticipated, but together the two men made a film that perfectly combined the glamour and the darkness they each brought to it. And in insisting on faithfulness to the source, Selznick also ensured *Rebecca* was as much du Maurier's film as it was his and Hitchcock's. But it would be the last time Hitch tolerated a producer with that level of control. He would never go back to Manderley again; that much is certain.

FOREIGN CORRESPONDENT

1940, b/w

**Based on the book *Personal History* by
Vincent Sheean**

United Artists

US

---

*A gripping return to action, adventure and espionage, with more
than its fair share of thrilling set-pieces and nail-biting tension.
Not that you'd know it from its bafflingly dull title; there's a very
good reason why* Psycho *wasn't called 'Motel Manager'.*

The 1940 Academy Awards saw *Rebecca* win Best Picture (as
the film's producer, David O Selznick took the Oscar home) and
Hitchcock receive the first of five nominations for Best Director
- an award he would never win. But the less-than-harmonious
experience the two men had making the film meant Hitchcock's
seven-year deal with Selznick was beginning to look more like
a sentence than a contract. So it was to their mutual benefit

when Selznick agreed to loan Hitch out to independent producer Walter Wanger, for a film based on journalist Vincent Sheean's memoir *Personal History*. It was an especially sweet arrangement for Selznick, who trousered a small fortune for doing literally nothing, but Hitch also profited. Not so much financially, but artistically, from the freedom Wanger gave him to make 'a Hitchcock picture' - a freedom he felt he'd been denied with *Rebecca*.

Wanger was a liberal who believed in the power of cinema as a force for change. He wanted to produce a film that opened American eyes to the war in Europe, just as Hitchcock had hoped to alert British audiences with *The Lady Vanishes*. Hitch, meanwhile, just wanted to make another preposterous caper, preferably at the kind of expense he'd only dreamed of back in England. Both men got their wish. *Foreign Correspondent* is a rip-snorting, politically charged adventure: arguably the seventh film in the classic thriller sextet, thanks to the presence of writer Charles Bennett, who worked on five of those six British features, and the shared themes of deadly international shenanigans offset by comic relief and the pursuit of a largely irrelevant MacGuffin. Its $1.5 million budget was 50% more than *Rebecca*'s and almost four times the cost of the average movie in 1940, allowing Hitch to devise some unforgettable sequences utilising outstanding sets and effects. In return for his investment, Wanger ensured his anti-isolationist message got through, and while it might occasionally feel forced (the final scene hits dangerously high levels of cringe), it helps the film become a time capsule of frustration at American neutrality in the early years of World War II.

Set during the pressure-cooker fortnight leading to the Nazis' invasion of Poland, *Foreign Correspondent* is the story of Johnny Jones (Joel McCrea), a jaded New York reporter who Hitchcock biographer John Russell Taylor describes as "stand[ing] in place of the average uncommitted American". Jones's (and, by association, America's) reluctance to acknowledge the threat of fascism receives a mighty slap in the chops when he's sent to London to interview a Dutch diplomat, and inadvertently uncovers a web of subterfuge that will lead to him clambering outside windmills and hotels to evade enemy agents, almost pushed from a 200-foot-high window, shot down over the Atlantic Ocean and subsequently nearly drowned: just another day at the office for a Hitchcockian hero.

Those events provide the opportunity for Hitch to pull off his most spectacular action to date. A shocking assassination outside the entrance to a peace conference ignites a belting 15-minute episode that would have provided contemporary audiences with a rush equivalent to the most pulse-pounding sequence in any modern action franchise. Hitchcock drenches his full-size Amsterdam city square set with rain, forcing the assassin to escape through a visually striking forest of bobbing black umbrellas and into a waiting car. Feeding Wanger's dream of transatlantic cooperation, Jones gives chase alongside painfully British fellow journo Scott ffolliott (who has been given that name solely so Hitch can punctuate the action with a comically elaborate explanation of its origin), and the assassin is tracked down to a windmill hideout. As Jones creeps around the dusty old mill - a stunning piece of set design by *Gone With The Wind* production designer William Cameron Menzies - Hitch breaks out familiar motifs like stairs and doubles to build suspense and reveal surprises. Permanently on the verge of discovery by the villains, Jones narrowly escapes being chewed up by the windmill's grinding cogs, but much as he tries he can't avoid getting caught up in the machinery of international intrigue and conflict.

The casting is a mixed bag. Joel McCrea makes a fair fist of Johnny Jones, whose character arc - from self-centred cynic to noble war hero - prefigures that of *Casablanca*'s Rick Blaine two years later, but McCrea is no Bogart. His co-star Laraine Day does what she can with the role of peace warrior Carol Fisher, but her initially independent character eventually devolves into little more than a love interest, defined only by her relationships with her villainous father and her heroic fiancé. Hitch was as unsporting as ever in later describing his leads as unsatisfactory, but as usual his supporting cast go a long way towards making amends. It's no coincidence that the best of them were all Hitchcock alumni. George Sanders (*Rebecca*) is silky smooth as the unflappable Scott ffolliott, but faces stiff competition in the suavity stakes from Herbert Marshall (*Murder!*) as another of Hitchcock's devilishly charming scoundrels. Meanwhile Edmund Gwenn (*The Skin Game*; *Waltzes From Vienna*) is amusingly improbable as catastrophically useless hitman Rowley. The scene atop Westminster Cathedral tower, in which Rowley attempts to send Jones to street level the quick way, is a literal high point and a true Hitchcock box-ticker: jet-black humour and wicked suspense combine with genuine anxiety in a key scene at a famous - and very tall - landmark.

Foreign Correspondent is a terrific standalone wartime thriller, but its confidence conceals the lack of self-assurance Hitch felt in his first years working in America; years he spent either repeating past glories (*Foreign Correspondent* and *Saboteur* both owe a heavy debt to *The 39 Steps*) or stepping outside his comfort zone with mixed results (much of *Rebecca*'s success was down to Selznick; *Mr & Mrs Smith* is a limp attempt at screwball comedy). But Hitchcock had proved he could handle big budgets responsibly, and *Foreign Correspondent*'s climactic plane crash alone showed he could apply everything he knew about camera placement, staging, special effects and editing to a grander canvas with breathtaking results. The film might not have single-handedly convinced the US to join the war effort -

that was 16 months and a deadly Japanese air strike away - but Nazi Minister of 'Public Enlightenment' Joseph Goebbels was concerned enough to label it "a masterpiece of propaganda", so it must have been doing something right.

MR. & MRS. SMITH

1941, b/w
Story by Norman Krasna
RKO Radio Pictures
US

Forget the Brad Pitt / Angelina Jolie actiongasm of the same name; this is a quite different musing on marriage starring Carole Lombard and Robert Montgomery. The unhappy couple are just as antagonistic, but where Brangelina sizzle, Carobert fizzle.

Still happy to maintain some professional (if not financial) distance from his star director, David O Selznick loaned Hitchcock out again - this time to Selznick's former studio, RKO Pictures. The one-year, two-film deal was perfectly agreeable to Hitch, primarily because RKO and producer Harry Edington more or less left him alone to make his pictures, but also because he got to work with Carole Lombard. Lombard (at that time the highest-paid star in Hollywood) and her husband Clark Gable were firm friends with Alfred and Alma, so when she asked him to direct her in a screwball comedy, he couldn't refuse. Hitch later told François Truffaut he'd agreed to it "in a weak moment," but when a beautiful woman asked Hitchcock for a favour, there was rarely any other kind of moment.

The story concerns the eponymous Smiths, a couple whose volatile three-year marriage turns out to be null and void due to a minor legal wrinkle. Ann (Lombard) expects David (Robert Montgomery) to rectify the situation immediately, but when he doesn't, the stage is set for a typically screwballian battle of the sexes. Nuptial hostilities escalate to critical mass until the finale, when the inevitable mutual capitulation occurs and everyone lives happily ever after despite clearly hating each other's guts.

Hitchcock's biographers are divided on just how enthusiastic he was about *Mr. & Mrs. Smith*. Donald Spoto says Hitch was "wild" about the idea, while Patrick McGilligan claims he "put on the happiest possible face" during filming. The truth is probably somewhere in between. In his book on Hitchcock's relationship with Selznick, Leonard J Leff points out that after the leisurely and eye-wateringly expensive production of *Foreign Correspondent*, Hitch saw his next project as a chance to scotch the potentially harmful Hollywood scuttlebutt that was painting him as incapable of working quickly and cheaply.

It's certainly true that Hitch didn't look back on *Mr. & Mrs. Smith* with much fondness, although he wasn't about to take responsibility for any failure. Ungraciously shifting the blame onto Norman Krasna's screenplay, Hitchcock told Truffaut: "Since I really didn't understand the type of people who were portrayed in the film, all I did was to photograph the scenes as written." While contemporary critics looked upon the movie more favourably, and it was a modest box office success, it's hard not to agree with Hitchcock's retrospective assessment. *Mr. & Mrs. Smith*'s script *is* dull, but Hitch's direction is similarly uninspired. His desire to knock it out as quickly as possible left no time to add the kind of Hitchcockian touches that might have elevated it beyond its source material, and the lack of subtext which had often gone unnoticed in his more inventively constructed 'slices of cake' is harshly illuminated by the film's perfunctory plot.

The most common complaint aimed at *Mr. & Mrs. Smith* is that Hitchcock had no business making a screwball comedy when it's so far from the suspense-laden thrillers that were his forte. But the assumption that he couldn't successfully turn his hand to other genres ignores his earlier success with romantic melodramas, his later dalliances with horror and his proven comedic skills. *Mr. & Mrs. Smith* shouldn't be compared to other Hitchcock films, it should be compared to contemporary romantic comedies; that's where it *really* suffers. And you don't need to look far - just a month either side of the release of Hitchcock's film in January 1941, audiences were spoiled with two vastly superior romcoms. George Cukor's *The Philadelphia Story* (December 1940) immediately lodged itself in cinemagoers' hearts and has so far refused to budge, while Preston Sturges' *The Lady Eve* (February 1941) wove a far more complex, sexier, funnier web of matrimonial mischief. *Mr. & Mrs. Smith*'s unlikeable characters and unimaginative situations also pale in comparison to screwball standards like *His Girl Friday* and *Bringing Up Baby*, both of which stand as bitter reminders that their effortlessly amiable lead actor Cary Grant was another of Hitchcock's irritatingly unavailable first choices.

Claims of *Mr. & Mrs. Smith*'s incongruity in the Hitchcanon also ignore the blindingly obvious. An entire film about a marriage on the rocks was a virtual sandpit for Hitch to play in (and, as ever, possibly an emotional outlet for personal issues), and in many ways this film is a companion piece to 1931's *Rich And Strange*. As in the earlier film, the husband makes an offhand comment early on which miraculously becomes a wish fulfilled moments later, and needless to say both men should have been careful what they wished for. In the same scene, Hitchcock delights at pointing out how married couples can never truly be honest with each other without hurting their spouse's feelings. Hitch's thinly veiled tirades at the ridiculousness of monogamy used to end happily, but would slyly suggest an inevitable return to animosity for his protagonists. *Mr. & Mrs. Smith* ends so abruptly and improbably positively that he doesn't need to imply anything - we simply don't buy it.

Also making an appearance, albeit somewhat obliquely thanks to the puritanical restrictions of the Production Code, is the prudish (to modern, non-religious minds) notion of sin which so often heated up Hitchcock's already-tight collar. Ann is aghast that David intends to sleep with her knowing they're not legally married; she's very much the kind of gal who insists on being wedded before bedded. Confusingly, Hitch doesn't make David's motives clear - we're unsure whether he's a calculating monster or a clueless idiot - so our reaction to Ann's extreme response is less sympathetic than perhaps it should have been.

There is at least one good gag that's another reminder you're watching a Hitchcock film: David miming away to a beautiful but oblivious woman in a noisy restaurant in an attempt to convince Ann, who's sitting too far away to realise he's not making a sound, that he's scored a hot date. It's a fun piece of silent comedy which, ironically, would never work in an actual silent comedy. But that's pretty much the extent of *Mr. & Mrs. Smith*'s laughs. Hitchcock would never again make a conjugal comedy; his experience with the Smiths convinced him that that joke isn't funny any more.

SUSPICION

1941, b/w

Based on the novel *Before The Fact* by Francis Iles

RKO Radio Pictures

US

SPOILER WARNING

Joan Fontaine just can't get enough of meeting and marrying handsome strangers with a mysterious past and possible wife-murdering tendencies. Not content with doing it in Rebecca, *she's at it again in* Suspicion. *When will she learn?*

"I always think of my murderers as my heroes," *Suspicion*'s crime novelist character Isobel Sedbusk tells Joan Fontaine's aghast heroine Lina McLaidlaw. If Hitchcock ever spoke through any of his characters, that line echoes louder and longer throughout his work than most. From *Blackmail*, through *Shadow Of A Doubt* and *Psycho* to *Frenzy* and more, Hitch was often more aroused by his killers than either their victims or their pursuers. And no wonder, when *Suspicion*'s chief suspect is played by the extremely arousing Cary Grant in the first of four collaborations with Hitchcock, three of which see the actor toying with a moral ambiguity few other directors encouraged him to express.

Grant plays society rogue Johnnie Aysgarth, who literally bumps into the mousy, bespectacled Lina on a train in a scene which privileges Lina's point of view. Grant often looks directly into camera as he begs Lina to help him pay for his ticket: a signal that we're heading into a Hitchcockian tunnel of subjectivity. As is mandatory in pre-sexual-revolution cinema, the couple marry after a comically short courtship, the highlight of which is a party where they dance a waltz - something Hitchcock has been sneaking into his recent films with curious frequency. Musicologist Jack Sullivan describes Hitchcock's waltzes as "used to embody collapsing worlds and dangerous charm": a description that perfectly characterises the ensuing plot of *Suspicion*.

Soon after the Aysgarths' honeymoon, Johnnie reveals he's a penniless freeloader, and his methods of bringing money into the household arouse a deepening uncertainty (a suspicion, you might say) in Lina. The decision to tell the story through her eyes means we're as much at the mercy of Johnnie's outlandish explanations as she is, and the constant shifts in his behaviour from reckless liar to devoted husband and back again induce a sympathetic emotional exhaustion in the viewer.

It's a bit of a leap of logic for Lina to suspect Johnnie might be planning to add 'murderer' to his catalogue of character flaws, but it's to Hitchcock's credit that we don't find this conjecture as implausible as it sounds on paper. The evidence is entirely circumstantial, but it mounts up convincingly enough - and our identification with Lina is strong enough - for us to share her fears. In the space of 100 minutes Hitch takes us from romance, through increasingly dark-edged comedy, to paranoid psychodrama. It's a wild ride, and one that could have been unforgettable if only the wheels hadn't come off at the end.

Suspicion's intended climax - in which Johnnie finally makes good on all the innuendo and bumps Lina off - was never going to get past the Production Code. Its insistence that no movie murderer could go unpunished, combined with the perceived refusal of audiences to accept Cary Grant as an uxoricidal maniac (although it was when Laurence Olivier was originally up for the role of Johnnie that this problem arose), resulted in a hastily rewritten ending. Just as Johnnie literally drives Lina to the edge, he reveals he's guilty only of fiscal incompetence; she pathetically apologises for being a terrible wife and they ride off into an unconvincing sunset.

While the denouement isn't universally despised, for most viewers it's a crushing anti-climax. The suspense that's built up isn't relieved, it's deflated. Ironically the film's primary weapon - its subjectivity towards Lina's point of view - is what cripples the ending. We've never known whether or not Johnnie has been telling the truth, piecing information together as Lina does, so it's hard to read his final revelations any differently. Perhaps that could be seen as deliberate; maybe he's still lying and Lina is doomed to a post-credits death, but that wasn't Hitchcock's intention. There's a strong feeling that if he'd had the time to write and shoot a last-act flashback that explained everything objectively, he would have. It's an identical deception on Hitchcock's part to *The Lodger*, which also went out of its way to make its hero look guilty as sin before casually and improbably revealing otherwise.

Until those closing moments though, *Suspicion* is a fun, captivating film. Many of Hitch's themes and motifs are present and correct: Lina is a blonde in danger (maybe), Johnnie a suave villain (possibly) and murder lurks around every corner (perhaps). Troubled marriages and useless police show up, and lots of brandy gets drunk. A fascination with looking is also detectable in Lina's long-sightedness. Her constant reaching for her glasses is almost fetishised, reinforcing the point that she can't clearly make out what's right in front of her: whether her husband is a lover or a killer. Not unconnected to that is a transference of guilt, wherein Johnnie is blissfully carefree regarding his misdemeanours while Lina's doubts about him plague her conscience, leading to her climactic, hair-tearingly frustrating apology.

Then there's the indelible moment when Johnnie brings Lina a glass of milk, which may or may not be deadly. Casting a sinister shadow straight out of German Expressionism and passing through that web of darkness and light that Lina keeps finding herself caught in throughout the film, Johnnie slowly ascends the grand staircase of so many Hitchcockian houses of horror. In his hand, a silver tray holding an attention-demanding glass of milk that sucks all the light from the shot like a potentially poisonous (but calcium-rich) black hole. It's another of Hitch's naughty tricks to make us suspicious of Johnnie, done by placing a light bulb *inside* the glass, which definitely makes it unsafe to drink.

As film #27 of 53, *Suspicion* sits smack in the middle of Hitchcock's feature filmography. It marks the first time he worked with two huge stars, and arguably the first male lead who could give Hitch what he wanted in terms of Hollywood prestige and three-dimensional characterisations. Biographer Patrick McGilligan suggests that "with Grant […] the heroes began to deepen in Hitchcock films, and the films deepened with them." It's arguable that it was actually Joan Fontaine's performance in *Rebecca* that truly set those wheels in motion, but McGilligan's belief that Hitch had reached a point where his narratives would become more psychologically complex is a suspicion the back half of his canon would happily confirm.

SABOTEUR

1942, b/w
Story by Alfred Hitchcock
Universal Pictures
US

Hitch goes back to war for this restless, cross-country adventure which, while rarely at home to logic, is boisterously patriotic fun. And in a world where all movie heroes are called Jack, John or James, Saboteur *provides welcome representation for every Barry out there.*

Hitchcock's seven-year contract with David O Selznick was crawling by at an agonising pace for the disgruntled director, who was increasingly irked by the amount of cash his boss was pocketing from loaning him out. Selznick, burned out after the exertions of *Gone With The Wind* and *Rebecca*, took a step back in 1941 and allowed Hitch to develop a story of his own choosing. Looking to his own back catalogue for inspiration,

Hitch considered remaking *The Lodger* with sound and for an American audience, until contractual entanglements and fractious negotiations over the rights scuppered the idea. The film he eventually settled on wasn't a remake in name, but if Hitch was hoping nobody would notice its similarity to his earlier work he was very much mistaken.

Saboteur is a slick Americanisation of *The 39 Steps*: an enjoyable wrong-man-on-the-run romp with memorable touches. But the earlier film's edge and propulsive nature don't quite survive the transatlantic crossing, and *Saboteur* becomes little more than a series of disparate ideas barely held together by clunky propaganda. Loaned out again (this time to independent producer Frank Lloyd), Hitchcock was given the freedom he treasured, but it's arguable that tighter reins on the director might have benefited the picture. Audiences lapped it up though, and Hitch cared little about the film's quality as long as it expedited the end of his contract with Selznick.

Barry Kane (Hollywood-handsome Robert Cummings) is a munitions factory grunt, wrongly - and quite improbably - accused of causing a fire that destroys his workplace and kills his best pal Ken. Hitchcock throws in a pair of dramatically abstract shots here: black smoke slowly creeping from the corner of the frame to eventually fill it, and the lunching factory workers standing up one row at a time in reaction to the conflagration, which makes no logical sense but looks great and increases the tension.

Branded a saboteur (as with *Sabotage*, we can substitute the word 'terrorist' for modernity's sake) by truly imbecilic officers of the law, Kane goes on the lam, schlepping from LA to New York on the trail of the real culprit: a rat-faced traitor called Fry (Norman Lloyd). Kane's odyssey takes in several suspiciously familiar beats: obliviously wandering into the charming villain's home; getting handcuffed; struggling to convince a blonde he meets en route that he's innocent; finding himself making an impromptu speech to a room of strangers, and engaging in a thrilling showdown at a famous landmark. The only major differences between all this and *The 39 Steps* are *a)* the individual episodes of Kane's adventure are connected by gossamer-thin narrative logic, rather than naturally flowing into each other, and *b)* the blonde (played here by Priscilla Lane) is called Pat, not Pam. Unfortunate bestie Ken, meanwhile, is completely forgotten about once Kane leaves LA and doesn't even warrant a mention in the credits.

In fairness, those episodes - while overwhelming in number - are a lot of fun. Highlights include Kane instigating a brief horseback chase which ends with him being lassoed (the closest Hitchcock ever came to making a western); effecting one of several escapes by tombstoning off an insanely high bridge; listening to a ruthless Nazi sharing his concerns over children's haircuts; (partially) foiling an act of terrorism, and ending the film dangling from the Statue Of Liberty's torch. Anybody would think Hitchcock was panic-stuffing his movie with every idea he'd ever had in case he never got to make another one. Sadly it's sometimes a case of quantity over quality: for example, to imply people being blown skywards by a bomb, Hitchcock simply tilts his camera down their bodies very quickly, which just looks weird. And in one of the torch-dangling shots, Cummings half-disappears under a matte painting.

The Japanese bombed Pearl Harbour during pre-production on *Saboteur*, so by the film's release the United States were at war. There was, however, a vocal minority of the American public who supported Germany, and the US government's previous policy of neutrality had done little to quell it. Reflecting this, Kane's two most interesting encounters are where the film briefly pauses for breath - and also to drive home its message that libertarianism (pointedly embodied by the climax's setting) is broadly preferable to totalitarianism.

In the first of those scenes Kane, seeking refuge in a forest cabin, meets a blind man and his niece Patricia - the aforementioned mistrustful blonde. Clocking Kane's handcuffs, Patricia immediately decides he's a bad guy and should be turned over to the law. Her mindset is fuelled by an unfounded fear based on appearances; she later tells Kane "You look like a saboteur... you have a saboteur's disposition", though it seems unlikely she's ever met one. Her uncle is less inclined towards such quick judgement, claiming that despite being blind he can 'see' Kane's innocence. "Are you frightened?" he asks Patricia, "is that what makes you so cruel?"

Later on, Kane and Patricia find themselves among a group of circus performers, including a bearded lady, conjoined twins and a dwarf: outsiders who know what it is to be feared by 'the normal'. They are also torn between helping Kane and blowing the whistle on him, and for any audience members who haven't been paying attention, the group's leader literally points out the situation's resemblance to "the present world predicament." He goes on to talk about sympathetic passivity, malignant fascism and ignorance-fuelled confusion, before celebrating American democracy by calling a vote which finds Kane innocent and finally convinces Patricia she's been, in her own words, "a dope".

There's no doubt that Hitchcock was horrified by fascism, and he did perform patriotic duties *outside* his films, but the deafening unsubtlety of *Saboteur*'s messaging betrays a shaky grasp of making effective political points *inside* them. And as New York Times critic Bosley Crowther pointed out in his contemporary review, asking audiences to trust their government and support the cause is a message in danger of being cancelled out by simultaneously portraying all authority figures - police, FBI and government agents - as thick-headed nincompoops.

That said, the idea of ignorance breeding fear, and destabilising malcontents fuelling hatred on a global scale, have persisted long after World War II's guns fell silent. Perhaps those calls for tolerance should have been even louder.

HITCHSPOTTING: ALFRED HITCHCOCK'S CAMEOS

Hitchcock's cameo appearances in his own films are baked into the mythology of cinema. They were born of necessity: legend has it Hitch needed someone to play a newspaper editor for one shot in *The Lodger*, and nobody fitted the bill as well as he did. But they soon became little jokes with which Hitchcock amused himself, and when he realised his public were playing along they became Easter eggs, hidden in plain sight for fans to spot as each new film was released. Before long the cameos played a key role in Hitchcock's self-promotion machine. They were like watermarks, stamping his films with a literal authorial presence alongside all those thematic and stylistic tropes that already signified them as his.

It seems unlikely that Hitchcock intended any meaning to be taken from his cameos, nor that he expected future generations to spend time studying them, and yet here we are. Their very ubiquitousness in his filmography invites investigation, and looking at them in the context of his career opens up a number of readings. For the purposes of this exercise, **Hitchology** has grouped the vast majority of the cameos into five categories: The Passerby, The Bystander, The Joker, The Musician and The Character. Some cameos fall into more than one category, and a couple (his silhouetted introduction to *The Wrong Man* and his final, obscured appearance *Family Plot*) don't comfortably fit into any.

Not all of Hitchcock's cameos are mentioned here. For a full list feel free to browse the internet, but proceed with caution: some lists are incomplete, several examples are unconfirmed, and some are just shots of a random extra who happened to be slightly overweight and losing his hair.

THE PASSERBY

For someone who never looked like he got a lot of exercise, Hitchcock spent a surprising amount of time scurrying hither and thither in his cameos. The majority of his on-screen appearances see him simply passing across the frame, and (fittingly, for a director whose films were rarely political) his trajectories are evenly split between leftward and rightward. Only in *Foreign Correspondent* does The Passerby dawdle slowly *towards* the camera, paying more attention to his newspaper than where he's going. In the earlier films, The Passerby is tricky to spot, although he does draw attention to himself in *The Lady Vanishes* as he marches through Victoria Station doing something weird with his head, like he might be choking on his own cigarette smoke.

Hitchcock probably amused himself editing his appearance in *I Confess*. A shot of him striding from right to left immediately cuts to a close up of a signpost marked "DIRECTION" pointing the opposite way; either the director can't take direction, or - given that the signpost leads us to a dead body - it could be that The Passerby is fleeing the scene of the crime. *Vertigo*'s cameo is curious thanks to the somewhat phallic object The Passerby is carrying: frequently mislabelled by viewers and writers as a bugle case (which would put this cameo firmly in the Musician category), the item was tentatively identified by Hitchologist Ken Mogg as a manual foghorn. Given the perpetually misty San Francisco setting and the shipyard location of the cameo, this seems a more likely explanation than the bugle theory. And *The 39 Steps* is notable for The Passerby's companion: the film's screenwriter Charles Bennett. It is of little surprise, given Hitch's tendency to publicly disregard his writers' contributions, that Bennett's cameo is almost entirely obscured by Hitchcock; the writer cast firmly into the director's shadow.

THE BYSTANDER

The Bystander is essentially The Passerby's lazier brother. He made a career of inconspicuously hanging around outside the likes of bookshops (*Suspicion*), drugstores (*Saboteur*) and 19th century Australian government buildings (*Under Capricorn*). In *Psycho* Hitchcock loiters outside the real estate office where his daughter Pat is playing Marion Crane's colleague Caroline; perhaps he's playing her father, and is waiting for her to finish work so he can show her his new cowboy hat? (This cameo is perfectly referenced in Gus Van Sant's 1998 *Psycho* remake, in which Van Sant takes Hitchcock's spot but appears to be on the receiving end of a severe reprimand from a Hitch lookalike.)

In 1956's *The Man Who Knew Too Much* The Bystander is part of a crowd being entertained by an acrobatic display in Morocco, but it's composer Bernard Herrmann who takes the meatier cameo, conducting the orchestra in the dramatic Albert Hall sequence. 12 years later, in *Frenzy*, The Bystander joins another crowd, this time on London's South Bank, to listen to a windbag politician extolling the cleanliness of the River Thames. Ever the political fence-sitter, Hitchcock is the only one who remains inscrutable while the rest of the crowd applauds the minister. Perhaps it's because Hitch knows full well that the bloated corpse of a murder victim could float past at any minute.

THE JOKER

Appearing almost as frequently as The Passerby, The Joker made his debut in *Blackmail*, providing some amusing background business as a London Underground passenger being harassed by an obnoxious child. The kid is among the first of Hitchcock's annoying screen brats, and - in a possible comment on the joys of fatherhood - makes his appearance less than a year after Hitchcock's own daughter Pat was born. Hitch continues to mug for the camera in *Young And Innocent* (as a photographer struggling with comically tiny equipment), *Stage Fright* (in a self-reflexive film about acting, he appears to recognise famous actress Jane Wyman in the street) and *Marnie* (where Hitch glances guiltily into camera on behalf of his larcenous lead character; apparently both of them are up to no good).

Lifeboat features Hitchcock's most ingenious cameo gag, in a newspaper ad for 'Reduco' - a fictional weight loss treatment inspired by the director's own recent health kick. This appearance was so popular it not only resulted in a flood of queries to Hitchcock's office asking where Reduco could be bought, it even gets a sequel: although it's out of focus in the finished film, *Rope* shows Hitchcock's famous profile - by now his official logo - in a neon sign advertising the fake wonder drug. *North By Northwest* boasts perhaps the funniest cameo (Hitchcock, virtually chasing his own credit off the screen, thoroughly fails to catch a New York bus), but the film also confused Hitchspotters with a familiar-looking passenger on the 20th Century Limited, this time wearing a dress. While the thought of Hitchcock cameoing in drag is a delicious one, the extra in question is actress Jesslyn Fax, who had appeared in *Rear Window* as the sculptress. Her thoughts on being mistaken for Alfred Hitchcock have gone sadly unrecorded.

The joke cameos were a reminder to audiences not to take anything they were watching seriously. Hitchcock certainly didn't: in the largely humourless *Topaz*, his wheelchair-bound character (being pushed by his real life assistant Peggy Robertson) inexplicably gets to his feet and strolls off without so much as a limp. But perhaps his most self-deprecating cameo occurs in the poorly-received *Torn Curtain*. Apparently left literally holding the baby in a hotel lobby, the infant appears to soil itself on Hitchcock's leg. The unperturbed director casually brushes off the offending unpleasantness. Everyone's a critic.

THE MUSICIAN

Hitchcock wasn't a musician, but he did like to talk about his manipulation of audiences in musical terms: "You might say I was playing them, like an organ," he told François Truffaut while discussing *Psycho*. Perhaps it was with this metaphor in mind that Hitch carried a violin case for his cameo in *Spellbound*, while smoking in a vaguely ostentatious manner. Two films later, Hitch seems to be playing the same character for his cameo in *The Paradine Case*. Still smoking in that affected way (and, interestingly, exactly replicating the walk from centre frame, towards camera and then exiting screen right, that he did in *Spellbound*), The Musician has now apparently upgraded to a cello.

The trilogy of increasingly cumbersome string instruments was completed by *Strangers On A Train*: no longer smoking, presumably because he had his hands full, Hitchcock manhandles a double bass onto a train. In a film packed to the sprockets with doubles, the use of the 'double' bass seems unlikely to be coincidence.

THE CHARACTER

Rarely do Hitchcock's cameo roles affect the films' plots, but on rare occasions he does take an active part in proceedings. That very first cameo in *The Lodger* sees Hitch in the role of newspaper editor, frantically gathering information on the mysterious serial killer threatening London's blondes, and thereby influencing the paranoid mood that permeates the film. There's a pleasing metatextuality in Hitchcock's debut onscreen appearance as a professional manipulator of words and images, eagerly feeding blood-curdling chills to a terrified but ravenous audience. His cameo in *Notorious* seems innocent enough at first - a party guest downing a glass of champagne - until you notice that Cary Grant has just remarked to Ingrid Bergman that if the champagne runs out, the villainous Claude Rains will go to the cellar for more, and for reasons too convoluted to go into here, that will lead to him rumbling Bergman as a traitor. So Hitchcock's boozy partygoer is in fact unwittingly ratcheting up the tension for Grant, Bergman and - of course - the audience.

Not content with wrestling a large musical instrument in *Strangers On A Train*, the actual Alfred Hitchcock makes another, subtler appearance in that film: the book Guy Haines is fruitlessly trying to read when his life is irreversibly derailed by Bruno Antony is *Alfred Hitchcock's Fireside Book Of Suspense*. Proof that Guy didn't get to read much of it lies in his catastrophic unpreparedness for Bruno's actions. And then there's the clock-winder in the songwriter's apartment in *Rear Window*. Why the songwriter requires a clock-winder remains a mystery, but in Hitchcock's brief skit he appears to offer some words of encouragement to the struggling artist. When the completion of the song accompanies the happy ending for all the film's characters (with the notable exception of the late Mrs Thorwald, the arrested Mr Thorwald and one unfortunate dog), it's almost as if none of it could have happened without Hitchcock. Which is, of course, entirely the case.

SHADOW OF A DOUBT

1943, b/w
Story by Gordon MacDonell
Universal Pictures
US

Hitch famously said it was television that "brought murder back into the home where it belongs." He was being disingenuous. If anyone made homicide a house guest it was Alfred Hitchcock, and the familial skullduggery of Shadow Of A Doubt *saw him at his most welcoming.*

Saboteur had turned a reasonable profit for Universal Pictures and Hitchcock's cachet was only increasing, so associate producer Jack Skirball wasted no time in securing the director's services from David O Selznick for a second picture. Delighted that prestigious playwright Thornton Wilder agreed to work with him at a time when he felt most writers of any worth looked down on his films, Hitchcock was emboldened to construct arguably his most mature work to date. Rich with detail and characters who behave like people rather than plot functionaries, *Shadow Of A Doubt* is further evidence of Hitchcock's evolving obsession with the psychological darkness that would come to define his greatest films.

Joseph Cotten stars as Charlie Oakley, a misanthropic misogynist on a misguided moral crusade to rid the world of rich widows. Hitchcock introduces him and his low-rent New Jersey surroundings in a series of shots culminating in Oakley lying on his bed, planning to escape the law by holing up at his sister's house in Santa Rosa, California. Hitch then repeats that series of shots 3,000 miles to the west, contrasting Oakley and his grim environment with his teenage niece, also named Charlie (Teresa Wright), and the twee Americana of Santa Rosa. Charlie lies on her bed in the same position as her uncle, dreaming of an end to the boredom of comfortable middle-class life, and concludes that inviting Uncle Charlie to come and stay is the perfect solution. Uncle and niece are immediately connected through framing and editing, but also through motivation: each offers a potential resolution to the other's predicament. She may not realise he's the notorious 'Merry Widow Murderer', but he is equally unaware of how smart and tenacious an investigator she is.

Hitch implies Uncle Charlie's malevolence from the moment he arrives in Santa Rosa. As his train pulls into the station, its stack belches thick black smoke into the air, suffocating the daylight and signifying impending danger as it did in *Saboteur*'s opening. This sulphurous cloud follows Uncle Charlie through the film like a toxic shadow: from the station, through the smoke rings blown from his cigar, to the exhaust fumes that almost kill Charlie in her garage. It's one of several motifs Hitchcock plays with here, including a liberal use of doubles (characters and shots are frequently paired and opposed) and the peak of his increasingly overt use of waltzes to signify impending catastrophic disruption.

The *Merry Widow* waltz, introduced under the titles with the aid of dancers from a bygone era (foreshadowing the film's nostalgic undercurrents), was written in 1905 and rearranged in various degrees of drama by *Shadow Of A Doubt*'s composer Dimitri Tiomkin. That abstract shot from the titles, entirely disconnected from the events of the film, reappears after the plot point that ends each act: first when Charlie suspects her uncle's "wonderful secret" may not be quite so wonderful, then when her suspicions are all but confirmed by a newspaper story about the Merry Widow Murderer, and finally after the climactic fight on the train. It's an entirely cinematic device that behaves as a leitmotif one minute and actively intrudes into the film the next. The tune inexplicably bleeds from a non-diegetic insert shot into Charlie's subconscious, actively prodding her to remember its name and realise the truth about Uncle Charlie.

The waltz inserts are experimental even for Hitchcock, but they're emblematic of what feels like a conscious effort to prove he wasn't a one-trick pony after *Saboteur* was criticised for its overfamiliarity. So in *Shadow Of A Doubt* we see an unusually successful marriage, the 'wrong man on the run' is an unseen minor character referred to only in passing, and there's no MacGuffin. And that's not all that's uncommon. Hitchcock boosts audience empathy by giving Charlie a recognisable, relatable family full of likeable characters, and he instils each of them with elements of his own personality. Joe (Hitch's middle name was Joseph) is a loving, hard-working father, obsessed with true crime and casually inventing murder techniques he'd never dream of using. Charlie's young sister Ann is precocious and exasperated by the limited wit of others, while Charlie herself is intelligent and easily bored by mundanity.

But it's Emma - Charlie's mother and Uncle Charlie's sister - who is the film's heart. One of few positive portrayals of mothers in the Hitchcanon, Emma shares her name with Hitchcock's own mother, who passed away during production. Emma's delight at her brother's visit, her reminiscences of how his temperament changed after a childhood accident (a detail from Hitchcock's own youth) and her sadness when he announces he's leaving are all deeply felt. When she involuntarily blurts out to her friends that her baby brother's presence reminds her of a time when she wasn't just her husband's wife, the script speaks heartbreaking volumes about growing old and the sacrifices women make for their families. Patricia Collinge, who plays Emma, wrote much of her own dialogue, which goes some way to explaining this uncharacteristic moment of authenticity in Hitchcock's otherwise fantastical worlds.

Further charm and credibility radiate from the real-life setting of Santa Rosa: a rare external location for Hitchcock, who usually preferred the controlled environment of a studio. Santa Rosa represents a sleepy, almost complacent normality and innocence ripe for dramatic disruption, and acts as ground zero for future squeaky-clean movie towns blighted by a cancerous evil. *Halloween*'s Haddonfield, *Blue Velvet*'s Lumberton and the eponymous setting of *Fargo* all share architects with the narrative conflict office of Santa Rosa's town planning department. But *Shadow Of A Doubt* is different, in that evil isn't lurking beneath Santa Rosa's surface. Like a vampire, it has to be invited in. It's an interesting inversion for Hitchcock, who criticised American isolationism in *Foreign Correspondent* and promoted tolerance of outsiders in *Saboteur*, but now seems to say that if you let a stranger through the door you've basically invited death to dinner.

After teasing us with are-they-or-aren't-they red herrings in *The Lodger* and *Suspicion*, Hitch finally unleashed his first genuine, murderous psychopath onto audiences with *Shadow Of A Doubt*. Charles Oakley may have been uncle to young Charlie, but to the likes of *Rope*'s Brandon Shaw, *Strangers On A Train*'s Bruno Antony, *Psycho*'s Norman Bates and *Frenzy*'s Bob Rusk, he was practically daddy.

LIFEBOAT

1944, b/w
Based on an idea by Alfred Hitchcock
20th Century-Fox
US

Lifeboat is a ticking time bomb of ethical quandaries, in which key tenets of western civilisation such as democracy and civil rights are tested to breaking point. Threats faced by the stranded characters include Nazis, starvation and a cockney accent to make Dick Van Dyke's toes curl.

1943's lucky winner of 'Who Will David O Selznick Loan Alfred Hitchcock Out To Next?' (first prize: Alfred Hitchcock, temporarily) was Darryl F Zanuck, production chief at 20th Century-Fox. Hitch was wary of working with Zanuck, whose reputation for sticking his oar into any given production was almost on a par with Selznick's. But Zanuck was, at that time, commissioned to the US Army Signal Corps, and therefore unlikely to be doing much in the way of oar-sticking while Hitchcock developed his next project, *Lifeboat*. So Hitch packed his bags again (it's a wonder he ever unpacked them while at Selznick International) and took up residence at 20th Century-Fox.

Hitchcock scratched two itches with *Lifeboat*. He was desperate to contribute to the war effort with his films (at 44 years old and over 20 stone in weight, he certainly wasn't about to contribute in person), hoping to tell a story that made important political and humanitarian points without becoming a clichéd 'message' picture. And on the technical side, he was fascinated by the challenge of making a film in a single, restricted location - in this case, as you may have guessed, a lifeboat.

The urge to experiment is a crucial factor in Hitchcock mythology. He was constantly finding new and inventive ways to achieve certain shots and effects, but *Lifeboat* presented arguably the riskiest filmmaking challenge Hitch had faced since he dragged British cinema into the sound era with *Blackmail*. If he couldn't sustain audience interest in the same few characters in the same place for over 90 minutes, *Lifeboat* would be sunk.

The tools Hitch used to achieve his goal were deceptively simple. Firstly, he storyboarded virtually the whole film in advance, allowing him to plan his shots carefully enough to avoid repetition. (Modern films are storyboarded to within an inch of their lives, but in the 1940s the practice was still rare.) Secondly, he had a terrific story to tell, with a whopping kicker. After a Nazi U-boat torpedoes a transport freighter bound for England from New York, a ragtag bunch of British and American survivors have their wits and morals tested when their lifeboat takes on one more passenger: the captain of the U-boat that attacked them, which has been destroyed in the firefight.

The lifeboat itself is crewed almost entirely with metaphors. Hitchcock told François Truffaut that earthy engineer Kovac (John Hodiak) represents communism, while stogie-chomping businessman Rittenhouse (Henry Hull) stands in for fascism. Tender nurse Alice (Mary Anderson) epitomises pacifism, and in his 2012 essay *Shelling The Lifeboat*, critic Bill Krohn draws a neat parallel between the English woman (Heather Angel) grieving for her baby boy and all the mothers of Britain who had lost sons to the war before America intervened.

Lifeboat, then, is much more than a simple survival story. It's a morality play set in a microcosm of contemporary society, intensified by a claustrophobic setting that forces characters to look inwards for their demons and their salvation. It's also a study of humanity, loss of innocence and complicity in violence during wartime, where moral compasses are as fragile as real ones. Ultimately though, it's Hitchcock's plea for unity amongst allies: the disorganisation and bickering of the British and American characters become their potential undoing when pitted against a prepared, cunning and committed enemy.

Meanwhile, Hitchcock's own preparedness paid off in spades. He overcame the challenge of the limited setting so successfully he would revisit it, with variations, in *Rope*, *Dial M For Murder* and *Rear Window*. And while *Lifeboat* isn't the most thrilling of Hitchcock's pictures, there are still moments of suspense. The audience is shown that Willi (Walter Slezak), the German U-boat captain, has a compass and a water supply which he doesn't reveal to the directionless, dehydrated allies, and our need for them to discover his secrets is almost as great as Hume Cronyn's need for a dialect coach.

That element of suspense is one of a handful of Hitchcockian tropes to surface in *Lifeboat*. Hitch's hunger for technical innovation is sewn into the very fabric of the film, and the desire to make a point visually is evident when the lifeboat's sail casts a sinister shadow across Willi's face at a key moment. Murder is still very much a travelling companion, and watch out for the stray boot, already imbued with morbid meaning, which becomes a powerful motif when deployed in the film's most harrowing scene. A potential new mini-motif is suggested in the opening sequence, which marks the third Hitchcock film in a row to use thick black smoke in an early scene to signify peril. Finally, there's the potent transference of guilt, which is all Willi's when he's declared a prisoner of war - but as the tables turn and events reach their ugliest, few of the allied characters survive with their halo intact.

One of those untarnished souls belongs to Joe (Canada Lee), notably the most substantial role for a person of colour in a Hitchcock film to date. Typically for mainstream early-to-mid-20th century western directors, Hitch's track record with Black characters is woeful, so Lee's appearance in *Lifeboat* is, ostensibly, a welcome one. Joe is the most morally sound person on the lifeboat, being the only one who doesn't take part in the film's horrific murder-by-angry-mob. Hitchcock biographer Patrick McGilligan notes that Joe's refusal to join what is effectively a lynching is loaded with significance. But any positive effects of Joe's presence are countered by his clumsy stereotyping as a religious, uncomplicated character who is routinely given orders and told to fetch stuff for the others. They're on a *lifeboat*; how far away can that stuff be?

Compounding an already problematic representation, Joe is also apparently the only one with the necessary skills required to steal Willi's compass. You could weakly argue that when wealthy, self-centred journalist Connie (Tallulah Bankhead) calls Joe 'Charcoal', it's an indictment of her appalling character (given nobody else calls him that). Sadly the era and conditions in which the film was made mean in truth, nobody would have batted an eyelid over it. It's a pleasant surprise that Joe survives to the credits, but it would be another 25 years before Hitchcock gave another Black actor a meaningful role in one of his pictures.

THE WARTIME SHORTS:
BON VOYAGE AND AVENTURE MALGACHE

1944, b/w

Stories by Arthur Calder-Marshall and
Jules François Clermont

Phoenix Films

UK

*Hitchcock's wartime shorts were a brief interlude in his feature
film career which reward close inspection. They are not, it should
be noted, knee-length trousers worn by Hitch between 1939 and
1945, which in all probability would not reward close inspection.*

As World War II dragged on, Hitchcock was bursting with
patriotic juices. He felt the urge to do more for the Allied cause
than just the feature-length calls for tolerance and transatlantic
co-operation he'd made in *Foreign Correspondent*, *Saboteur* and
Lifeboat. Handing post-production duties on the latter film

to Alma and 20th Century-Fox's Darryl F Zanuck (recently returned from his own national service), Hitch flew to England to join his friend Sidney Bernstein, then head of the British Ministry of Information's film division. Bernstein had arranged, with David O Selznick's predictably grudging permission, for Hitch to direct two half-hour films aimed at French audiences and designed to promote the work of the Resistance. While made in England, both shorts would be in French, and would employ French actors and technicians who had sought refuge in the UK.

Despite his brief, Hitchcock found it virtually impossible to churn out straightforward propaganda. Aided and abetted by screenwriter Angus MacPhail, Hitch couldn't help adding narrative flourishes which obscured the very message he'd been tasked to get across. He may not have furthered the Allied cause as much as he'd hoped to, but the wartime shorts proved to be a notable (and often overlooked) chapter in Hitchcock's own evolution.

Bon Voyage is a satisfyingly twist-laden spy drama, in which RAF gunner John Dougall (John Blythe) is questioned in London by the Deuxième Bureau (the French equivalent of MI6) after escaping Nazi-occupied France with the aid of French Resistance fighters. Dougall's story is shown in flashback, but then pulled apart and fleshed out by his French superior, who reveals to Dougall - in further flashbacks, which fill the gaps in his story - that he's been an unwitting stooge for the Nazis all along.

While Resistance fighters are shown in the film, and one of them is seen paying the ultimate price for their patriotism (it's implied the others suffered a similar fate), Hitchcock was so taken with the tropes of the spy genre that the actions of his ostensible heroes are subordinated to noirish lighting, convoluted passwords, dastardly betrayals and other melodramatic and romantic examples of subterfuge. If anyone thought Hitch had got all this out of his system with 1936's *Secret Agent*, they too had been double-crossed.

Bon Voyage's elaborate structure toys with the nature of truth to the point where we're not even sure the final version of events we hear is an honest one. It's a natural progression for Hitchcock, who was finding new and sophisticated ways to enhance his carefully-planned drip-feeding of certain information to characters and viewers. Hitch enjoyed the conceit so much he contemplated a feature-length version which never came to pass, but echoes of it can be found in the similarly rug-pulling flashback sequences of *Stage Fright* and *Vertigo*.

Aventure Malgache, meanwhile, is an entirely less thrilling prospect, whose most engaging aspects are to be found in its metafictional grace notes. In the film's prologue, two French actors are preparing for a play backstage at a London theatre. Clarus (Jules François Clermont) is a former lawyer and Resistance soldier, whose co-star (Paul Bonifas) is struggling to find the right way to portray his villainous character (why he's left it until 20 minutes before the curtain rises to work out his part is a mystery). Clarus tries to help his friend by recounting the story of Michel, a rotten Vichy police chief with whom Clarus tangled while stationed in Madagascar four years earlier.

We're in flashback territory again, but the story unfolding this time displays none of the vitality of *Bon Voyage*. In stultifying, mostly static shots, reams of dialogue are rattled off which require a moderate grasp of the political complexity of World War II-era Madagascar if you've any hope of following the plot. It essentially boils down to Clarus and Michel bickering and betraying each other against a background of French citizens trying to escape the island to fight alongside the British. By the film's present-day (i.e. 1944) epilogue, Clarus's co-star has learned enough about Michel to successfully depict his own treacherous rogue character.

The most interesting elements of *Aventure Malgache* are even more unlikely to be picked up by modern viewers than by contemporary audiences. Firstly, Jules François Clermont, playing Clarus, is telling his own true story: the actor was also known as 'Clarus' and the events described in the film actually happened to him. Secondly, Paul Bonifas plays both the unprepared actor and, in flashback, dastardly officer Michel. While this visual gag is heavily signposted (Clarus comments at length on how much the other actor resembles his old nemesis), it's still likely to go unnoticed by audiences not fluent in French; there are so many subtitles to read, there's little chance to get a good enough look at the characters' faces to spot it.

Sadly, any pro-Resistance sentiment Hitchcock was aiming for with *Aventure Malgache* is buried under its dull, barely penetrable story. So unsuccessful was Hitch's attempt at propaganda in the film, and so morally murky were its characters and plot, that it was never even released to its intended audience. In fact it barely saw the light of day until the BFI restored and released it in the early 1990s.

And yet for anyone interested in Hitchcock's evolving techniques, *Bon Voyage* and *Aventure Malgache* are more than just footnotes in his career. Both shorts feature framing devices: they're stories within stories, which play games with the audience. *Bon Voyage* literally interrogates the storytelling process, foregrounding the ways in which a narrator can manipulate an audience by including or excluding vital information. Whether Hitchcock intended it or not, it's almost as much of a commentary on filmmaking as *Rear Window* would be. Meanwhile, the twin roles for Paul Bonifas in *Aventure Malgache* make you wonder if Clarus has mentally replaced the real Michel with his actor friend, and if so, what else from his recollections has been modified?

With these gentle applications of the 'unreliable narrator' device, Hitchcock began to realise the power he had to control audiences' emotions. As he grew older and his films drifted away from thrilling, surface-level adventures towards more psychologically complex themes, Hitch would build on the formal and narrative experimentation of the wartime shorts to construct some of his best work.

SPELLBOUND

1945, b/w

Based on the novel *The House Of Dr. Edwardes* by Francis Beeding

Selznick International Pictures

US

Hitchcock takes a voyage into the subconscious for an eerie murder-mystery which marks the first of three collaborations with Ingrid Bergman, one of his many dream women. Gregory Peck, meanwhile, plays an analyst suffering from a severe identity crisis. Alternative title: Doctor Who?

Psychoanalysis was big business in 1940s Hollywood. Film-makers experiencing the assorted anxieties and neuroses that came with working in the industry were increasingly turning to therapy as a method of treatment. One high-profile advocate was David O Selznick, who believed the time was right for *Psychoanalysis: The Movie*, and that there was only one director who *a)* could pull it off, and *b)* was conveniently under contract to him. Alfred Hitchcock was certainly curious about the process, having briefly flirted with it in his 1930 film *Murder!*, but to him it was more an excuse to smuggle wild stories and avant-garde imagery into mass entertainment than a chance to make an expensive ad for analysts.

So after five years of a contract which had seen Hitchcock loaned out to other studios no fewer than six times, Selznick brought him back into the fold for only their second picture together. *Spellbound* succeeded in bringing psychoanalysis to the masses, but only in a laughably oversimplified way. It hardly matters: Hitchcock biographer Patrick McGilligan claimed "the bottom line was creating a mystery with a pair of sexy stars that would clean up at the box office," and that's exactly what *Spellbound* did. Bemoaning the film's absence of convincing psychiatry is like complaining that RoboCop isn't seen doing enough paperwork.

Ingrid Bergman stars as Constance Petersen, a doctor at a mental health facility and perhaps the quintessential Hitchcockian icy blonde. (Despite the curious similarity of their names, she's the polar opposite of Hitch's previous female lead character, *Lifeboat*'s hot-blooded hack Constance Porter.) Constance's clinical, pragmatic nature predictably melts when dishy new supervisor Dr. Edwardes (Gregory Peck) turns up, and within hours of meeting they fall in love. Their first kiss is unexpectedly accompanied by a dissolve to an abstract image of a series of doors opening. It's just one example of *Spellbound*'s recurring motif of doors and doorways, which - in the film, at least - usually represents psychological barriers to be broken down: an opening caption references "the locked doors of [the] mind"; Hitch frames Bergman and Peck within a doorway from each other's point-of-view in the build up to the kiss; a light glimpsed underneath a door takes on different meanings in two separate scenes, and with that kiss, Edwardes is opening doors into hitherto unexplored rooms of Constance's psyche. No doubt Hitchcock, one of cinema's dirtiest old men, had other potential Freudian symbolism in mind for Constance's private areas to which Edwardes now has access.

A minor stumbling block in the romance appears when Constance discovers Edwardes is an amnesiac imposter who's misplaced his identity (all he knows are his real initials: 'JB') and who thinks he may have killed the real Dr. Edwardes. Having diagnosed 'JB' as suffering from a guilt complex and convinced of his innocence, Constance takes it upon herself to solve his mysteries using professional psychoanalysis and amateur detective work. Hitchcock would dismiss *Spellbound* to François Truffaut as "just another manhunt story wrapped up in pseudo-psychoanalysis," which is technically accurate, but undersells the fun to be had watching Constance piecing the mock-doc's story together using skills apparently gleaned from *Dream Interpretation For Dummies*.

The film's psychotic centrepiece is the dream sequence designed by preposterously-moustachioed surrealist Salvador Dalí. It's a little jarring to see Dalí's phantasmagorical nightmares gatecrash Hitchcock's glossy melodrama, but the fusion of the two artists somehow works. Perhaps the key image is that of a man using giant scissors to chop up curtains decorated with huge eyeball designs - iconography evoking at least three readings. Textually it provides a clue to 'JB''s past, but the imagery also recalls the ocular trauma of Dalí's own 1929 film *Un Chien Andalou*. Meanwhile the symbolism of voyeurism, violence and cutting - in both the stabbing and the editing senses - is a coded reference to Hitchcock himself.

Spellbound also provides a rare portrayal of a professional woman as the lead in a Hitchcock film. Constance features in almost every scene, and Hitch's camera frequently takes her point of view - notably when she's patronised by large groups of men (fellow doctors in one scene, policemen in another) or seduced by Gregory Peck's mentally ill but undeniably sexy murder suspect. Constance faces a barrage of misogyny throughout the film, not all of which the script feels obliged to condemn (the cuddly, Freudian mentor she loves and respects tells her "the mind of a woman in love is operating on the lowest level of the intellect," which is frankly a bit much). Yet she proves every chauvinist wrong, solves the mystery, saves the helpless man's life and sanity, and presumably lets him into those previously-locked rooms on her own terms: a significantly more positive outcome than that experienced by many of Hitchcock's heroines.

Alongside all this, *Spellbound* comes loaded with the familiar beats that by now virtually spell Hitchcock. Constance is the blonde in danger, juggling murder, suspense, a charming villain, ineffectual police and an entire textbook's worth of guilt, both real and assumed. Hitch makes time for several train sequences and portentous staircase scenes, squeezes in a few doubles in the forms of Edwardes / 'JB' and the symbolic figures of 'JB''s dreams, and gets to play with several outlandish, oversized props. Sharp objects imbued with menace are also back after a long break (a letter-opener, a cutthroat razor, scissors), and two types of glasses are on loan from 1941's *Suspicion*: the tumbler of possibly-drugged milk and the heroine's spectacles, which must be repeatedly removed and replaced to signify her efforts to clearly see the truth. And in a welcome switcheroo, Hitchcock gender-reverses his 'wrong man' theme, so it's the man on the run who doubts his own innocence, while the woman is positive he's no killer.

Hitchcock was among the first to admit his attempt to represent the nuts and bolts of psychoanalysis was a little clunky. So it would prove again 15 years later, when Norman Bates is analysed by the world's most expositionally verbose therapist in *Psycho*. But Hitch was now at a stage where the deadly thrills of his characters' internal torments appealed more to him than any external threats. It would be when offering up cases for audiences and critics to analyse, rather than attempting the job himself, that Hitchcock left us truly spellbound.

NOTORIOUS

1946, b/w

Story by Alfred Hitchcock and Ben Hecht

RKO Radio Pictures

US

The stars aligned for one of Hitchcock's greatest achievements, and few shone as brightly as the elegant threesome of Ingrid Bergman, Cary Grant and Claude Rains. You can't say no to Notorious, *no matter what Duran Duran sang.*

World War II was drawing to a close as Hitchcock and screen-writer Ben Hecht began work on *Notorious*, with regular input from Hitch's boss, David O Selznick. The end of the war wasn't the end of fascism though, and resilient Nazi cells scurried underground to plot their next moves. Hitchcock and Hecht used the political situation as a backdrop for the story of a woman recruited by a man as a government honeytrap and forced to sleep with a Nazi, while all three parties grapple with agonising feelings of love, jealousy and betrayal. Or, as Hitch modestly described it, "the old conflict between love and duty." His version is snappier, to be fair.

It was a stressful time for Selznick, who was wrestling with lavish western *Duel In The Sun* and a marriage that was on its last legs. Although he wanted to make *Notorious* with Hitchcock, Selznick realised selling it to another studio would mean one less plate to spin and a financial boost for his other, cash-guzzling project. It wasn't long before RKO Pictures became the film's new owners.

This was ideal for Hitchcock, who for the first time became his own producer. The autonomy he was suddenly granted seemed to focus his efforts, and *Notorious* is his first American film to recall the efficiency of his British thrillers. It's an entirely fat-free script, meticulously constructed and executed so not a single shot, edit or line of dialogue is superfluous. The mid-section is a masterclass in piling up suspense, while the lead characters' love triangle is the most grown-up (and, psychologically speaking, fucked-up) of all his films thus far. Making good on the promise of *Shadow Of A Doubt*'s sophisticated characterisations and boasting the kind of psychological complexity *Spellbound* only thought it was offering, *Notorious* marks the point where Hitch finally realised his potential for weaving exquisite drama around flawed, fascinating people.

It didn't hurt that those people were played by the best in the business. Ingrid Bergman's Alicia Huberman is low on self-esteem and high on booze (assuming the guilt of her Nazi father, she'd make a fascinating case for Bergman's *Spellbound* psychoanalyst), while Cary Grant - as in *Suspicion* - is cast against type as the flinty Devlin, an emotionally stunted government agent who thinks nothing of placating a drunk, upset Alicia by knocking her out cold. As Grant's biographer Mark

Glancy remarks: he's a sadist; she's a masochist. And *they're* the romantic leads.

Devlin inconveniently falls for Alicia just before he's ordered to send her undercover to woo her Nazi ex-boyfriend Alex Sebastian, to whom Claude Rains lends a sympathy and humanity that Hitch and Hecht deliberately deny Devlin. This is indeed "a very strange love affair," as Alicia and Devlin self-destructively bury their emotions, almost appearing to enjoy the bitter animosity the situation forces them to spit at each other. And underneath all this, the story of a woman manipulated and mistreated by a man - who's confused by sexual attraction, jealousy and an inability to express himself emotionally - is one that several of Hitchcock's leading ladies would recognise as all too similar to their own dealings with the director.

Aside from the plot's psychological intricacies, *Notorious* is a fascinating case study of Hitchcock's technical and storytelling dexterity. His balance of subjective and objective viewpoints allows us to identify strongly with Alicia (the hair in her eyes when driving drunk; her woozy, hungover view of Devlin; the poison-infused blurring of her treacherous husband and mother-in-law), while he dispenses privileged information to the audience about the villains that intensifies our fear for her safety. Watch, too, as scene after scene ends with a narrative punchline followed by a gentle fade, either to black or into the next scene: the audience equivalent of being socked in the jaw by Cary Grant then considerately placed in a prone position to recover before the next wallop.

Nowhere is Hitchcock's ingenuity more apparent than in the iconic party scene, which is bookended by two close-ups of keys that epitomise Hitch's fetishisation of objects to anchor the narrative. (See also the camera pushing into a door lock, a similar shot of ersatz wine bottles, and the dramatic foregrounding of a coffee cup - linked, via its deadly contents, to identically-framed vessels in *The Lady Vanishes*, *Suspicion* and *Spellbound*.) The party begins with a remarkable 35-second crane shot down the Sebastians' sweeping staircase (a house isn't a Hitch-home without one) that zeroes in on the key secreted in Alicia's hand, stolen from her unwitting husband, which will unlock the wine cellar and reveal his deadly secret. It's an echo of *Young And Innocent*'s ambitiously long move, which also picks out the crucial detail in a crowded room for the audience's benefit.

Much of the scene unfolds without dialogue, recalling Hitchcock's prowess as a silent, visual storyteller. Devlin's tense investigation of the wine cellar, the dwindling supplies of champagne upstairs that could lead to his discovery, and Sebastian's realisation that his wife has double-crossed him are all buttock-clenchingly suspenseful acts of directorial mischief enhanced by minimal exposition. The choice of shots and cuts in the latter of those moments is impeccable: as the truth dawns on Sebastian, overhead angles and long shadows tell us he's in as much danger from his Nazi comrades as Alicia is.

The silence of that three-minute sequence is ended with a single word: "Mother." Hitchcockian trope-spotters won't fail to notice Madame Sebastian, who follows the prototype set out in *Easy Virtue* and the substitute figure of *Rebecca*'s Mrs Danvers to become the next step in the evolution of Hitchcock's domineering matriarchs. Madame Sebastian is the protective mother whose love for her son renders the *de facto* villain a little more human. Jealous of Alex's girlfriends and (justifiably) suspicious of Alicia, she's essentially a pre-mortem version of *Psycho*'s Mrs Bates. Plus she gets the film's best line, delivered to her son when he reveals he's inadvertently married an American agent and fears his Nazi friends will kill him for it. "We are protected by the enormity of your stupidity," she tells him, comfortingly. And they say a boy's best friend is his mother.

THE PARADINE CASE

1947, b/w

Based on the novel by Robert Hichens

Vanguard Films

US

SPOILER WARNING

This stodgy legal drama betrays its chaotic production. When a lawyer falls for his potentially murderous client, sympathy goes out of the window – shortly followed by logic, clarity and the will to carry on watching. But the blame doesn't rest entirely on Hitchcock's shoulders...

For the third time in as many films, Hitchcock tackled a story about rational people suddenly finding themselves struggling to balance duty with unexpected and overwhelming feelings of love. After the cod-psychoanalysis of *Spellbound* and the knottier psychological issues of *Notorious*, Hitch was eager to further explore the dark side of his protagonists' psyches. Sadly the third film in any trilogy is rarely the best, and instead of another thought-provoking rollercoaster of emotional imbroglios and cutting-edge filmmaking, we got *The Paradine Case*.

Charismatically-challenged lawyer Tony Keane (Gregory Peck, whose advantageous woodenness in *Spellbound* cripples him here) takes the case of Mrs Paradine (Alida Valli, equally lifeless), who's accused of her husband's murder. Rapidly and improbably falling in love with his client, Keane defends her to the hilt while his wife Gay (Ann Todd) quietly seethes away in the film's corners. Suspecting Mrs P had an affair with her husband's valet Latour (Louis Jourdan), Keane jealously paints the unfortunate manservant as the likely killer in court, only for Latour to kill himself out of shame. Mrs Paradine, bitter at Keane for causing her lover's suicide, turns on him and admits to the murder, which is an unexpected and unhelpful development for her defence team. Having lost both the case and the chance to shack up with a murderess, Keane exits court a failure, whereafter his wife forgives him everything. Gay's final remark to her husband that he really could do with a shave was probably meant as a tender reconciliation, but instead comes off as the oddest non-sequitur in the Hitchcanon.

The psychological mechanics of the story are right up Hitchcock's alley, and should have provided him with plenty to get his teeth into. Instead, The Paradine *Case* is a humourless, lifeless slog, any notions of character complexity buried under acres of turgid dialogue and forgettable performances. Court cases were never Hitchcock's forte (he deliberately and succinctly avoided showing one in *Murder!*, much to its benefit), and this one occupies almost the entire second half of the film. The circumstances of the murder, never shown but recounted by witnesses, are so tediously complex that even Hitch himself admitted to François

Truffaut that he "never truly understood the geography of that house or how she managed the killing." A similar quandary had lain at the heart of Howard Hawks's *The Big Sleep* just a year earlier, but that film's narrative befuddlement was rendered irrelevant by its red hot leads and crackling dialogue. Peck and Valli, sadly, could not hope to match the sizzling chemistry of Humphrey Bogart and Lauren Bacall.

While there are a handful of Hitchcockian themes scattered about the place (murder; a love triangle or two; a troubled marriage; transference of guilt), there's very little remarkable camerawork or cutting to speak of. The courtroom might count as one of Hitch's famous single locations, but nothing that takes place within it comes close to the brilliance of *Lifeboat* or *Rope*. What's also frustrating are the early ideas that go nowhere, despite ostensibly appealing to Hitchcock's sensibilities. Keane is described as being anti-establishment in his youth; now he's trying to exonerate a society woman so she can lunch at the Savoy again. Notions of class like these were Hitchcock's bread and butter in his British films, but it's never mentioned again, despite the exaggeratedly upper class company Keane keeps. This includes Charles Laughton's disgusting, lecherous judge - just about the film's only interesting character, simply because he's so revolting - who leers over Keane's wife, dragging the camera with him to linger over her bare shoulder. Moments like these feel like setups for payoffs that never happen.

Curious audiences don't have to look far to find the source of *The Paradine Case*'s woes. Hitchcock's wife Alma may have received a rare on-screen acknowledgement in the opening titles for 'adaptation', but a far more chilling credit, dripping with vanity, reveals the film's true villain: 'Screen Play by the Producer David O Selznick'. Selznick had owned the rights to

The Paradine Case since the 1930s, and was determined to get it made after several false starts earlier in his career. His ill-advised, ego-driven decision to script the film led to a disastrous production experience. He would frequently bash out scenes the night before they were due to be filmed, delivering them the next morning for a disheartened and increasingly unenthusiastic Hitchcock to shoot.

Hitch's frustration was presumably enormous, but it must have paled in comparison to the relief he felt at completing this, the final film in his contract with Selznick. It had been a tumultuous seven-year-long arrangement, strewn with successes and failures, but an absolutely critical stage in the director's career. Despite *The Paradine Case* (which - incredibly - cost Selznick more than *Gone With The Wind* and made only a fraction of its budget back on release), Hitchcock was well on the way up in Hollywood. His temporary employer, professionally and personally knackered, was heading in the opposite direction. Selznick desperately tried to keep hold of Hitchcock, offering him another, more generous contract, but Hitch had other plans.

For years Hitchcock had been in discussion with his friend Sidney Bernstein about setting up their own independent production company, Transatlantic Pictures. Finally the time had come for Hitch to break free from Selznick, the man who'd brought him to the US, and go it alone. Success was far from assured - Transatlantic had no guaranteed finance for their ventures - but Hitch had tasted autonomy when he self-produced *Notorious* and wanted more. Transatlantic's proposals included a modernised version of *Hamlet* starring Cary Grant, which would sadly drown in legal wranglings, becoming one of cinema's most tantalising lost projects. But Hitchcock had grown used to the slings and arrows of outrageous fortune, and the time had come for him to take arms against his sea of troubles. Silently cursing Selznick for cutting a scene in *The Paradine Case* which involved following the characters in one experimentally long, unbroken shot that moved through different sets, Hitch pocketed the idea. He knew his next producer would give him enough rope; he just needed to make sure he didn't hang himself with it.

ROPE

1948, colour
Based on the play by Patrick Hamilton
Transatlantic Pictures
US

Hitchcock's first independent film was also his first in glorious Technicolor, and his first to star Jimmy Stewart (Cary Grant, aptly, was tied up). But they're not Rope's *only experimental elements: Hitch set himself a formal and technical challenge like nothing he'd tried before.*

As the titles make clear, this isn't just 'Rope'. This is 'Alfred Hitchcock's *Rope*'. Having finally untethered himself from David O Selznick's restrictive bondage, Hitch awarded himself his first possessory credit for the debut film of his new production company, Transatlantic Pictures. The credit announces Hitchcock's independence, but it's also a huge step in the promotion of his brand as an auteur. Already better-known to the public than most directors, Hitch wanted to ensure it was *his* name audiences remembered. Writers? Pfft. Actors? Whatever. There's a reason nobody calls *Psycho* 'An Anthony Perkins Movie'.

Rope was the kind of hugely experimental project no sane studio exec would have greenlit, but Hitch *was* the studio exec now, and he couldn't resist a challenge. For his next trick, he hit upon the idea of filming Patrick Hamilton's single-setting play in one long, continuous take - or at least the illusion of it: the cameras' capacity for only around ten minutes of film at a time necessitated some cinematic sleight-of-hand. Sadly, audiences didn't give a toss about the story or the technique, and *Rope* was a flop.

But the film has enjoyed a critical reappraisal, which is easier when viewing it in the context of Hitchcock's filmography. Its form is a logical extension of the technical innovation seen in *Blackmail* and *Lifeboat*, while its themes - among the darkest, most intriguing Hitchcock ever explored - further the psychological complexity he was examining in his work. If we take the time to untangle it, *Rope* might just be a masterpiece.

Young, wealthy intellectuals Brandon (John Dall) and Phillip (Farley Granger) strangle their 'friend' David because they're convinced of their moral superiority over humanity, and therefore believe they have the right to decide who lives and who dies. Then, purely for kicks, they throw a party for David's friends and family, serving dinner from a trunk concealing his slowly-chilling corpse. It's the epitome of Hitchcock's famous theory, wherein suspense is created by the audience knowing a bomb is about to go off while the characters remain blissfully unaware: the constant threat of discovery tightens around *Rope*'s characters and audience like a noose.

Equally daring is Hitchcock's method. In going for the long-take approach he ties one hand behind his back, denying himself the full power of editing and the subjective point-of-view shot, instead weaving his camera in and out of the action. The parallel between art and artist is striking: here's a film about two men so full of themselves they try to get away with an incredibly risky stunt just to see if they can, directed by a man so full of himself he tries to get away with an incredibly risky stunt just to see if he can.

To clarify: *Rope* is neither shot in one take nor presented as such. The film contains ten edits, alternating between five 'invisible' cuts (where the camera pushes inelegantly into a character's back, filling the frame with black so the film reel could be changed), and five 'visible' cuts from one character to another. There's a certain irony in the 'invisible' cuts being blindingly obvious while the 'visible' ones are easily missed, but it's churlish to focus on them. In keeping his camera mobile, Hitchcock is still able to use varying shot sizes to dramatic effect; in fact, some of the slow tracks from wide shots to close-ups (and vice versa) are loaded with portent. And when he does sit still - as in the nail-biting, two-minute-long, static shot of the housekeeper clearing things off the trunk so she can open it to put some books inside - the result is as suspenseful as anything in the Hitchcanon.

Rope's technique isn't for everyone, but criticism of it tends to overshadow the content, which is succulent with macabre drama. It's an examination of the smug entitlement of the over-privileged, and as such will always be relevant. Hitchcock intended the film as a refutation of fascist interpretations of Nietzsche's 'superman' theories: the idea someone could be above the law due to genetic or intellectual superiority. Sadly those ideologies haven't gone away, and we see them today in everyday prejudice against minorities and lower classes.

Brandon is a narcissistic psychopath; a true nephew to *Shadow Of A Doubt*'s Uncle Charlie in his homicidal misconceptions, and Phillip is weak and in thrall to him. Both are compelling ghouls, but it's James Stewart, cast wildly against type as their former mentor Rupert Cadell, who really raises *Rope*'s game. Rupert is ostensibly the protagonist, turning detective to uncover the murder as you'd expect the all-American hero of countless feelgood movies to. But Hitchcock saw a darkness in Stewart, and wasn't afraid to tap into it. It's Rupert's sociopathic teachings that radicalised the sycophantic Brandon and Phillip in the first place, and his attempt to extricate himself from his terrible responsibility in the film's electrifying final speech is chilling. If proof were needed of Rupert's unforgivable monstrousness, watch him brazenly navigate the party with two massive ice creams all to himself.

As an almost incidental backdrop to all this, Brandon and Phillip are Hitchcock's most overtly gay couple, even though their sexuality is never mentioned. It's fascinating because their relationship is so matter-of-fact you want to congratulate Hitch for not making a big deal of it, but it's not long before you realise it's hardly a positive representation. Like *Rebecca*'s Mrs Danvers before them and more ambiguous examples in later films, Brandon and Phillip can be read as villains whose crimes are arguably linked to their queerness: Hitchologist Robin Wood suggests *Rope* associates "homosexuality with the unnatural, the sick, the perverse - with 'evil' and fascism". Whether or not you agree, it's hard to deny there are no obviously gay heroes in Hitchcock (although *The Lady Vanishes*' Caldicott and Charters might just qualify).

Hitchcock's first step into independence may not have been a roaring success at the time, but its divisiveness makes it eternally worthy of inspection. First viewings of *Rope* are usually tricky, but subsequent visits reveal textual layers that reward the curious. One thing's for sure: Alfred Hitchcock rarely did what anyone expected him to. Which might explain why, when critics and audiences clearly expressed a disregard for his talky film full of long takes, he immediately went off and made another one.

UNDER CAPRICORN

1949, colour

Based on the novel by Helen Simpson, and the play by Margaret Linden and John Colton

Transatlantic Pictures

UK

True to its name, Hitchcock's Transatlantic Pictures jetted from Hollywood to Borehamwood for Under Capricorn, *recreating 19th century Sydney in Hertfordshire's MGM-British studios. Ingrid Bergman has difficulty down under, as the past catches up with her beneath the titular tropic.*

Hitchcock's appetite for a challenge sometimes looked more like gluttony for punishment. Despite being hopelessly out of his comfort zone on previous historical dramas *Waltzes From Vienna* and *Jamaica Inn*, he decided the second film for his own production company Transatlantic Pictures would be another period piece. He also intended to shoot it in long, unbroken takes, despite a total lack of audience interest in the technique in his previous film, *Rope*. What could possibly go right?

It seems like an odd career choice in retrospect, but at this time Hitchcock's options were limited. Despite his impressive track record, Transatlantic was a fledgling independent without the funds to secure more bankable properties to adapt. Hitchcock had owned the rights to *Under Capricorn* since 1945 and saw it as a star vehicle for Ingrid Bergman, with whom Hitch had become somewhat besotted. He'd secured her services and waited patiently for her availability, and was delighted just to have her in his film, given every studio in Hollywood wanted her.

Not unconnected to this was the choice to use long takes and minimal edits again. Biographer Patrick McGilligan claims the director thought the approach would impress Bergman. If so, Hitch couldn't have been more wrong. The pressure of long, emotional dialogue scenes, and the logistical mechanics required to pull off the process, drove the actress round the bend. If Hitchcock hoped Bergman would leave her neurosurgeon husband for a film director, his wish came true - unfortunately for him, it was Italian neorealist Roberto Rossellini's arms she ran into. It wouldn't be the last underachievement of the Alfred Hitchcock school of charm.

Under Capricorn seems almost aggressively anti-Hitchcockian on the surface. A dour costume drama set in the British colony and convict dumping-ground of 1830s Sydney, Australia, it's heavy on dialogue and light on incident: a two-hour melodrama that's around three parts melo to one part drama. But on closer inspection, a handful of Hitchcock's favourite tropes reveal themselves. A marriage is put under strain when one of the unhappy couple assumes the guilt for a crime committed by the other, and the arrival of a handsome third party leads to a good old-fashioned love triangle. Ingrid Bergman plays Lady Henrietta 'Hattie' Flusky, the woman torn between her foul-tempered, Heathcliffian husband Sam (Joseph Cotten, deploying a face that could sour milk) and old flame Charles Adare (Michael Wilding), described by the film's marketing as "The most exciting 'other man' you ever met!", but in truth about as tempting as the milk Joseph Cotten's face just soured.

Seasoned Hitchwatchers should spot the shared elements between *Under Capricorn* and the self-replicating director's previous films. Like *The Paradine Case*, an upper-class heroine falls for a stable boy with deadly consequences: a return to the love-bridging-class-divides theme that characterised many of Hitch's silents. The primary location with a shady reputation is noted by a coachman: "There's something queer about that place," he says of the Fluskys' house - a virtual rearrangement of *Jamaica Inn*'s equally sceptical cabbie's remark, "There's queer things going on there". Meanwhile severe, jealous housekeeper Milly echoes *Rebecca*'s Mrs Danvers, and her poisoning of (and denial of the house keys to) Ingrid Bergman's character recalls *Notorious*. That's not the only Bergman callback: at the climax she chooses a selfless fate over her heart's desire, as she did in *Casablanca*. Although given Michael Wilding is no Humphrey Bogart, fewer hankies are required here.

Then, of course, there's the return of *Rope*'s long takes. Hitchcock doesn't attempt the illusion of an unbroken shot in the same way with *Under Capricorn*, instead scattering handfuls of shots of six, seven or eight minutes' length across a film otherwise traditionally edited. But without that formal thread running through the whole film, the technique doesn't quite gel. Where *Rope*'s camera prowled impatiently around its characters in real time, virtually willing the bubble of suspense to pop, *Under Capricorn* seems more concerned with showing off its very long sets and its actors' abilities to remember reams of dialogue at a time. Bergman's confession speech, in a shot clocking in at almost nine minutes, is an acting *tour de force* in and of itself, but does nothing for the film's already torpid pace.

And yet the mixture of extreme long takes and classical continuity editing feels like it might be an attempt to finesse *Rope*'s experimental style, rather than a half-hearted reproduction of it. Twice in *Under Capricorn*, Hitchcock ends a lengthy, uncut, dialogue-heavy scene by unexpectedly cutting to a character we didn't know was in the room. Both times the cut evokes surprise and shifts the scene up a gear, which speaks not only to the power of the cut, but also to the impact of withholding it for as long as possible. Hitch would use long takes and hidden cuts in the future (see *Frenzy* for a chilling example), but sparingly and for maximum effect.

Sadly no amount of technical bells and whistles can counterbalance *Under Capricorn*'s dull, meandering story; little wonder Joseph Cotten referred to it as 'Under Cornycrap'. Twenty-five minutes of near-inconsequential waffle elapse before Bergman, the film's lead, makes her entrance. The Fluskys' misery infects the whole film, sapping any attempt at humour: possibly the three harridan cooks are intended as comic relief, but they're fighting a losing battle. Brief and effective moments of visual storytelling, such as the beautiful close-up of Sam excitedly clasping a ruby necklace before deflatedly concealing it when Hattie says she doesn't need jewellery, are few and far between. And regardless of the costume design's accuracy, it's hard to concentrate when Ingrid Bergman often looks like she's wearing an elaborately decorated wedding cake.

Under Capricorn isn't without its charm, but audiences and critics struggled to find it. The film performed so badly the Bankers' Trust of New York, who loaned Hitchcock the cash to make it, repossessed it. His third consecutive flop, it remains one of Hitch's least-seen films - although a small army of admirers make strong arguments for its reappraisal. Unfortunately that comes several decades too late for Transatlantic Pictures, which began to quietly fade away after just two movies. Its future projects were transferred to Warner Brothers, who had distributed *Rope* and *Under Capricorn*, and Hitchcock dutifully worked on those while licking his wounds.

THE TROUBLE WITH HITCHCOCK

Hopefully, by the time you've seen a good few Hitchcock films, you'll be aware that he was truly a master of the art of cinema: a technical wizard and a witty, innovative storyteller with a unique voice. But a full understanding of Hitchcock involves an awareness of his dark side. Watch a few more of his films and you'll soon realise that he sometimes used that voice in ways that would be unacceptable today, and weren't necessarily all that acceptable at the time. Do some background reading on the man himself, and you'll find out that just as he sometimes failed with his art, he wasn't always successful at being a human being.

It's fair to say that, like the vast majority of his contemporaries working in mid-20th century mainstream western cinema, Alfred Hitchcock was not a leading proponent of diversity and inclusion. People of colour rarely come off well in Hitchcock's films, either by being reduced to stereotypes (*Downhill*,

The Ring, *Champagne*, *Lifeboat*) or by their near-total absence (pretty much all the rest, except *Topaz*). Hitchcock's most significant representation of disability consists of a single - and arguably clichéd - scene in *Saboteur* featuring a blind character (*Rear Window*'s wheelchair-bound Jimmy Stewart really doesn't count). And thanks to Hollywood's Production Code, which forbade positive portrayals of homosexuality in American films from the mid-1930s to the late '60s, gay or bisexual people in Hitchcock are few and far between. When they do appear, their sexuality is heavily coded rather than explicit, and is usually associated with villainous or morally questionable characters (*Murder!*, *Rebecca*, *Rope*, *Strangers On A Train*).

You can make all the arguments you like for Hitchcock working in 'a different time', and the Production Code - along with the similarly puritanical National Legion of Decency - were certainly responsible for holding back many of the progressive ideas filmmakers may have had. But it's worth remembering that Hitchcock spent his career constantly pushing technical and narrative boundaries in cinema, becoming one of pop culture's most powerful and influential figures. And yet he chose *not* to use that power and influence to push social boundaries by standing against the prevailing winds of prejudice against minorities. Tales of his battles with the Production Code over how violent *Psycho*'s shower scene could be are legion; less common are stories of him fighting to portray positive gay characters.

Easily the most complex relationship Hitchcock had, both on screen and off, was with women. He was capable of friendliness and respect towards the women in his life, and while female colleagues undoubtedly formed a small minority of Hitchcock's team, some of them were among his closest collaborators: his wife and most trusted ally Alma; script supervisor, personal assistant and associate producer Peggy Robertson, and writer (and producer of his TV series) Joan Harrison. That said, some Hitchcock biographers claim his interest in the blonde, attractive, impeccably stylish Harrison wasn't exclusively professional.

Hitchcock's relationships with his leading actresses were, to say the least, varied. He was close friends with Carole Lombard, Grace Kelly and Ingrid Bergman (despite alleged unrequited feelings for the latter two), but he also treated several female stars with a contempt and cruelty that have earned him a reputation as one of cinema's leading misogynists. Vera Miles, who Hitchcock excitedly signed to a five-year contract in 1955, found herself shunned by her director when she became pregnant and couldn't star in *Vertigo* as he'd meticulously planned. Hitchcock channelled his frustration over Miles into his treatment of Kim Novak, who suffered a similar ordeal to her *Vertigo* character: fashioned and shaped into the image of a dominating man's previous obsession, her biggest crime was that she wasn't Vera Miles.

But it was Tippi Hedren who appears to have suffered the worst of Hitchcock's dark side. Like Vera Miles, Hedren was signed to a lengthy contract with Hitchcock, with the intention that she would become a star of his designing. Her experience making *The Birds* was arduous, to say the least: she spent a week having angry gulls thrown at her face for the climactic sequence. But it was during the production of *Marnie* that, Hedren told biographer Donald Spoto, Hitchcock paid her an undue amount of attention which overstepped several lines and caused the actress great distress. When he reportedly forced himself on her, her rebuttal infuriated him, and Hedren found herself on the receiving end of a career-crippling cold shoulder. Despite tentative plans to work together again, they never did so.

The representation of women in Hitchcock's films is no less complicated than his relationships with their real-life counterparts. Plenty of his pictures feature progressive and positive female characters who frequently outwit and triumph over their male counterparts, but they're largely overshadowed by the shocking graphic and sexually-charged violence he visited on some of them in the name of entertainment, particularly in his later films. This contrast has resulted in fascinating analysis by feminist film theorists like Laura Mulvey, Tania Modleski and Camille Paglia, but perhaps *The Guardian* journalist Bidisha Mamata most succinctly and entertainingly outlined the trouble with Hitchcock's women, categorising them in a 2010 article as "the vamp, the tramp, the snitch, the witch, the slink, the double-crosser and, best of all, the demon mommy. Don't worry, they all get punished in the end."

As time passes, Hitchcock's attitudes slip further into a past that will soon be unrecognisable. It's important to understand the social context of the period in which he lived and worked, but it's equally important to keep interrogating and re-evaluating his representations of minorities in order to see how far we've come, and how far we still have to go. His treatment of certain women also can't be ignored, because to do so is to give a free pass to that behaviour, making it harder to eradicate today. Alfred Hitchcock was an exceptional artist, but he was also part of a problem with which the film industry, and the world at large, is still living.

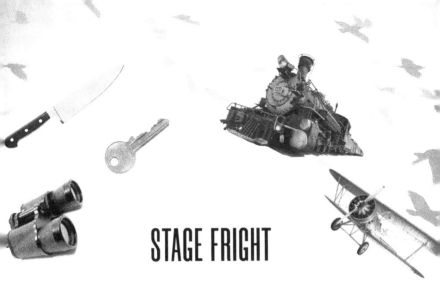

STAGE FRIGHT

1950, b/w

Based on the novel *Man Running* by Selwyn Jepson

Warner Brothers

UK

SPOILER WARNING

*"Here you have a plot, an interesting cast… even a costume,"
remarks Alastair Sim's character in this mischievously self-
reflexive film. Actors and acting get the Hitchcock treatment – not
least the director's own daughter, whose character he ungraciously
names 'Chubby Bannister'.*

Three flops in a row would send any director running for cover,
and Hitchcock was no exception. Although he was relatively
unfazed by commercial failure, Hitch's decision to return to
the breezy comedy-thriller stylings of his late British period
after three experimental disappointments feels very much like
reaching for a comfort blanket. And a well-worn comfort blan-

ket it was: after *Foreign Correspondent* and *Saboteur*, this was his third such nostalgia trip since leaving the UK a decade earlier.

In truth, work on *Stage Fright* was well underway before his previous film *Under Capricorn* tanked at the box office, but Hitch already knew he badly needed to recapture old magic. And he almost did: *Stage Fright* is loaded with charm, humour and weapons-grade female star power, but its weak plot and mixed tone relegate it to mid-tier Hitchery. And one narrative decision in particular proved contemporary audiences weren't quite ready for some of Hitchcock's storytelling skullduggery.

Set in London and the home counties, *Stage Fright* sees doe-eyed Jane Wyman as Eve Gill, an aspiring actress caught up in another of Hitchcock's improbable plots. Eve is in love with Jonathan (Richard Todd), but Jonathan is in love with stage and screen diva Charlotte Inwood (effortlessly brought to life by stage and screen diva Marlene Dietrich). The film kicks off at speed with Eve helping Jonathan escape the police, who are after him for a crime he says he didn't commit - the murder of Charlotte's husband. So far, so wrong-man-on-the-run again. Eve's increasingly convoluted attempts to clear Jonathan's name, and to point investigating detective Wilfred Smith (Michael Wilding) in the direction of Charlotte, the apparent killer, form the bulk of the plot.

We're immediately in familiar Hitchcock territory, both narratively and geographically. The resourceful woman coming to the rescue of the accused man after a murder involving an actress is all very *Young And Innocent*, as are the circumstances of the murder, which becomes the MacGuffin - a virtual irrel-evance that merely lights the plot's fuse. *Stage Fright*'s theatrical setting recalls *Murder!*, *The 39 Steps* and all those British thrillers that used showbiz as a backdrop for passion, jeopardy and violence. Hitchcock's fondness for the working classes returns, with rich depictions of maids, barmaids and barflies, and his love for the eccentricities of his countrymen drenches the already-soaked garden party scene - which, incidentally, allows for a sly callback to *Foreign Correspondent*'s sea of bobbing black brollies. An extended skit in which Alistair Sim's character attempts to procure a doll from a batty shooting gallery assistant (played by Joyce Grenfell and credited, wonderfully, as 'Lovely Ducks') is a delightfully nutty aside.

But the Hitchcockian concern that gets top billing in *Stage Fright* is the artifice of art: the overlapping dynamics of acting and lying, and the duplicitous mechanics of storytelling. Here's a film that opens with the slow raising of a theatre's safety curtain to reveal an entirely cinematic scene: a high-angle shot of London's St Paul's area. It's a fun sight gag, but it also sets up the film's bookend climax, in which another safety curtain is lowered, this time to even more dramatic effect - quickly, and onto the villain's prone body. Watch carefully, too, for the elaborate camera move that tracks Jonathan into Charlotte's house. Hitchcock follows him through the doorway, then has him reach behind to close the door - a physical impossibility given the camera's in the way, but lighting and sound effects complete the deception. Hitch would reuse this device in *The Wrong Man*, and reverse it in *The Birds*.

Then there's Eve, the actress forced to assume false identities *offstage* in order to fool other characters. First she pretends to feel faint to attract Detective Smith, then she claims to be a reporter to get close to Charlotte's housekeeper. Finally she transforms into a maid, *within* her role as investigative journalist, as part of a long con to trick Charlotte into admitting her guilt. Inevitably the layers of subterfuge are unsustainable, and Hitchcock knows how much his perverse audience is enjoying the heroine's suffering.

The film's most significantly devious plot device, though, is the early flashback sequence narrated to Eve (and us) by Jonathan, explaining his innocence. It drives Eve to great lengths to protect Jonathan, until the emotionally crushing moment (shortly before a physically crushing moment) when he reveals it was all a gigantic whopper, and that he *did* kill Charlotte's hubbie. The false flashback was Hitchcock's idea (it didn't feature in the book on which the film is based), and Alma and scriptwriter Whitfield Cook tried to talk him out of it. Hitch stood his ground and paid the price: audiences were appalled that the film had lied to them, and it became *Stage Fright*'s most negative talking point.

But unreliable narrators in cinema had been around since at least 1920's *The Cabinet Of Dr. Caligari*; Akira Kurosawa's *Rashōmon* - released the same year as *Stage Fright* - boasted four of them. Hitchcock himself had already used one in his wartime short *Bon Voyage*. In the context of *Stage Fright*'s blurring of actors and liars, Jonathan's porky is entirely consistent. It enhances the otherwise relatively standard storytelling, adding metatextual layers to a film that arguably doesn't deserve them. Unfortunately, nobody wanted that from Hitchcock, and he regretted committing what audiences saw as a betrayal of their faith.

If the fake flashback can be condemned at all, it's as an example of *Stage Fright*'s focus on plot mechanics over people - a common criticism of Hitchcock's work. Despite a talented cast, it's hard to care about any of the characters. Moreover, the structure doesn't allow for much in the way of suspense: nobody's ever in mortal danger, so the film becomes a black comedy (to be fair, it is *very* funny) with an incongruous murder suspect popping up every now and again to frown solemnly. Still, there's much to enjoy, not least a lip-smacking femme fatale role for

Marlene Dietrich, still firing on all cylinders despite being past the peak of her cinematic fame. But she wasn't the only one in need of a hit: Hitchcock's attempt at a return to former glories had failed. Fortunately there was light at the end of the tunnel, if only he could get back on the right track.

STRANGERS ON A TRAIN

1951, b/w

Based on the novel by Patricia Highsmith

Warner Brothers

US

Two men with a loco-motive for murder are pitted against each other in this first-class return to form for Hitchcock. While the characters' relationship is decidedly antagonistic, Hitch met a collaborator for life in cinematographer Robert Burks, who elevates the material to genuine art.

After five years without box office success, it seemed like Hitchcock's nose for a great property was a bit bunged up. But when the master of suspense - as he would soon be nicknamed - happened upon the debut novel by a writer who would one day be referred to as the *mistress* of suspense, he sensed a soulmate; a partner in crime fiction. The talents of two gifted storytellers converged so naturally, it was as if Alfred Hitchcock and Patricia Highsmith had planned his latest caper together. Criss-cross.

Another big name appears in *Strangers On A Train*'s opening credits, but you can dismiss the contribution of ostensible co-screenwriter Raymond Chandler as easily as Hitchcock did (although the small matter of Chandler's unused script didn't stop Warner Brothers using his name in their marketing). Instead, the film's achievements were in no small part thanks to three virtually unsung women: screenwriter Czenzi Ormonde, who was somewhat unfairly forced to share the 'Screen Play by' credit with Chandler; Barbara Keon, an associate producer of David O Selznick's who had followed Hitch out of Selznick's shadow, and Hitchcock's wife Alma, who had a hand in almost all her husband's screenplays.

Together, these talented writers reshaped Highsmith's study of whether murderous intent is a product of nature or nurture into a classically Hitchcockian text on the fragility of order, especially when tested by a lethally effective agent of chaos. It is perhaps a by-product of Hitchcock's love of order that he took the lion's share of credit for his best films, neatly finessing his own brand. But without Ormonde, Keon and Reville on board, *Strangers On A Train* would never have left the station.

Hitch frequently explored the dramatic effects of dumb luck on an unsuspecting average Joe, but rarely was that idea of malevolent fate embodied as purely or successfully as it was in Robert Walker's lunatic in a lobster-print tie, Bruno Antony. Bruno's apparently random assault on the cosy existence of terminally dull tennis player Guy Haines (Farley Granger) begins with implied inevitability: Hitchcock cuts between shots of the two men's feet, striding towards each other as if drawn together. The occasional cutaway to intersecting railway tracks mirrors the convergence of their paths.

They're heading for the same train, and once aboard, the strangers' ominous meet-cute establishes their respective obstacles in life - Bruno's disdainful father and Guy's recalcitrant, estranged wife Miriam. Their chit-chat takes a surprisingly sinister turn when Bruno suggests he and Guy solve their problems by swapping murders: "What is a life or two, Guy? Some people are better off dead." If there were such a thing as the Hitchcock Cinematic Universe, Bruno would definitely have been in the same house at prep school as *Rope*'s conceited killers Brandon and Phillip.

From this exquisite exposition, *Strangers On A Train* gathers steam all the way to the end of the line, a thrillingly staged climax on a runaway merry-go-round - the last in a series of ordinarily tame experiences, sent hurtling violently out of control by Bruno's presence. But en route, the film stops to show off some of Hitchcock's greatest moments of visual storytelling. It's no surprise that after this beautifully-shot picture, with its crisp contrast of narratively appropriate darkness and light, Hitch collaborated with cinematographer Robert Burks 11 more times. Burks understood Hitchcock implicitly, and his translations of the director's ideas are among cinema's finest images.

But it's not just that *Strangers* looks good. The pictures tell the story so clearly that, once you know the premise, you could arguably mute the rest of the film and still understand everything that unfolds. Perhaps the most accomplished fusion of thematic idea and visual flair comes when Bruno appears outside Guy's apartment to update him on the progress of his deadly plan. Hitchcock divides the frame with an iron gate: Bruno admits his crime from behind the bars (common movie shorthand for a guilty party), while the innocent Guy stands in the open. But as Guy's complicity in Miriam's murder dawns on him, that deeply Hitchcockian idea of transference of guilt takes hold. Bruno reminds Guy of his unwitting part in the plot, at which point Hitch shoots *both* characters through bars. But the gate is between them; there's a chance Guy is still on the right side of that divide. Then the police arrive, and Guy aligns himself with Bruno behind the bars to hide from them. Guy's assumption of Bruno's guilt is complete. In a brief, simple masterclass of blocking and staging, Hitchcock visualises the dialogue, accentuating the moment at which Guy realises his life will never be the same.

Strangers On A Train is packed with unforgettable imagery like this. Bruno chillingly watching Guy (and, crucially, the camera) from the steps of the Jefferson Memorial, and later from an oblivious tennis crowd, are nightmarish vignettes in which Hitch exploits the power of subjective point of view. More objectively, Hitchcock and Burks stage dramatically stylised tableaux in which figures recede into the background (most notably at the end of the record store scene and in Senator Morton's sitting room), echoing the perspective of train tracks disappearing into the distance. And Miriam's murder - reflected in her fallen glasses in a shot that recalls Hitch's beloved German Expressionism - is a grotesque distortion of a grotesque act. It also marks a shift from Hitchcock's previous fetishisation of spectacles, which connote character in *Suspicion* and *Spellbound*, to a more practical plot function here.

Bruno is, of course, the id to Guy's superego: the personification of Guy's basest desires, carrying out the morally repugnant ideas any sane person would keep locked away in the darkest recesses of their conscience. It's as if Guy has conjured Bruno up from a deep psychological pit - any modern remake would surely deploy a twist ending wherein they're revealed to be the same person. And while that idea (and Robert Walker's flawless performance) makes Bruno extremely watchable, it's clear Hitch was far more interested in him than any of the other characters. Guy and his girlfriend Ann are so rigid with tedium they're consistently overshadowed, even by most of the supporting parts. *Strangers On A Train*'s writing team, who were also destined to be eclipsed by the man at the centre of everything, must have sympathised.

I CONFESS

1953, b/w

Based on the play *Nos Deux Consciences* by
Paul Anthelme

Warner Brothers

US

SPOILER
WARNING

---

*It's a Canadian stand-off between love, the church and the law
in this Quebec-set tale of the price of priestly passion. Method
actor Monty Clift is as devoted to his craft as his character is to
God; Anne Baxter and Karl Malden round out the congregation.*

Unfolding in French-speaking Quebec City, *I Confess*'s opening
montage features a quick succession of road signs that read
'DIRECTION', each one accompanied by a stab of violins
from Dimitri Tiomkin's ominous score. To Canadian drivers
the signs merely display useful traffic instructions, but to Alfred
Hitchcock, they're a huge in-joke. The fourth and final sign
points directly to the open window of a house, and the camera

follows it to find a fresh corpse inside. Cinematography, editing, music and audience have all been manipulated by Hitchcock's own 'direction', a fact he gleefully - and literally - signposts.

Sadly there isn't much more visual fun, or indeed much fun of any kind, to be found in the remainder of *I Confess* (unless you count a priest whose bike keeps falling over, which is about as funny as it sounds). But what the film lacks in laughs, it more than makes up for in Catholic guilt. The transference of guilt is one of Hitchcock's most frequently recurring themes, and this is his starkest depiction of it. Critic Bill Krohn said of Hitch's films that "guilt is everywhere, and as easy to catch as a cold." In *I Confess*, there's an epidemic.

The aforementioned cadaver belongs to lawyer Villette, recently bumped off by church caretaker Otto Keller in a fatally bungled robbery. Keller, overcome with guilt, immediately confesses the crime to his priest and employer Father Michael Logan, played by a breathtakingly handsome Montgomery Clift. Thanks to a wrinkle in Catholic ritual that prevents a priest from disclosing anything heard in confession, Logan must now bear the weight of Keller's awful admission alone. Keller, now considering himself absolved of his sins, has transferred his guilt to Logan.

Unfortunately, Logan is already suffering from the guilt of a past affair with a married woman, Ruth Grandfort (Anne Baxter), who was being blackmailed over the affair by Villette. Still more guilt is piled onto the shame-stricken priest by Inspector Larrue (Karl Malden, as that Hitchcockian rarity: a smart cop), when a convoluted set of circumstances lead to Logan becoming Larrue's prime suspect in Villette's murder. The weight of real, transferred and assumed guilt becomes almost too much for Logan to bear, symbolised by Hitchcock in an uncharacteristically on-the-nose shot of Logan dwarfed by a statue of Christ carrying his cross.

Almost every main character struggles with varying degrees of guilt at some stage of the story, and while *I Confess* remains a middling Hitchcock, the Catholic-born-and-raised director arguably assumed more guilt than was necessary when he later claimed he shouldn't have made the film. There's much to admire, not least Robert Burks's noirish photography, especially in the *Third Man*-esque early scenes. Note the latticed window that separates Father Logan and Keller during the latter's confession, which places Keller behind figurative bars but also pointedly casts its shadow onto Logan, recalling the similar transference-of-guilt scene in *Strangers On A Train*. It's also a rare treat in terms of location filming, although no amount of unwitting Quebecoise extras gawping into camera can stop the city coming off as a little sterile. At least Hitchcock allows his director of photography a cameo of sorts: Logan walks past a cinema showing Humphrey Bogart in *The Enforcer*, which Burks also shot.

It's no great mental leap to imagine *I Confess* filmed as a straight whodunnit from the point of view of dogged investigator Larrue, but this is Hitchcock, and Hitchcock couldn't give a stuff about whodunnits. It's far more interesting for him to feed us necessary information when it has the most dramatic impact, rather than when the plot would traditionally demand it. Telling us Keller is the murderer in the opening minutes allows Hitch to focus on the emotional weight of revelations like Logan and Ruth's affair, and the torment of Keller's wife Alma - herself carrying guilt that becomes unbearable. And Hitch shifts narrative subjectivity between Logan, Larrue and Ruth throughout the film, even allowing it to take on characters' emotional states. Ruth's flashback to her affair may appear cheesy for Hitchcock, with its slow motion, soft focus and lush score, but as Hitch scholar Robin Wood explains, it's merely representative of the nostalgic, romantic ideal Ruth dreams of and hopes in vain to regain.

Hitch had hoped to retain the play's ending, in which Father Logan is hanged for crimes he didn't commit, but neither the Production Code nor Warner Brothers were about to let that happen. While it would have provided a crushingly downbeat ending to rival that of *Vertigo* or the generally grim mood of *The Wrong Man*, the abandoned climax might at least have been more memorable than the one we get. A rote, final-act chase is half-heartedly executed, and having painted himself into a corner of Canada with no famous landmarks, Hitch is forced to stage the chase in a fancy hotel. Keller improbably kills his wife to stop her blabbing, shortly before confessing himself, simply because the film has run out of plot. Meanwhile Ruth, watching her true love anxiously walk into a room to face a desperate, armed murderer, chooses that moment to go home with her unloved husband and doesn't even return when, seconds later, shots are fired.

Despite its somewhat weak story and a lead actor who, much to Hitchcock's annoyance, internalised his emotions to the point of spending much of the film frowning like he's trying to mentally solve a quadratic equation, *I Confess* remains a worthy entry in the Hitchcanon. Blondes, murder, love triangles, unhappy marriages and wrongly accused men are all to be found within, and it's powered by layered - if not particularly complex - ideas around guilt and religion. Unfortunately it's neither suspenseful nor thrilling, and those are the qualities audiences now demanded from Hitchcock's films. Hitch complained to his friend Sidney Bernstein at the time that he had become 'typed' as a certain kind of director, but rather than deny his instincts, it was at more or less this point that Hitchcock chose to lean into that reputation. If suspense and thrills were what audiences wanted, he was ready to answer that call.

DIAL M FOR MURDER

1954, colour
Based on the play by Frederick Knott
Warner Brothers
US

An unfaithful wife. A jealous husband. A perfect murder. Except it's not: everything that can go wrong for vengeful cuckold Tony Wendice does. He's a charming Hitchcock villain so we'll allow him a little sympathy, but he never deserved a wife like Grace Kelly.

The early 1950s saw Hollywood bending over backwards to haul audiences away from their new-fangled 'television sets' and back into cinemas. New colour processes, stereophonic sound and wider screens were all part of the drive to render the cinematic experience unbeatable. In 1953, another wacky enhancement proved temporarily successful: 3D. That spring, Warner Brothers hit paydirt with camp horror *House Of Wax*, a film that brought the nascent 3D craze to the mainstream despite being directed by Andre de Toth, a man who famously possessed only half the optimum number of eyeballs required to fully appreciate the effect of 3D cinema.

Alfred Hitchcock did not suffer from the same depth perception issues as de Toth; in fact he could see deep enough into the future to recognise 3D as a passing fad. So when Warners insisted he make the fourth film of his contract with them in the format, he was unenthusiastic. But Warners weren't asking, they were telling, so *Dial M For Murder* became Hitch's first and only foray into stereoscopic vision. Released a year after *House Of Wax*, at the waning of 3D cinema's short-lived 'golden era', Hitchcock's film barely screened anywhere in its dimensionally-enhanced form. As a 'flattie', though, it was a success, and remains something of a minor classic to this day.

Watching *Dial M* in plain old 2D, you'd be hard-pressed to spot the moments where the extra visual plane added much. That's because Hitch wasn't interested in visual gimmickry that (literally) foregrounded the artifice of cinema; he wanted to pull audiences into his films, not the other way round. It does, however, explain the omnipresence of a green table lamp in the foreground of a disproportionate number of shots in the first act. Take a swig of brandy each time you see it and you'll be struggling to even find M on your telephone, let alone dial it. Grace Kelly's desperate heroine Margot, reaching out into the audience for the nearest sharp object, is the only evidence that 3D was ever a consideration: an intended dramatic close-up of a finger in a telephone dial, which required a giant wooden digit and a similarly huge phone to be built to facilitate the 3D effect, lasts a smidgen over two seconds.

As the third of Hitchcock's four single-location films (allowing for minor excursions outside the flat it's set in), *Dial M For Murder* presented him with more challenges than just convincingly poking the odd limb out of the screen. It's very obviously a stage adaptation, although Hitch does everything he can to make Cinema out of it. He cuts around characters like he's being paid by the edit, always looking for an unexpected angle from which to photograph his subjects. Shots range from floor-level to overhead: watch Ray Milland's insidious plotter Tony Wendice outline his plan to hapless patsy Swann (Anthony Dawson) while the camera dispassionately observes from above, as if the frame is the back of an envelope on which Tony is sketching instructions.

It's also impossible to ignore the wildly expressionistic scene in which Hitchcock elides an entire court case by using a head-on shot of Margot, as slivers of dialogue, coloured lights and shadows swirl menacingly around her. And there's an echo of *Rope* and *Under Capricorn*'s long takes curtailed by a potent edit: Tony's apparently innocent chat with Swann includes a two-minute unbroken shot filled with innocuous dialogue, which ends when talk suddenly turns to murder and Hitchcock cuts to Swann's stupefied reaction, mirroring that of the audience.

The script's deft handling of crosses, double-crosses and double-reverse-countercrosses - committed by characters *and* storytellers - allows Hitchcock to take an unusual approach to the opposing elements of mystery and suspense. What he does and doesn't let us know is vital to *Dial M*'s impact. No fan of whodunnits, wherein characters are often several steps ahead of the audience, Hitch nevertheless enjoys surprising us with Tony's plan to have Margot bumped off, after we thought we were the ones with the privileged information about her affair. And knowing the plan in detail means we're back in nerve-jangling suspense territory when it's being carried out. But when things go wrong for Tony, the ensuing investigation by Chief Inspector Hubbard (John Williams) dares us to keep up. Your chances of solving the mystery in advance depend greatly on your ability to keep track of a series of keys, moved around the story like chess pieces. Hitchcock's decision to hide the most crucial movement of a key, underneath a casual shot of Margot sleeping, shapes the entire audience experience for the next hour: a powerful demonstration of the manipulative function of editing.

Simultaneously, our knowledge that Tony is guilty creates the suspense of desperately wanting Hubbard to realise it. The balancing act between mystery and suspense is incredibly delicate, yet Hitch gleefully plays around with it. Tony's realisation that his watch has stopped threatens to throw his entire plan into chaos, and Hitchcock exacerbates the anxiety with tense music and a shot of a telephone exchange slowly shifting its gears. And yet none of this affects the plot: Tony's phone call goes ahead as planned, just a little late. The only reason for the manufactured suspense is to play with audience identification: for a brief moment we're desperate for the villain's plan to succeed. Similarly, we're fed a juicy red herring when Margot's lover unwittingly works out the truth of Tony's scheme, only to abandon it as far-fetched. Hitch plays us like a fiddle, and it's impossible not to admire his musicianship.

Dial M For Murder ends gloriously, with a scene of deliciously smug moustache-combing. Retrospectively, it's a perfect metaphor for the position Hitchcock was then in. He'd pulled off a potentially leaden stage adaptation in style, and at the same time was working on no fewer than three future projects. He didn't know it, but he was about to enter a decade of filmmaking in which he would create some of the most important, iconic and influential works of art that cinema would ever produce. And as for those audiences for whom even 3D movies weren't enough to drag them away from their TV sets... well, Alfred Hitchcock would soon present something for them too.

REAR WINDOW

1954, colour

Based on the short story *It Had To Be Murder* by Cornell Woolrich

Paramount

US

Neighbours can be murder, as James Stewart discovers from his room with a view. Rear Window *boasts achievements great and small: the apartment block set is hugely impressive, but the kiss with which Grace Kelly introduces herself is unforgettable.*

In 1954 Hitchcock left Warner Brothers for Paramount, who granted him a freedom that led to a tipping point in his career. After nearly 30 years in which he'd directed almost 40 films and steadily built his own brand to the point of being as famous as his stars, Hitchcock finally had sufficient clout to do as he pleased. He gathered a trusted creative team who perfectly understood his vision, and picked his favourite actors without studio heads nixing his expensive choices. He was exactly where he wanted to be, and this long-desired contentment birthed a new filmmaking maturity. Almost everything Hitch made from this point on was characterised by a slick Hollywood sheen that belied multiple layers of psychological depth and seductively dark themes. Exhibit A: *Rear Window* - a glossy, charming, battle-of-the-sexes romcom featuring murder, suicide and a severed head in a flowerbed.

Set entirely in a New York apartment, presenting a huge technical challenge for Hitchcock and with a prominent role for James Stewart, *Rear Window* is arguably a jazzier, younger sibling to *Rope*. But whereas that film deliberately eschewed the benefits of editing, *Rear Window* takes the polar opposite approach. Stewart plays L.B. 'Jeff' Jefferies, a daredevil photographer stuck in a wheelchair with his leg in plaster after getting too close to the action on his last assignment. With no action to get close to while housebound, Jeff resorts to ogling his neighbours across the courtyard, eventually suspecting - as you do - that one of them may have bumped off his wife.

That's *Rear Window*'s plot, but that's not what *Rear Window* is about. The murder mystery is certainly suspenseful, gripping and quite gruesome in its details, but it's merely a distraction from two big themes which had consumed Hitchcock since he first picked up a megaphone. With its prying protagonist and its subplot about Jeff's rocky love life, *Rear Window* is the purest distillation of Hitchcock's fascination with voyeurism, and of his belief in the insurmountable romantic incompatibility of men and women.

Hitch appeals to the voyeur in all of us when he places us in Jeff's position with his subjective point-of-view shooting and cutting. He knows we're all tempted to spy on our neighbours, and he knows we love to indulge in a little consequence-free voyeurism every time we go to a cinema to sit in the dark and watch people's lives unfold in the most intimate ways, just as Jeff does in his apartment. When Jeff wonders if perhaps there *hasn't* been a murder, we share his disappointment. What does that say about us? It's precisely the kind of deliciously uncomfortable position Hitch loved to put his audience in.

A key element of Hitchcock's voyeurism is his editing. A student of Russian montage, Hitch was well aware of the power of the 'Kuleshov effect' - the idea that any reaction shot of an actor is as dependent on the shot they're reacting to as it is on the actor's performance. Hitchcock's films, and *Rear Window* in particular, are full of shots of characters looking, followed by a shot of what they're looking at, followed by a reaction shot. Combine this with the subjectivity of giving the audience only Jeff's point of view, and our experience of the film's events is at the mercy of his reactions. Think about the infinite combination of shots and reaction shots that Hitchcock *could* have cut together, and you get some idea of the power of editing to shape narrative.

Meanwhile, Jeff is in the improbable situation of being annoyed that his girlfriend Lisa (an impossibly radiant Grace Kelly) wants to give herself to him entirely. He's trying hard to convince himself she's too good for him, while she's trying to tie him down to a less dangerous career. If two people this perfect can't get it on, suggests Hitchcock, what hope do the rest of us have? Jeff's dissatisfaction is exacerbated by his voyeurism, and Lisa complains that the only way Jeff will pay her any attention is if she moves across the courtyard where he's constantly looking. Little do either of them know she will eventually do just that, and that's when Jeff will indeed finally take an interest in her.

As Jeff and Lisa bicker and banter away, possible versions of their relationship echo throughout the apartments across the courtyard. A newlywed couple's marriage is threatened by the wife's insatiable libido; a lonely woman sets a dinner table for an imaginary date just as Lisa arranges a meal for a man who's barely present; a husband looks after and argues with his invalid wife, reversing the roles of Jeff and Lisa's partnership. The lead couple seem to reach an understanding at the film's climax, just as the other relationships in the block resolve. But a sly coda suggests otherwise, Hitch somehow ending his film on a simultaneously triumphant and bleak note.

Quite apart from these themes, there's so much more going on in *Rear Window* that it remains one of Hitchcock's most dissected films. Note, for instance, how events *outside* Jeff's apartment seem to be intertwined with what happens *inside*: Jeff and his nurse discuss marriage, just before the newlyweds arrive. Jeff and Lisa have their biggest argument; moments later, Jeff hears a scream that signals the extreme culmination of another couple's spat. A detective talks about poking into the case a little, shortly before we see a neighbourhood dog on the verge of uncovering vital evidence. Is Jeff somehow the cause of everything that happens? That chimes with another interpretation - that Jeff is Hitchcock's surrogate, sitting in his chair, naming his characters and piecing together their stories from short scenes in rectangular frames - most of which are virtually silent, in a reminder of Hitch's early career. It's surely no coincidence that the film is bookended with the raising and lowering of blinds, like the curtains of a cinema screen.

Rear Window remains an undisputed masterpiece to this day, and it ignited an extraordinary phase in Hitchcock's career. Critics and audiences alike were now his voyeurs, watching him night and day, desperate to see what he might do next. And while his on-screen relationships never ran smoothly, many filmgoers were now forming love affairs with Alfred Hitchcock that would last forever.

TO CATCH A THIEF

1955, colour
Based on the novel by David Dodge
Paramount
US

Cary Grant plays the professional burglar, but it's Grace Kelly who steals his heart as they trade saucy banter along France's Côte d'Azur. Hitchcock leaves the oppressive heat of Rear Window's *New York behind for a bright and breezy romantic comedy that's lighter than air.*

The blinds of L.B. Jefferies' rear window had barely closed before Hitchcock skipped off to the French Riviera for his next picture. Still making the most of the autonomy recently granted to him by Paramount, Hitch wrangled all his professional pals and whisked them away to one of the world's most glamorous and exclusive beauty spots. Together they laughed, joked, generally had a massive jolly at the studio's expense and even found the time to knock out a film in between martinis. Unsurprisingly, the result was a thing of mesmerising elegance, but as light and frothy as the foam that gently lapped up onto the beaches of the Croisette.

To Catch A Thief sees Cary Grant (teased out of semi-retirement by the prospect of swanning around the Côte d'Azur with Grace Kelly) as former jewel thief John 'The Cat' Robie. Robie is the prime suspect in a fresh batch of ruby robberies, and determines to prove his innocence: set a thief to catch a thief. Is he another of Hitchcock's wrongly-accused men? Wealthy tourist Francie Stevens (Kelly) doesn't think so, and uses every weapon in her considerable arsenal of feminine wiles to get him to confess.

On first viewing, the mystery of whether or not Robie is as clean as he claims to be drives the film's suspense, and the ambiguity Hitchcock draws from Grant's smooth, sardonic demeanour keeps you guessing. But return visits suffer a little when you know the truth, and what's left is a beautiful but flawed piece in the Hitchcock collection. Without that enigma, every scene feels slightly longer than necessary, the lead characters' courtship takes an age to catch fire and certain plot developments reveal themselves as baffling or meaningless. But *To Catch A Thief* does provide a welcome breather in Hitch's filmography: a European escape offering a brief respite from all the antagonistic marriages and ugly murders - although, inevitably, even the crystalline Mediterranean is muddied by the corpse of one unfortunate soul.

The film's beauty is its standout feature, and the rolling hills, golden beaches and shimmering waters of Provence are in constant competition with Grant and Kelly for most stunning attraction. Aerial shots of an early car chase show off the French countryside (filming from a helicopter was still rare in the 1950s, and Hitch made the most of it), while the primary colours of a Nice flower market burst from the screen. But Hitch is far more interested in his leading lady, and iconic costume designer Edith Head has a ball (literally, in the finale) helping Grace Kelly look at least 40% of the film's $2.5 million budget. Cary Grant is no slouch either, his chestnut tan making the most of his natural movie star features. His own wardrobe choices include a sharp Bondian tuxedo, some dashing checked shorts and a timeless Milk Tray Man getup for rooftop-scrambling. The jury's still out on those striped tops.

Kelly seals her position here as a key figure in Hitchcock's work. To him she personified the icy blonde, so often associated with his work, whose cool surface gave way to a fiery sexuality once she crossed the magical threshold that separated the rest of the world from the bedroom. This was, of course, an entirely reductive viewpoint for Hitchcock to take, and he was living out an adolescent wish-fulfilment fantasy he never outgrew. After Kelly retired from acting to become Princess Grace of Monaco in 1956, Hitchcock's disappointment would echo throughout the rest of his career, fascinatingly but uncomfortably reflected in how he treated his actresses and how his male characters treated their female counterparts.

For now, though, everyone was having a romp. John Michael Hayes, writing his second of four consecutive Hitchcock films, gifted the cast warm characterisations and a steady stream of wicked, censor-baiting *double entendres*. Hitch opens the film by cutting off Lyn Murray's jaunty theme mid-phrase with a piercing scream, fusing apparent horror with humour once again. And the fun he has with cutaways to orgasmic fireworks during Francie's seduction of Robie is palpable, if clatteringly unsubtle. Hitch even unwittingly created a signature look for his late '50s Paramount films when the studio imposed the VistaVision process on him. While the new technology allowed him to capture incredible wide shots of the Riviera in razor-sharp deep focus, close-ups tended to blur the backgrounds too much, so rear projection had to be employed back in the Hollywood studio. This gave rise to an aesthetic that inadvertently drew attention to itself, and although it's occasionally jarring in some films, it would work perfectly for the reality-blurring layers of *Vertigo*'s warped world.

To Catch A Thief is light on Hitchcock's usual tropes, but recognisable elements peek through the hairline fissures in the film's glossy surface. Francie's mother, while far from the monstrous matriarchs of *Rebecca*, *Notorious* and *Psycho*, is a formidable and grounding character, and Hitch's interest in socio-economic disparity shows itself in every well-heeled character flashing jewels along the Riviera while concealing a working class background from which they escaped by nefarious means. Everyone, as Robie proposes, is a thief of some kind. And try not to be too distracted by the picnic scene, and Francie's offer of a leg or a breast, not to notice the three-minute-long unbroken shot that's only cut into when the leads finally kiss - an editing technique previously seen in *Rope*, *Under Capricorn* and *Dial M For Murder*, to name but a few.

It was around this time that the critics of French film magazine *Cahiers du Cinéma* - most notably Éric Rohmer, Claude Chabrol and François Truffaut - began publishing their theories on Hitchcock (among other directors) as an *auteur*, and arguing for and against his value as a serious artist rather than a pure entertainer. Hitch, of course, had always considered himself a serious artist, no matter how much he played it down. After three decades of filmmaking, he was finally being understood. It's ironic that it happened just as he embarked on a brief run of some of his most lightweight pictures, but it wouldn't be long before Hitchcock entered a phase of his career that would feed the minds of critics and scholars for generations to come.

THE TROUBLE WITH HARRY

1955, colour

Based on the novel by Jack Trevor Story

Paramount

US

SPOILER WARNING

Four people find love thanks to a series of complications arising from a fresh corpse, which is inconveniently blighting the melancholy beauty of a Vermont autumn. Hitchcock skilfully juggles comedy, death and sex, but fumbles audience satisfaction.

The sudden attention Hitchcock received from the upstart critics of French film magazine *Cahiers du Cinéma* was not only gratifying to his ego; it may have also saved his box office bacon when *The Trouble With Harry* was released. A dark comedy about an irksome corpse to which nobody shows the slightest respect, the film tanked in the US but found a home in French cinemas for over a year. The European sense of humour was perhaps more in tune with Hitchcock's idea of a joke than

America's was, but renewed critical interest in the director's work may also have provided a boost in ticket sales east of the Atlantic.

Those critics positing Hitch as an *auteur* would no doubt have clocked *The Trouble With Harry*'s familiar Hitchcockian tropes. There's an entire graveyard's worth of morbid humour, an ineffectual police officer (tellingly the only character invented for the film who wasn't in the source novel), and the familiar assumption of guilt that shifts between the three characters who think they've inadvertently caused Harry's terminal trouble. But the one element that most clearly signifies this as an Alfred Hitchcock joint to savvy modern audiences wouldn't have even occurred to contemporary critics: the unmistakable sound of composer Bernard Herrmann.

While Truffaut *et al* would have lapped up Herrmann's perfect score, which drifts between doom-laden horns and chirpy strings with Hitchcockian deftness, they couldn't have known it would be the first of an extraordinary eight-film collaboration. Herrmann's music would become as integral to the Hitchcock experience as icy blondes and wrongly accused men, his scores going down in history as the aural equivalent of Hitch's unforgettable imagery. And like Hitchcock, Herrmann wasn't afraid to repeat himself: *The Trouble With Harry*'s music carries over snippets of his cues from radio docudrama *Crime Classics*, and the overture bears an uncanny resemblance to his own score for J Lee Thompson's *Cape Fear* seven years later.

Despite the amusing premise of a body that won't stay buried, and a romantic lightness of touch carried over from *To Catch A Thief*, *The Trouble With Harry* is deceptively macabre. Death stalks the entire film: there's Harry, of course, oblivious to the shenanigans he's causing while quietly decomposing; there's the poor rabbit, shot by Captain Wiles and swung around by little Arnie as an undignified bargaining chip; there's Miss Gravely (note the name) casually mentioning her father's eye-watering fate at the hands of a threshing machine; and there's the town of Highwater itself, as beautiful but dead as the rust-tinted leaves on the New England trees. If all that reaping isn't grim enough for you, don't forget Shirley MacLaine's young single mother Jennifer has been widowed not once but twice, making you wonder if John Forsythe's amorous artist Sam isn't tempting fate by pitching himself as her third husband.

But as surely as death lurks in the margins of John Michael Hayes's script, its Freudian opposite, sex, also lies suggestively between its lines. When Sam first meets Jennifer and immediately proposes painting her nude, the fact he doesn't get slapped into next week suggests she's not entirely averse to the idea. Certainly the unspeakably saucy notion of a double bed as something the couple would find "very practical" would have been ever so suggestive to 1950s audiences. Even the ancient Captain Wiles, contemplating courtship with the middle-aged Miss Gravely, describes her to Sam as "a preserve that has to be opened" while Harry's mortal remains lie inert at his feet. It's as if the abrupt appearance of one stiff has aroused a similar sensation in Highwater's menfolk, and Hitch gets off on the idea as much as they do. Sex and death go hand in hand throughout the Hitchcanon, but usually with disturbing effect; rarely are they treated as frivolously as here.

Sadly, neither problematic cadavers nor psychoanalytical subtexts were of much appeal to audiences (except, of course, the French), and Hitch had another relative failure on his hands. It's not hard to see why *The Trouble With Harry* was virtually pronounced dead on arrival. In her debut role Shirley MacLaine has charm to spare, but John Forsythe delivers his lines like a low-budget Cary Grant (little wonder: Grant and Grace Kelly were early suggestions for the roles of Sam and Jennifer, but the film is too small for such star wattage). The lack of a charismatic antagonist (at least one that's breathing) leaves the plot unfocused, and the various excuses for Harry's frequent burials and exhumations aren't convincing enough to justify the comedy that's meant to arise from them. Even the doctor's final analysis - that Harry died of natural causes - seems hard to swallow: given the deceased had a weak heart, surely being battered around the head by two angry women - wielding a milk bottle and a sturdy hiking shoe respectively - would have *some* bearing on his newly-inanimate state?

Crucially, though, the trouble with *The Trouble With Harry* is that it's even stagier than some of Hitchcock's actual stage adaptations, with all its exposition delivered in lengthy dialogue scenes rather than with the director's usual visual flair. For someone who famously saw no value in "photographs of people talking", this film certainly contains a lot of static shots of people yakking away.

As usual though, Hitch couldn't care less if the film flopped. While he was personally fond of *The Trouble With Harry* he wrote it off as "an expensive self-indulgence" and, still in a flush of prolificacy, moved on to the next project. He'd tried to do something audiences wouldn't expect, and he'd succeeded, but audiences had repeatedly indicated they didn't want the unexpected from Hitchcock. They wanted to see something they'd seen before, reimagined but not altered beyond recognition, preferably with beautiful, major stars in the lead roles. For his next film, Hitch would comply with his audience's demands to the letter.

HITCHBOX: ALFRED HITCHCOCK'S TV TAKEOVER

In early 1955 Lew Wasserman, head of media conglomerate MCA and Hitchcock's friend and agent, came up with one of the shrewdest wheezes in Hitchcock's lifetime: to stick him on the telly. And thus, *Alfred Hitchcock Presents* was born - a weekly anthology series showcasing half-hour tales of what can only be described as the unexpected. The show ran for seven seasons before doubling in length and rebranding as *The Alfred Hitchcock Hour* for its final three years.

Understandably, Hitchcock was involved only to a certain extent; his previous collaborator Joan Harrison was initially executive producer (today she'd be called showrunner). But Hitch would be front and centre of every episode, performing droll, increasingly silly intro and outro sketches written by James

Allardice. These sardonic appearances, which almost always involved brazenly belittling the show's commercial sponsors, injected Hitchcock's image into the homes of millions on a weekly basis, making him the most famous and recognisable film director of the time. Brand Hitchcock took a giant leap forward: he even had his own theme tune - Gounod's *Funeral March of a Marionette* - which is just about the most perfect representation of Alfred Hitchcock in musical form.

At a time when no film director would dream of going near cinema's snotty punk cousin television, Hitch embraced it, directing 18 episodes (and two more for other contemporary series) of his choosing. While these budget- and time-restricted episodes were hardly the ideal platform for Hitch to replicate his cinematic magic, it's interesting to investigate them in the context of his usual themes. Predictably, murder and marital woes pop up most often, with variations on the theme of guilt a close runner-up. Stylistically, the TV series is unsurprisingly much more basic than Hitchcock's features, but he still managed to sneak in some of his customary shooting and editing devices.

Hunting down and watching the Hitchcock-directed episodes is far from essential viewing, but completists gonna complete. So if you've developed full-blown Hitchitis, then here's what to expect from his adventures in television…

REVENGE

Season 1, Episode 1
First broadcast October 2 1955
Script: Francis Cockrell
Story: Samuel Blas

Ralph Meeker and Vera Miles are newlyweds; he comes home to find her unconscious after a mysterious attack. Typically Hitchcockian police incompetence leads Meeker to take matters into his own hands, with hilarious consequences (just kidding, the consequences are tragic). It's easy to see why *Revenge* appealed to Hitchcock: a blonde in danger, useless cops, ugly murder and ironic transference of guilt all show up. And in the standout moment (unsurprisingly, a murder scene), the camera waits nervously outside a hotel room, watching the horror unfold via shadows in a mirror, and Hitch's brand of stylish voyeurism makes its small screen debut.

BREAKDOWN

Season 1, Episode 7
First broadcast November 13 1955
Script: Francis Cockrell & Louis Pollock
Story: Louis Pollock

There's a certain audacity in taking an actor of Joseph Cotten's calibre and having him do nothing but stare blankly into space for 20 minutes. Cotten plays a stone cold businessman who goes from emotionless to motionless when a car crash leaves him in a paralysed state of panic. Hitchcock busts out some formal experimentation, telling the story almost entirely through Cotten's internal monologue and by cutting around static shots of him and his limited perspective. With its singular point of view and self-imposed restrictions, this might just count as one of Hitch's single-location dramas; the location being Cotten's mind.

THE CASE OF MR PELHAM

Season 1, Episode 10
First broadcast December 4 1955
Script: Francis Cockrell
Story: Anthony Armstrong

Tom Ewell plays a businessman discombobulated by the unwelcome appearance of his doppelgänger in this frustrating episode. The idea of a mysterious double turning a man's ordered life upside down obviously appealed to Hitchcock, possibly planting the seed for *North By Northwest*, but the mystery here is a supernatural one that's never fully explained. Outside his wheelhouse and feeling those limits on time and money, Hitch fails to fully convey the terror of the situation. The conceit is gripping but the execution left wanting; the story would be better served by the Roger Moore-starring 1970 feature-length adaptation *The Man Who Haunted Himself*.

BACK FOR CHRISTMAS

Season 1, Episode 23
First broadcast March 4 1956
Script: Francis Cockrell
Story: John Collier

Boasting a loveless marriage, a long-planned murder, comedic suspense and a lip-smacking twist, this is the first Hitchcock-directed episode to actually feel like a mini Hitchcock film. John Williams is the hen-pecked husband with a flawless plan for a wife-free retirement which, inevitably, isn't quite as flawless as it seems. Hitch relishes the complex audience manipulation, asking us to identify with someone who's planning something truly awful right up to the point where he does it. Now we're complicit, and all we can do is wait for justice to prevail so we can be absolved of our own guilt.

WET SATURDAY

Season 2, Episode 1

First broadcast September 30 1956

Script: Marian Cockrell

Story: John Collier

Rope's Cedric Hardwicke plays a devious patriarch forced to protect the family name after his hysterical daughter murders her lover with a croquet mallet; John Williams is the unfortunate patsy to whom Hardwicke shifts the guilt. This is among the least successful of the Hitch-directed episodes, although it's not entirely his fault - the story unfolds neatly enough over two acts but then ends abruptly without a conclusion, which Hitch is left to spell out in his closing monologue. The lack of imagination in writing and direction is unsettling, but familiar themes would tickle the Hitchcock pickle for his next episode.

MR BLANCHARD'S SECRET

Season 2, Episode 13

First Broadcast December 23 1956

Script: Sarett Rudley

Story: Emily Neff

Just two years after *Rear Window*, Hitchcock directed this lesser tale of a nosey parker with an overactive imagination who suspects the neighbour of doing a Thorwald and bumping off his wife. Hitch enjoys the repeated setups and debunkings of each far-fetched theory, and encourages the audience to suspect everyone in the story of one crime or another at some point. The brief, hilariously overacted fantasy sequence plays out like every movie murder he'd ever criticised. A gentle episode with a darker edge provided by our own expectations, *Mr Blanchard's Secret* throws metatextual light on the effect of crime fiction on suspicious minds.

ONE MORE MILE TO GO

Season 2, Episode 28
First broadcast April 7 1957
Script: James P Cavanagh
Story: FJ Smith

An ordinary citizen commits a crime in the heat of the moment; unequipped to deal with the consequences, their getaway is hindered by a traffic cop who doesn't realise the protagonist's darkest secret is in the car with them, and things only go less smoothly from there. If that sounds familiar, it's because writer James Cavanagh would go on to pen the first draft of the similarly-plotted *Psycho*. Hitch plays to his silent era strengths in the dialogue-free first act of this episode, deploying the kind of evocative shot choices (point-of-view, sweaty close-ups and portentous foregrounding of the car's corpse-laden boot) which he usually reserved for the big screen.

FOUR O'CLOCK

Season 1, Episode 1 (of Suspicion*)*
First broadcast September 30 1957
Script: Francis Cockrell
Story: Cornell Woolrich

A watchmaker suspects his wife of having an affair, so makes the obvious and logical decision to fix things by planting a time bomb in the house. Naturally complications ensue, plans go awry and tables are turned. Have none of these people seen a Hitchcock film before? This is Hitch on autopilot, as if explaining how to do suspense to a class of primary school children. There's a ticking clock in almost every scene, increasingly tighter shots of the bomb trigger (an alarm clock, set to literally go off at 4.00) and an ironic climax, all of which Hitchcock could have done in his sleep.

THE PERFECT CRIME

Season 3, Episode 3
First broadcast October 20 1957
Script: Stirling Silliphant
Story: Ben Ray Redman

A somewhat talky two-hander, but when half of those words are delivered via the mellifluous tones of Vincent Price you can forgive Hitch for having him bang on for an entire episode. Price plays a Holmesian detective whose cunning is challenged by a visiting lawyer; while the episode plays out like a Conan Doyle short story for the most part, its climax takes a grimly Hitchcockian turn. Like John Dall in *Rope*, Price gets to ruminate on murder as a statement or an art form, and you can't help but wonder why he never popped up as one of Hitch's cinematic silver-tongued villains.

LAMB TO THE SLAUGHTER

Season 3, Episode 28

First broadcast April 13 1958

Script and Story: Roald Dahl

Vertigo's Barbara Bel Geddes wallops her old man to death with a leg of lamb not much smaller than she is, then cooks it and serves it up to the investigating police, who are Hitchcockian levels of incompetent. Bel Geddes is a chillingly calm murderer and murder-cover-upper, and Hitch delights in the incongruity of the mousy pregnant housewife as hubby-killer so much that he rewards her with a final shot so satisfying, he pocketed it for later use in *Psycho*. This was Hitchcock's favourite of his TV outings, but it's a slight tale and there's a strong whiff of Roald Dahl starting with the title and working from there.

DIP IN THE POOL

Season 3, Episode 35

First broadcast June 8 1958

Script: Robert C Dennis

Story: Roald Dahl

A morality tale which proves cheats never prosper; nor, for that matter, do gamblers, liars, bad husbands, boozehounds or men in loud jackets, as one poor sap who happens to be all of the above discovers on a cruise ship. Keenan Wynn plays the improbably-named Mr Botibol (thanks, Roald Dahl), a walking compassion repellent who nevertheless doesn't quite deserve the fate dealt to him by the story's final twist. Hitch enjoys shifting our sympathies though, and knows full well we wanted Botibol to get everything his dispassionate creators could throw at him. Anybody would think we're the bad guys here.

POISON

Season 4, Episode 1

First broadcast October 5 1958

Script: Casey Robinson

Story: Roald Dahl

Harry develops a bad case of snake fright when a venomous krait inconveniently nestles in his PJs, and he daren't move lest it sinks its fangs into his gut. Harry's pal Timber (*Rear Window*'s useless detective Wendell Corey) spends the evening deeply unsympathetic to Harry's plight, so let's hope for his sake their roles are never reversed, hmm? Hitchcock enjoys wringing suspense out of both the unseen critter in the bed and Timber's hair-pulling ambivalence, and Roald Dahl gives his characters enough backstory to lace their words with sinister meaning; it seems there's more than one poisonous snake in the room.

BANQUO'S CHAIR

Season 4, Episode 29

First broadcast May 3 1959

Script: Francis Cockrell

Story: Rupert Croft-Cooke

A wily copper sets up a dinner party with the specific intention of eliciting a murder confession from one of the guests. The twist is as old as time - or maybe it originated in the source play, written in 1930 - but it lends the episode a spooky (if un-Hitchcockian) gracenote. John Williams pretty much reprises his *Dial M For Murder* character, and Hitchcock repeats an editing trick from that film: a long, unbroken wide shot full of idle chit-chat that cuts to a dramatic close-up on the word 'murder' when the Inspector reveals the purpose of the gathering to his befuddled guests.

ARTHUR

Season 5, Episode 1
First broadcast September 27 1959
Script: James P Cavanagh
Story: Arthur Williams

Laurence Harvey narrates the story of how his eloquent Hitchcockian villain came up with a rather extreme solution to the problem of an unwelcome house guest (don't try this at home: an industrial meat-grinder and hungry chickens are required). Hitchologist Michael Walker draws parallels between this episode and *Lamb To The Slaughter*: food and murder are once again intertwined, an unfaithful partner is unceremoniously dispatched and the police are inept. At least the subtextual unpleasantness is counterbalanced by the unintentionally comical sound effect used to denote the death cry of both a chicken and a human, despite sounding nothing like either.

THE CRYSTAL TRENCH

Season 5, Episode 2
First broadcast October 4 1959
Script: Stirling Silliphant
Story: AEW Mason

The titular trench refers to a glacier, which claims a victim in Act I and spits it out again 40 years later in Act III, along with an unwelcome secret. Hitchcock's warped love triangle theme is given a chilly twist here, with one of its points encased in an icy tomb but still exerting a powerful influence over the living - much like the spirit of the first Mrs de Winter in *Rebecca*. A languid episode, memorable for Patrick Macnee's suspiciously accurate forecaster of glacial motion, who predicts the emergence of the body to within a few hours, four decades in advance.

INCIDENT AT A CORNER

Season 1, Episode 27 (of Startime*)*
First broadcast April 5 1960
Script and Story: Charlotte Armstrong

An elderly crossing guard is unexpectedly accused of child molestation, his family squabble over how to deal with it, and in due course almost every character jumps to a ridiculous conclusion. Hitchcock's wrong man makes one of his few appearances in a TV episode, although he's not on the run because, at 68 years old, he'd probably bust a hip. But he does shoulder the guilt for a crime he didn't commit, and that guilt is subsequently bounced around between a series of characters - all of whom are, typically, guilty of something else, even if it's just sticking their head in the sand.

MRS. BIXBY AND THE COLONEL'S COAT

Season 6, Episode 1

First broadcast September 27 1960

Script: Halsted Welles

Story: Roald Dahl

Marital infidelity is the catalyst for a gentle but amusing episode in which the titular Mrs Bixby receives the titular coat from the titular Colonel, only for Roald Dahl to twist events towards a satisfying bit of petard-hoisting. Hitch ensures that, true to Dahl's intentions, none of the main characters are at all likeable - not even a cuckolded husband is entirely sympathetic - but nevertheless keeps things light and breezy, despite a lengthy prologue in which he promises another season of amateur murders. And considering how Hitchcock's subversive women usually end up, the episode lets Mrs B off lightly.

THE HORSEPLAYER

Season 6, Episode 22

First broadcast March 14 1961

Script and Story: Henry Slesar

Hitch moves in a mysterious way, his wonders to perform, and having a primetime pop at hypocrisy and moral lapses in the Church was certainly a bold choice. He gets away with gently undermining piety though, thanks to the subtly irreverent entertainment he slips under the noses of God-fearing viewers everywhere. Claude Rains is, as always, eminently watchable as the priest trying to plug the holes in the chapel roof, and his furtive glances skyward when presented with a less-than-holy solution are delicious. Meanwhile, Hitchcock's cherished theme of Catholic guilt drips from the episode like the rain through Rains's rafters.

BANG! YOU'RE DEAD

Season 7, Episode 2
First broadcast October 17 1961
Script: Harold Swanton
Story: Margery Vosper

Five-year-old wannabe outlaw Jackie is wandering round town with a loaded revolver, blissfully unaware of its deadly potential and brandishing it like the toy he thinks it is. Hitchcock stretches the tension to unbearable lengths, delivering in spades the lessons in suspense he'd been preaching in cinemas for years. Sound plays a big part too: a noisy drinks machine and a backfiring car help pile on the anxiety. Hitch felt so strongly about the subject matter of this unusually socially conscious episode that his usual flippant closing monologue is replaced with a sombre public service message about gun control in the presence of children.

I SAW THE WHOLE THING

Season 1, Episode 4 (of The Alfred Hitchcock Hour*)*
First broadcast October 11 1962
Script: Henry Slesar
Story: Henry Cecil

Hitchcock's career as a television director ends with a whimper, as John Forsythe leads an uneventful courtroom drama (Hitch really should have learned to avoid them by now) about a driver accused of manslaughter after a hit and run accident. There's no suspense, given we don't know the truth until it's revealed in a humdrum twist, and the only fun to be had is from the performances of the witnesses: a stereotypical teenage blonde, a drunk, an obstinate war veteran, a pompously righteous berk and a sad mother. Forsythe ends the episode smiling, but nobody seems to care about the poor bugger who died.

THE MAN WHO KNEW TOO MUCH

1956, colour

Based on a story by Charles Bennett and D.B. Wyndham Lewis

Paramount

US

As fantasy parents go, Doris Day and James Stewart's Mom and Pop McKenna are hard to beat. Sure, he's arrogant and ignorant and she'll bellow popular hit songs in your ear, but if you're kidnapped by dastardly communist agents, they're your guys.

If Hitchcock was guilty of frequently repeating himself, here's his biggest crime: a literal remake of one of his own films. It's another odd career decision, and the reasons cited over the years for him making it are legion and often contradictory - as are opinions regarding which is the superior version. It's a somewhat futile debate that demeans the work of a cultural icon, and supposes that one piece of art can somehow be compared to another made under entirely different technical and financial circumstances, so let's not go into it here. Besides, the 1934 version is obviously better and anyone who thinks otherwise is clearly mad.

Still riding the wave of his slickest, glossiest period of film-making, Hitchcock presents James Stewart and Doris Day as Ben and Jo McKenna, the atypically glamorous everyman and everywoman tangled up in international espionage and intrigue when their son Hank is kidnapped during a family holiday in Morocco. The film's plot is virtually identical to that of its precursor, although Hitchcock is uncharacteristically languorous with his storytelling here. Forty-five minutes longer than the original, the extended duration of the remake (bafflingly not called *The Man Who Knew Too Much Too*) brings pros and cons. Characters are more fully realised and motivations are more complex, but improvisational acting and a lengthy narrative red herring - which descends into incongruous farce - render the film a little flabby.

It's Hitchcock's third relatively superficial picture in a row, somewhat deflating the promise of the psychologically rich *Rear Window*, but there are enough typically Hitchcockian stylistic touches to prove he wasn't entirely resting on his laurels. The Albert Hall sequence alone is a *tour de force* of visual story-telling: the 1934 version had already called back to Hitchcock's career in silent films, but the '56 vintage adds extra wordless vignettes like the emotional reunion of Ben and Jo, in which all their dialogue is entirely obscured by the dramatic *Storm Clouds* cantata playing in the Hall. And in the tense climax at a foreign embassy where Jo belts out *Que Sera, Sera* in the hope that Hank - held captive somewhere in the same building -

will hear it, Hitchcock's camera follows Jo's voice as it carries through corridors and up winding stairs to her son's hiding place. This sequence of shots, accompanied by the fading sound of Jo's singing, is a remarkably effective melding of sound and image: less efficient than a simple cut from Jo to Hank, but more suspenseful because with each cut her voice gets quieter, and we know we have to reach Hank before it disappears entirely.

Jo's singing is crucial to the plot. It's the remake's equivalent of the original's Jill Lawrence being a crack shot with a rifle: less Chekhov's Gun than Chekhov's Chart-Topping Pop Earworm. But more than that, Jo's former career as a singer feeds into *The Man Who Knew Too Much*'s portrayal of gender politics in married couples. Jo has reluctantly forsaken a life on the world's stages to be a wife to Ben and a mother to Hank, and it clearly rankles (it also echoes the mother in *Shadow Of A Doubt*, who wistfully recalls a time when she wasn't just her husband's wife). Meanwhile Ben is a successful doctor, the bread-winner of the family despite the fact that Jo probably out-earned him as a singer. (Jo's friend's comment to her about Hank, that she "hope[s] he looks like you and has a doctor's brain", is staggeringly insulting even for the 1950s.)

But Ben bungles his investigation into Hank's kidnapping at almost every turn: he inexplicably keeps information from the police even *before* he's blackmailed to keep quiet, he entirely misunderstands the vital 'Ambrose Chapel' clue, and - most unforgivably - he reveals a terrifying god complex when he uses his medical knowledge to sedate his own wife before telling her their son's been abducted. In his book on the film, Murray Pomerance suggests there's a narrative necessity for Jo to be drugged at this point: Hitchcock needs the emotional wallop of her later scream at the Albert Hall, he says, and full-blown hysterics earlier in the film would dilute that impact. That may be, but Hitch comes dangerously close to losing audience sympathy for Ben, and probably would have done so with any other actor.

So the only time Ben uses his professional skills in the film is to repress Jo's motherly instincts, whereas the only time Jo uses hers is to wield those instincts like a weapon and rescue their son. When she realises Ben's 'Ambrose Chapel' blunder and takes off on her own, she seizes control of the narrative right through to the Albert Hall and the embassy climax, where she achieves her own goal of successfully combining her profession with motherhood. All her husband is required to do is kick a door in and push a bad guy down the stairs, and there's no reason to believe she couldn't do that too, given the opportunity.

The feminist subtext is admittedly subtle (maybe even accidental: according to author Bill Krohn, Hitchcock found the career/motherhood conflict "old hat" and wanted to play it down in favour of comedy), but it's part of a wider discourse about Hitchcock's portrayal of women, which is often characterised as misogynistic. Feminist scholar Tania Modleski argues that "Hitchcock is [neither] utterly misogynistic nor [is he] largely sympathetic to women", but instead that he is ambivalent towards femininity, and 1956's *The Man Who Knew Too Much* seems to represent that argument in microcosm. Jo saves the day, but Hitch can't bring himself to make a point of it.

There would be more complex and controversial female characters to come in Hitchcock's remaining films, and their psychological states would be better served by those films' plots than Jo McKenna's is. *The Man Who Knew Too Much* is the film that cares too little, preferring trivial thrills to anything more intellectually fertile, but it's hard to criticise it for that - many of Hitch's earlier thrillers took the same approach. In fact it remains one of his best-known films, and plenty of fans prefer it to the original. They're wrong, of course, but that's a futile debate which demeans the work of a cultural icon, so let's not get into it here.

THE WRONG MAN

1956, b/w
Based on a true story
Warner Brothers
US

Hitch briefly pops back to Warners for a final, contract-fulfilling picture as rich in irony as it is devoid of colour. "An innocent man has nothing to fear," a New York cop tells wrongly-accused protagonist Manny Balestrero. Clearly New York cops don't watch many Alfred Hitchcock films.

Fresh from the comfort of remaking one of his own films, Hitchcock does a handbrake turn into the unexpected world of *The Wrong Man*. Stark black-and-white photography, a spoken introduction from Hitch himself, a script faithful to a true story and a complete absence of warmth or humour all point to this film's incongruity in the Hitchcanon.

If the glamour of the preceding Paramount films felt like a globe-trotting holiday (the French Riviera! New England! Morocco! London!), *The Wrong Man* is the depressing return to real life, and all it may throw at you.

Henry Fonda plays bewildered bass player Manny Balestrero, whose unfortunate physical resemblance to a serial hold-up artist earns him a weeks-long nightmare when he's mistakenly fingered for two robberies. Worse, his wife Rose (Vera Miles) suffers a complete mental breakdown as a result of Manny's troubles. It's a bleak and gloomy story which doesn't even offer any relief when Manny's finally exonerated. Rose's descent into madness becomes the focus, and while a suspiciously upbeat ending sees the Balestrero family walking off into a bright Florida sunset, a cursory search for their true story reveals that Rose lived for nearly 60 years after the events of the film without ever fully recovering. But it's also Hitch's most empathetic picture. We care more about these people, their lives upended by the theft of 271 measly dollars, than any of his characters caught up in murder or war. In no small part is that thanks to Fonda - even more convincing as a Hitchcockian everyman than James Stewart - and Miles, whose portrayal of a woman losing her mind is chilling.

Hitchcock's common transference-of-guilt theme is obvious here. Manny is forced to assume the real robber's guilt before inadvertently transferring it to Rose, who - in a mentally delicate state - blames everything on her own perceived failure as a wife, and collapses under the weight of imagined guilt. But *I Confess* was The One With All The Guilt, so *The Wrong Man* becomes the most thorough representation of Hitch's fear of the law. Here the police aren't just ineffectual, they're hair-tearingly incompetent, lazy and callous, leaping to conclusions based on the flimsiest of evidence and a sound belief that accused people are guilty until proven innocent. It isn't even police work that saves Manny in the end - just sheer, dumb luck. Like a child picking at a scab, Hitch almost fetishises the dehumanising procedural parts of the story: the fingerprinting, the handcuffs, the arraignment. He films the investigating officers in oppressive close-ups, stretching the claustrophobia of the situation to unbearable levels. If the oft-told tale of him being locked in a cell for five minutes as a child is true, this feels like Hitchcock trying to exorcise long-festering demons on the screen.

Opting for an almost documentary-style aesthetic, Hitch paints himself into a bit of a corner where he doesn't quite have room to bust out many technical flourishes. But look closely and there's still magic there. Manny's train ride at the beginning sees him reading the Daily Press, and in a quick sequence of shots Manny checks out the betting odds for the horse racing, an ad for a new family car, another ad for a savings bank, then the betting odds again. Those few, dialogue-free shots efficiently set up Manny's situation; he doesn't even glance at the unwittingly significant front page headline 'QUEENS HOLDUP'. Later, when Manny's briefly banged up, Hitch dramatically launches his camera into his cell through the door's tiny service hatch to watch him pace about, before suddenly reversing the move. The implication is the cell's so cramped, you can't even fit a camera in there, and you wonder how the shot was achieved (the answer: a wide-angle lens and a foreshortened set). Perhaps the most memorable expressionistic effect is during Manny's desperate prayer for intervention, where Hitch slowly dissolves a close-up of Manny into a shot of the actual criminal walking slowly towards camera so that his face blends into Manny's. It's a virtuoso shot that encapsulates his essential problem - that he's virtually indistinguishable from the true villain - while also segueing into a solution that feels like a miracle, precipitated as it apparently is by a prayer.

Often overlooked in considerations of *The Wrong Man* is another unusual element for Hitchcock: it's a story about immigrants in America, of which Hitch was but one. The Balestreros are of Italian descent, their lawyer Irish, their doctor German. The hotel owners and guests they rely on for alibis are Italian, they talk to a Spanish-speaking woman in one of the alibis' apartment buildings, and the store owners who catch the real crook are Germanic. All these people help Manny in some way, whereas his accusers and the police are significantly not identified as immigrants (barring the prosecuting assistant D.A., who in real life had an Italian surname which was substituted for another - that of Hitch's editor George Tomasini). While the film's true-story nature may have necessitated this ethnic range of characters, it's a potent ingredient in a story where the system is looking for someone to blame for social ills, and fingers are quickly and easily pointed at the outsiders.

Social relevance, though, was never a concern of Hitchcock's. *The Wrong Man* didn't kick off a slew of films about the immigrant experience. But as Donald Spoto notes in his biography of Hitchcock, what does become a primary theme at this point is "mental trauma over confused identities". Something about Manny Balestrero's story didn't just appeal to Hitch as the basis for one film; it may have triggered an idea that would inform the very essence of most of his late masterpieces.

Delays to Hitchcock's next film may have allowed that notion to percolate; if so, no bad thing. *The Wrong Man* was his sixth film to be released in just two and a half years, and 1957 would be only the third year in Hitch's three decades as a director in which he didn't have a new picture in cinemas. But another extraordinary period of productivity was on the horizon. One that audiences weren't quite ready for, and which, looking back, seems incredible to comprehend. Alfred Hitchcock was about to reach arguably the highest point of his entire career.

VERTIGO

1958, colour

Based on the book *D'entre Les Morts* by
Pierre Boileau and Thomas Narcejac

Paramount

US

ESSENTIAL
HITCHCOCK

SPOILER
WARNING

---

*High anxiety saturates this tall tale within a tall tale, with
manipulated actors and sadistic directors in both. Vertigo's
storytelling audacity and refusal to limit the depths to which
it plunges its characters make it Hitchcock's most awful,
brilliant achievement.*

The key to appreciating *Vertigo* is to understand that it's total
bunkum. "There's no straight story there," Martin Scorsese
said of the film. "It's all mood. Tone. Emotion. Beauty. Fear."
On the surface it's yet another suspenseful murder mystery, but
that surface is gossamer thin. Everything in *Vertigo* is below the
surface. Its most tragic and twisted ideas are implied rather than

explained, and the more you dwell on them, the further down you sink. And there is much to beware in its murky depths: desire, obsession, possession, control, cruelty, guilt. Psychological states so bizarre there aren't even names for them (except perhaps 'Hitchcockian'). The crushing inevitability of fate, of being trapped for eternity in a macabre cosmic loop. It's also, in no small way, about Alfred Hitchcock.

The story, as Scorsese says, is far from straight. Acrophobic ex-detective Scottie (James Stewart) is hired by old acquaintance Gavin Elster to shadow his apparently possessed, possibly suicidal wife Madeleine (Kim Novak). Scottie and Madeleine fall in love, but their affair is abruptly curtailed when she leaps to her death from the top of a mission bell tower, Scottie unable to stop her due to crippling vertigo. He sinks into guilt-induced melancholia, which is only relieved when he meets the suspiciously Madeleinesque Judy (Novak again). Little does he know she's the same woman, who'd been hired by Elster to pose as Madeleine and dupe Scottie into witnessing her apparent suicide. Turns out it was the *real* Madeleine Scottie saw plummet from the tower - killed by her own husband, Elster. Obsessed with his lost love, Scottie forcibly makes Judy over in Madeleine's image, finally finding peace regardless of Judy's protestations. But secrets rarely stay buried, and when Judy's is exposed, it spells disaster for everyone.

See? Total bunkum. Elster's plan is riddled with flaws, and it's ludicrously improbable that any of it works at all. But Hitchcock couldn't care less: he's far more interested in the perverse psychological torture the characters put each other (and themselves) through, and how to render that in the most cinematically effective way. His primary tool is to permeate the whole film with an intangible, ethereal quality; a dreamlike mood where every frame feels like it might be haunted. It's this elusive strangeness that keeps pulling viewers back to the film, fuelling every rewatch as they try to grasp exactly what's going on.

How Hitchcock achieves *Vertigo*'s uncanny atmosphere feels like dark magic, but boils down to nuts-and-bolts filmmaking techniques and narrative sleight of hand. Unconventional camera angles, stylised lighting effects and diffusing filters lend the film its oneiric aura. To visualise Scottie's vertigo, cinematographer Robert Burks zooms in while pulling his camera back, telescopically stretching space in ways the brain struggles to process. Hitchcock often shoots Madeleine in frames *within* the film frame (doorways, arches, mirrors), distancing her from reality and hinting at her existence as merely the image of a person. And in the bookshop scene, while the owner recounts an increasingly tragic story to Scottie, the light level gradually - almost imperceptibly - dims, to the point where the characters inexplicably stand in a crepuscular gloom. It's as if the grim nature of the bookseller's tale has slowly sucked all the light from the world.

Meanwhile, the script delights in finding opportunities to disconcert. The prologue leaves Scottie dangling precariously from a gutter several storeys up and never explains how he got down; similarly, while Scottie trails Madeleine, she disappears from a hotel room, the owner claiming not to have seen her despite Scottie watching her enter. While the plot's biggest mysteries are eventually revealed, this one never is, enhancing the general air of inscrutability.

The most impactful reveal - the kind most films save for their climax - comes a good half-hour before *Vertigo*'s credits roll. It's Judy's unsurprising but devastating flashback and confession that she was Madeleine, and that she loves Scottie as she did when she played the part of the possessed woman. (The theme of possession is multi-layered here: while 'Madeleine' was supposedly possessed by her great grandmother,

Judy-as-Madeleine was possessed by Elster. Soon Judy will be possessed by Scottie *and* by her performance as Madeleine, which comes back to haunt her in terrible ways. When Scottie tells 'Madeleine' no-one possesses her, he couldn't be further from the truth.)

Screenwriter Sam Taylor's idea to place the reveal at this point is the most Hitchcockian thing he could have done. Crucially, Judy only reveals the truth to the audience, not to Scottie - through whose eyes we've been looking for the last 100 minutes. Now the final act becomes unbearably suspenseful as we wait for Scottie to discover the truth, and as we empathise with Judy we begin to fathom the insanity of what she's been - and is still going - through. It's one of the most wrenching perspective shifts in cinema, perfectly demonstrating the manipulative power of point-of-view storytelling.

Manipulative storytelling isn't just what makes *Vertigo* work, it's stitched into the plot. It's the *modus operandi* of Alfred Hitchcock and Gavin Elster: both men spin a far-fetched yarn just about believable enough to pull us, and Scottie, into the storyteller's world, and both men know exactly how to elicit specific reactions from their audience (you can bet Elster told Judy *precisely* where to stand and find her light in Ernie's restaurant). But in a darker example of art imitating life, Hitchcock's habit of moulding actresses into the image of perfect, unattainable women, then becoming obsessive and controlling over them, is mirrored in both Elster's and Scottie's brutal insistence on transforming Judy into Madeleine. Ingrid Bergman and Grace Kelly would have sympathised with Judy; Kim Novak got a taste of her character's pain. Hitchcock shunned Vera Miles when her plans contradicted his, and Tippi Hedren would later bear the brunt of his obsessions harder than any of her predecessors.

Unpalatable as these metatextual considerations are, they only enhance *Vertigo*'s - and Hitchcock's - mythology. The film's intricate spirals of psychological complexity, perfectly represented in Saul Bass's hypnotic titles and Bernard Herrmann's whirlpool score, exist inside and outside the diegesis and make *Vertigo* an endlessly fascinating subject for analysis. That's why the film is often cited as Hitchcock's finest achievement, and in many critical corners is considered nothing less than the greatest film of all time. Not bad for total bunkum.

NORTH BY NORTHWEST

1959, colour

Story by Alfred Hitchcock and Ernest Lehman

Metro-Goldwyn-Mayer

US

ESSENTIAL HITCHCOCK

Hitchcock's slickest, most exhilarating version of The 39 Steps *is an odyssey of entertainment from beginning to shamelessly puerile climax. Cary Grant's final collaboration with Hitch sees him unleash his comic chops; his drunk acting alone makes this the director's funniest picture.*

If *Vertigo* is Alfred Hitchcock's most psychologically dense film, heaving with angst and tragedy and inviting infinite psychoanalytical readings, then it's easy to view its immediate follow-up as a reaction to that. A film about a nobody who stands for nothing, *North By Northwest* is pure surface entertainment. But what a surface: as slick, glossy and beautiful as *To Catch A Thief*, thanks in no small part to its ravishing leads. If *Thief* proved good looks aren't everything, though, *North By Northwest* fixed that issue and then some. The flawless construction of its script and Hitchcock's breathless direction make it the perfect entertainment machine.

To say it's not about anything isn't entirely fair, even if Hitch implies it by waiting *two hours* to casually reveal the MacGuffin and then ditching it as soon as possible. Like all Hitchcock's wrong-man-on-the-run thrillers, of which this is surely the epitome, it's about the fragility of order; the terrifying knowledge that a tiny event, entirely out of your control, could have life-changing consequences. But it's also about growing up: just as morally barren Roger Thornhill (Cary Grant, arguably at the height of his powers) must become less selfish, less reliant on his mother and less responsibility-phobic, the film - a smarter, sexier version of its older siblings *The 39 Steps* and *Saboteur* - is a dazzling showcase for Hitchcock's filmmaking maturity. And last but by no means least, it's about investing in a really sturdy pair of underpants, on the off-chance you might find yourself wearing them for four days straight.

That idea of helplessness in the face of an indifferent universe finds its visual manifestation in a series of high-angle shots. Movie shorthand for a (usually uncaring) god's eye view, *North By Northwest*'s top shots embody the cheery notion that our lives are insignificant specks at the mercy of forces beyond our control. Outside the United Nations where a violent twist of fate sends Thornhill scurrying off like a panicked ant; in a room of government agents casually condemning him to death; at a deserted bus stop where the threat of that death comes from the sky; and as the villainous Vandamm (James Mason) contemplates dealing with his treacherous lover "from a great height": all these moments of dark powers engineering someone else's destiny see Hitchcock hoik his camera to a conspicuous altitude. The result is a film even more vertiginous than *Vertigo*.

But such visual motifs, rich as they are, are mere decoration for Hitchcock. *North By Northwest*'s true beauty lies in Ernest Lehman's script, co-written - as always - by Hitch. Despite being the director's longest film to date, it contains some of his most economical storytelling. The most impressive examples bookend the film: the setup and execution of advertising executive Thornhill being mistaken for intelligence agent George Kaplan, which lights the fuse for the entire adventure, is breathtakingly efficient, while the climax is equally zippy - wrapping up all loose ends in less than a minute from when all appears lost for our hero. Meanwhile the exposition revealing the first act's big mystery is in and out in under three minutes - and, crucially, comes before the audience tire of being as confused as Thornhill. In the airport scene where Thornhill finally learns the truth, Hitchcock even drowns out the dialogue with a passing aeroplane because we don't need to hear it - if we did, it would take much longer to deliver.

By now a master of suspense *and* surprise, Hitch again perfectly balances both here. His decisions regarding the dispensing of information to the characters and the audience are unquestionable, and the constant alternation of being one step ahead of or behind Thornhill is what keeps us glued to his plight. This is most effectively accomplished in our shifting perceptions of Eve Kendall (Eva Marie Saint): first we assume she's just someone Thornhill meets on a train, then we learn she's in league with Vandamm (a surprise for us; suspense as we wait for Thornhill to find out), then we - and he - discover the truth (another surprise for everyone, leading to more suspense surrounding *her* fate). Eve's situation echoes that of Ingrid Bergman's Alicia in *Notorious*, although Hitchcock is less interested in the psychological toll on Eve because this film isn't about her. But with hindsight the scene at Chicago's LaSalle Street station, where she packs Thornhill off to his fateful non-meeting with Kaplan, becomes laced with tragedy.

Stylistically, Hitch still isn't afraid to fall back on his experience as a silent filmmaker: the famed crop duster episode is one of cinema's most outstanding sequences, comprising ten increasingly electrifying minutes with no score and almost no dialogue. It's a masterclass in editing (like *Rear Window*, its impact is derived from the protagonist looking, what he sees and how he reacts) and composition (the minute-long opening high wide shot; the two men facing each other across the empty road; Thornhill legging it from a malevolent biplane). It all emphasises the anxiety of a man who feels safer in the urban jungle of New York than America's wide open spaces - for which he is literally unsuited - and uses that tension to ramp up the thrills. The film is also full to bursting with familiar narrative tropes: blondes, charming villains, love triangles, MacGuffins, murders, set pieces at famous landmarks, ineffectual cops, trains, failed marriages, mothers and mistaken identities all jockey for space in Hitchcock's most quintessentially Hitchcockian picture.

So: a sharp-suited hero, a national-security-threatening villain flanked by deadly henchmen, a beautiful but inscrutable woman, thrilling chases and inventive set-pieces: it's little wonder *North By Northwest* is often cited as inspiration for the James Bond films, which arrived in style just three years later. The helicopter attack on 007 in 1963's *From Russia With Love* certainly looks familiar, and a line can be drawn between the verbal foreplay across the table of a train's dining car in *North*

By Northwest and 2006's *Casino Royale*. But *North By Northwest* is more like a Bond film from the girl's point of view, with Cary Grant as the Bond girl and Eva Marie Saint as the secret agent using sex to further the mission. Regardless, Hitch would leave others to shake and stir the spy movie. He was about to casually revolutionise a different genre altogether.

PSYCHO

1960, b/w

Based on the novel by Robert Bloch

Paramount

US

ESSENTIAL HITCHCOCK

Hitchcock's fascination with psychological aberrancy and crises of identity reaches a shocking crescendo. The violence might seem tame by today's standards, but nothing prepared 1960's audiences for what they saw in Psycho. *An actual toilet! Being flushed! Whatever next?*

As the sixties approached, movie audiences and their appetites were changing. Sex and horror were the new gods. But those audiences were fed a diet of cheap, trashy scares: fast food frighteners like *A Bucket Of Blood*, *The Man Who Could Cheat Death* and *The Screaming Skull*, while high-end horror at the time was served up by the likes of *The Bad Seed*, *The Mummy* and *The Fly*. Hitchcock noted all this and wondered, with characteristic humility, what it might be like to do horror *really well*. So, to usher in the 20th century's most culturally seismic decade, he crafted a film so shocking it shifted the very tectonic plates on which cinema rested. And as if to top all its contemporaries at once, it featured a bucket of blood, a man who cheated death, a screaming skull, a bad seed, a mummy *and* a fly.

Psycho is the Hitchcock film *everyone's* heard of, and the one inextricably linked with his name. It's a textbook example of his ability to take a pre-existing property and make it exquisitely, unmistakably Hitchcockian. Which is surprising, because it's that rare Hitchcock film that doesn't stray far from its source, a slim novel by author Robert Bloch.

With hindsight, the Hitch/Bloch interface seems inevitable. The book boasts a murder or two, a $40,000 MacGuffin, a little voyeurism, a controlling mother and some psychologically complex transference of guilt. All Hitch had to do was change the female murder victim's hair colour from dark to blonde, transform the pudgy, middle-aged antagonist into a handsome charmer, throw in some memorable business on a staircase, and bosh: an almost complete Hitch-package. Yet despite Hitchcock and writer Joseph Stefano adapting the book relatively faithfully, it's the movie that endures as an iconic cultural artefact; the novel has been relegated to a mere footnote in the film's history. That's because while Bloch's book was perfectly adequate, Hitchcock exploited the tools of filmmaking to forge an extraordinary, indelible and exclusively cinematic experience.

That said, the first thing to strike you isn't Hitchcock's creation, nor Bloch's. It's Bernard Herrmann's jolting, frantic, strings-only music ("a black-and-white score for a black-and-white film", as Herrmann described it), which triggers massive anxiety before Saul Bass's equally jagged titles even begin. The contribution of Herrmann's music to the film's success can't be overestimated; it's no coincidence he gets the penultimate credit in *Psycho*'s titles, rather than the usual placement that sees composers subordinated to cinematographers, editors, writers and various flavours of producer.

Having ratcheted up the tension during the titles, Herrmann brings melancholy and disquiet to *Psycho*'s early scenes, in which frustrated secretary Marion Crane (Janet Leigh) impulsively pilfers a small fortune from the office. But as she hits the road for the long drive to her lover Sam (John Gavin), Herrmann steps on the antsy gas again. These driving scenes allow for efficient, effective storytelling. Marion *imagining* the fallout from her crime visibly exacerbates her paranoia, while maintaining a propulsive momentum that would have been lost by showing that fallout. Meanwhile the windscreen wipers, thrashing back and forth in time to the music and cut together with increasingly tighter shots of Marion, raise our empathetic stress levels. Hitch delivers some neat foreshadowing here too: the driving rain and slashing wiper blades prefigure another shower to come, and Marion's grim smirk, delivered straight into camera, will be echoed by two more characters before the film's end.

After a pit stop at a perfectly innocent motel and a totally normal chat with its definitely sane proprietor - birdlike manchild Norman Bates (Anthony Perkins), pop culture's prototypical incel - Marion decides to come clean, both literally and figuratively. And that's when Hitchcock gave the movies a heart attack from which they've never recovered.

Psycho's shower scene is an endlessly fascinating technical *tour de force*. Watch how Hitchcock forces you into Norman's point-of-view as he spies on Marion, implicating character, director and viewer in a moment of sinful voyeurism that reaches back, through the film's opening snoop into a post-coital hotel scene, to the first shots of Hitch's debut feature *The Pleasure Garden*. Note the visual motif of the circle, previously deployed in *The Ring*, and found here connecting the peephole, the toilet bowl, the shower head, the screaming mouth, the plughole and Marion's unseeing eye.

Listen to Herrmann's music (as if you have a choice), initially the aural equivalent of slicing knife thrusts, before coming to represent Marion's gradually-slowing heartbeat. Think about those 50-odd, virtually meaningless individual pieces of film which, when cut together at breakneck pace, imply a shocking violence they never actually show. Wallow in outright terror: a purely emotional response evoked entirely by the cold mechanics of filmmaking. Then relax as Norman cleans up the mess, and notice that barring a few screams and a crucial, distant line of dialogue, nobody speaks from the moment Marion says her final, ironic "good night" for nearly 17 minutes, because Hitchcock never retired as a director of silent cinema. And there's still nearly an hour to go!

The remainder of *Psycho* can't compete with what's already transpired, but it has a good stab at it. The film doesn't appear 100% interested in the charismatically-challenged Sam or Marion's snippy, hard-to-like sister Lila (Vera Miles), but Martin Balsam's dogged investigator Arbogast is fun, and Perkins is formidable as the gradually-disintegrating Norman: the slow push in to his face after he dispatches another car into the swamp is deliciously chilling.

Psycho wraps up with a torrent of exposition; a gutful of psychiatric waffle aimed at the simplest audience member. The Freudian overtones are an extension of similar themes found in earlier films like *Murder!* and *Spellbound*, but *Psycho*'s ending is not Hitchcock's best. It hardly mattered: clunky epilogue notwithstanding, the film was a phenomenal hit, sealing Hitch's rep as the world's most famous director. But irony lay in wait. Having finally wowed audiences with a film that *wasn't* another twist on the wrong-man-on-the-run subgenre he'd made his own, Hitch discovered all anyone wanted now was another

Psycho. He would dutifully deliver a couple of variations on the theme, but nothing satisfied them like this. The jury will remain out forever, but it's possible Alfred Hitchcock had made his last masterpiece.

PSYCHO PSEQUELS AND PSPIN-OFFS

Several Hitchcock films have inspired remakes, or at least alternative adaptations of their source material, but it's telling that the best of them is the one Hitch made himself: 1956's *The Man Who Knew Too Much*. Fewer Hitchcock films got sequels: *The Lady Vanishes* generated further adventures for its bumbling English stereotypes Charters and Caldicott, while the less said about *The Birds II: Land's End* (1994), the better. But thanks to a combination of explosive success, an everlasting impact on cinema and the strange inscrutability of its characters, *Psycho* is responsible for more ripples in the cinematic swamp than any other Hitchpic.

The *Psycho* Cinematic Universe comprises sequels, prequels, remakes and docudramas made for the big and small screens; some directly connected to the 1960 film, and some surprisingly revisionist takes. And regardless of quality, they're arguably all of interest to Hitchologists. They cast a different light on what makes a Hitchcock film Hitchcockian, simply by association: more often than not, these films demonstrate how unique Hitch's approach was by the success of their creators' decisions to imitate or avoid the Hitchcock touch.

So to what extent are these films, which are by their very nature derivative, deserving of their attachment to such a ground-breaking original? How close do they hew to the magic of Hitchcock? And, arguably most importantly, which of them are actually pretty good and which of them are *Psycho III*? Time to check back in at the Bates Motel.

PSYCHO II (DIR. RICHARD FRANKLIN, 1983, US)

22 years after that unfortunate business with the shower, Norman Bates (Anthony Perkins) is released from psychiatric hospital a free man, much to the consternation of Vera Miles's bitter Lila. Norman returns home, apparently sane, but it's not long before 'mother' reappears and the knives are out for assorted visitors to the Bates Motel and its accompanying house of horrors. Thanks in no small part to its own predecessor, *Psycho II* arrived in the midst of a cinematic bloodbath, competing with franchises like *Halloween* and *Friday The 13th*, as well as the grand guignol of Italian *gialli* and Brian De Palma's own brand of Hitchcockery. That it more or less holds its own in this gore-soaked field is testament to its refusal to retread Hitch's footsteps, instead pinging the *Psycho* mythology off in unexpected directions.

Director Richard Franklin, an admirer and friend of Hitchcock, lacks his hero's efficiency, subtlety and gift for suspense, and *Psycho II* misses a distinct directorial voice that De Palma could have provided had he been given the gig. But Franklin and writer Tom Holland craft a reasonable mystery-thriller with enough nods and winks to the original to satisfy fans: there's a mid-film twist (less traumatic than *Psycho*'s but just as unexpected), interesting spins on Hitchy tropes like voyeurism and domineering mothers, and a neat addition to the original film's bathroom-based circular motifs. On its own terms though, and if you can forgive the arguably unnecessary franchising of a cultural masterpiece, *Psycho II* is a bold and - crucially - thoroughly entertaining tribute.

PSYCHO III (DIR. ANTHONY PERKINS, 1986, US)

Anthony Perkins directs the third film in a decreasingly necessary franchise, in which Norman Bates gets involved with disillusioned nun Maureen (Diana Scarwid, introduced in a *Vertigo*-referencing opening) and repellent drifter Duane (Jeff Fahey). Norman's feelings for Maureen naturally conflict with Mother's principles and, to cut a mercifully short story even shorter, lots of people die unpleasantly.

Perkins clearly watched *Psycho* a lot in preparation for directing the threequel, but seems to have learned nothing beyond how to replicate a few cool shots. Callbacks to Hitchcock's original are numerous, lurching from fun (Norman, on Cabin #1's messy bathroom: "I've seen it worse") to lazy (a murder in a phone box feebly mimics the shower scene). And Perkins' nuanced acting from *Psycho* has deserted him: he's indelibly *the* Norman Bates, but he's in an inexplicable hurry to get his lines out here. In that sense at least, Perkins the director shares Hitchcock's ambivalence towards his actors' craft. Sadly Perkins the actor doesn't have a good enough director to disguise his inadequacies.

By now the series is much less interested in fascinating characters and peculiar relationships than its mounting bodycount. Nor does it care much for its own internal logic: *Psycho III* clumsily undoes its predecessor's surprising take on Norman's family history in a rushed, sloppy finale. It's unclear to what extent the film realises it's silly trash, but if Perkins wanted *Psycho III* to be taken seriously, he probably should have rethought the sex scene in which Jeff Fahey's idea of foreplay involves moodily waggling a table lamp in front of his genitals.

PSYCHO IV: THE BEGINNING (DIR. MICK GARRIS, 1990, US)

In a further attempt to mangle its own mythology, straight-to-TV sequel-slash-prequel *Psycho IV* blissfully ignores everything from *II* and *III*, rendering this one of cinema's most frustrating franchises. The prequel element does little more than flesh out details we learned in *Psycho*, and is only really memorable for starring Henry Thomas (Elliott from Steven Spielberg's *E.T.*) as young Norman. The scene in which his mother screams about his penis only being good for "making wee-wee" also lingers in the memory, but for all the wrong reasons.

Norman's backstory is told by present-day Norman (Anthony Perkins again), in a framing device that sees him calling a radio talk show to reminisce over his unusual childhood. Norman, now married and facing impending fatherhood, fears his unborn baby will inherit his mental illness, and a fascinating intellectual debate around the idea of nature versus nurture is skilfully avoided by the uninspiring screenplay. *Psycho IV* may feel like an insult to Hitchcock, but the fact it was written by the original's scriptwriter Joseph Stefano actually goes a long way to proving Hitch's powers as a co-writer.

While less slashy than its predecessors, *Psycho IV* still follows the apparent rule that all *Psycho* sequels must include a handful of shots copied from the original, but done less well to remind audiences how much better Hitch was at this stuff. The final moments threaten a potential 'Son Of Psycho' follow-up we're thankfully yet to witness, but if the series has taught us anything it's to beware, because history has a habit of repeating itself.

BATES MOTEL (DIR. RICHARD ROTHSTEIN, 1987, US)

A feature-length pilot for a TV series that never happened (not to be confused with the identically-named series that *did* happen), *Bates Motel* is less a sequel to *Psycho* than merely *Psycho*-adjacent. In the 27 years Norman was incarcerated, he befriended Alex West, a young man in the same institution who also saw off an abusive parent. When Norman dies, Alex inherits the Bates Motel and house, moving in when he's re-leased from the institution. In much the same way as the *Psycho* franchise should probably have been left to rot but foolishly wasn't, Alex ignores all common sense and renovates the motel.

Bud Cort plays Alex with the same wide-eyed innocence and permanent look of surprise he used to great effect in Hal Ashby's 1971 film *Harold And Maude*, and he's about all that keeps you watching. Writer-director Richard Rothstein parps out a limp story that mostly resembles a home improvement show before improbably morphing into an episode of *Scooby-Doo*: someone's trying to scare Alex off the valuable Bates land, and it's either the ghost of Mrs Bates or a more corporeal force.

We're so far away from Hitchcock now that we'd need binoculars to see him. Rothstein's writing and direction is lifeless, and nothing that made *Psycho* unique is evoked beyond its setting, which could have been any old spooky house and motel. A jaw-droppingly incongruous subplot is introduced 20 minutes before the end that hints at the direction the series would have headed; you might say it must be seen to be believed, but in actual fact you really mustn't see it at all.

PSYCHO (DIR. GUS VAN SANT, 1998, US)

For reasons best known to himself, director Gus Van Sant re-made *Psycho* in 1998 using almost exactly the same script and shot construction as the original. Reaction among cinephiles ranged from mild bafflement to frothing outrage, but the moviegoing masses (peculiar creatures who somehow did not know Hitchcock's film by heart) accepted it as just another pre-millennial slasher. It's more a conceptual art experiment than anything else - probably a failed one, but curious nonetheless - that asks the question: can you make a film 'Hitchcockian' by doing everything exactly as Hitchcock did, or do you literally need to be Alfred Hitchcock?

Psycho '98 is set in '98, so it updates some archaic dialogue and achieves things Hitchcock could only imply, like an uncut aerial swoop across the Phoenix skyline, and Norman (Vince Vaughn) clearly taking matters into his own hands while snooping on Marion (Anne Heche). These changes are less egregious than others: Vaughn gives Norman an annoying nervous laugh, and Julianne Moore's Lila flirts with him a little. Most noticeably, Van Sant sticks surreal cutaways into the two murder scenes (a cow stares at the audience in confusion in the middle of Arbogast's killing; the audience returns the sentiment). These stylistic tics complicate Van Sant's experiment, branding the film as his own despite him going to extraordinary lengths to do otherwise.

It's hard not to feel some warmth towards something so clearly in awe of the original, but ultimately it's fascinatingly pointless. *Psycho* '98 is like Norman Bates himself: the child dresses up as the parent, but is doomed to be dominated by its power and endurance.

HITCHCOCK (DIR. SACHA GERVASI, 2012, US)

Perhaps the most Hitchcockian thing about *Hitchcock* is that it pretty much ignores most of the book on which it's based: Stephen Rebello's terrific *Alfred Hitchcock and the Making of Psycho*. The construction of *Psycho* is covered, but in condensed, bite-sized scenes, while the central narrative instead focuses on Alfred and Alma's less-than-perfect marriage - another Hitch trope of which the man himself would no doubt have approved. Trying hard to cram in all but the most salacious titbits regarding Hitchcock's obsession with his leading ladies and Alma's relationship with Whitfield Cook (if such an affair ever happened, it would have been over ten years earlier than depicted), *Hitchcock* comes across as a visual compendium of the most memorable passages from the director's many biographies.

As great an actor as Anthony Hopkins is, the inches of padding required for him to play Hitch muffle his performance a little, and his accent occasionally veers into Michael Caine territory. Helen Mirren, meanwhile, is a suspiciously glamorous Alma, but then maybe that's exactly how Whitfield Cook made Alma feel. There are enough details here to delight and infuriate Hitchologists in equal measure: you'll enjoy every familiar reference to *Psycho*'s creation, but might find yourself screaming at the telly louder than Janet Leigh when, for example, the filming takes place at Paramount rather than Universal. But this is a harmless, diverting accompaniment to *Psycho*, whose high point - like its inspiration - is the shower scene and its impact.

BATES MOTEL (TV SERIES)

Five seasons of ten episodes each, 2013-2017, US
Developed by Carlton Cuse, Kerry Ehrin and Anthony
Cipriano

If *Psycho IV*'s take on the Bates saga left you colder than Norma's corpse, then here's an alternative prequel that balances fealty to Hitchcock's original with a laudable desire to do its own thing. Transposing the story to the present day, *Bates Motel* is an enjoyably trashy experience that doesn't take itself too seriously, piling one improbably dramatic incident on top of another until it threatens to collapse under the weight of its own ridiculousness. The show settles into a groove in its final two seasons (arguably the first three could have been condensed into one), and having spent most of its running time convincing you it's leading up to the events of *Psycho*, it instead collides with the movie in an inspired way before peeling off and taking the characters in unexpected directions.

Moon-faced Freddie Highmore doesn't much resemble Anthony Perkins' Norman (weirdly, co-star Nestor Carbonell really, really does), but he makes the character his own, while Vera Farmiga brings complexity to - and evokes sympathy for - Norma, whose own backstory is as troubled as her son's. The show gifts Norman a brother and a selection of improbably attractive girlfriends, but appeases viewers who might find those elements inconsistent by frequently nodding and winking to *Psycho* (and other Hitchcock films) in character names, dialogue and certain shots.

Bates Motel's approach to mental health issues is about as sensitive as *Psycho*'s - i.e. not very - but it is a little more sophisticated, as you'd expect with over 50 years of psychiatric research and understanding over its source material. And that appreciation of its audience's awareness is carried through to the storytelling, where expectations are occasionally upended almost as shockingly as they were in 1960. Those are the most Hitchcockian moments, and the ones that stand out in a series which - perhaps wisely - rarely attempts to emulate the style of its progenitor.

THE BIRDS

1963, colour

Based on the short story by Daphne du Maurier

Universal

US

Like Shadow Of A Doubt's *Uncle Charlie,* The Birds' *Melanie Daniels brings chaos to a sleepy California town in this story of men and women, mothers and children, and birds and bees. Hitchcock, meanwhile, ends his most diverse purple patch in technically breathtaking style.*

Through their phenomenal reaction to *Psycho*, audiences sent Alfred Hitchcock a message that struck him like a kitchen knife between the eyes: they bloody loved horror. The bloodier, the better. Keen to satisfy that thirst but not to repeat himself, Hitch teamed up with screenwriter Evan Hunter for another bold experiment. While *The Birds* would feature classically Hitchcockian interplay between its male and female leads and typically virtuosic technique, it would also boast cutting-edge special effects, a wildly ambitious soundtrack and a complete lack of big names. The film's only stars would be the birds themselves. And, of course, Alfred Hitchcock.

The Birds follows Melanie Daniels (Tippi Hedren), a spoiled socialite who migrates from a battle of the sexes to a battle of the species when her flirtation with dishy lawyer Mitch Brenner (Rod Taylor) is sidetracked by an unexplained avian apocalypse. Under siege from winged bastards in the usually peaceful harbour town of Bodega Bay, Melanie and Mitch fight for their lives against the angriest of birds, while simultaneously negotiating the psychological wreckage of their emotionally chaotic lives.

Hitchcock delays *The Birds*' airborne horror for a potentially patience-testing amount of time, but there's enough richness and enjoyment in the first hour's characterisations and playful interactions to fill an entire romcom. As usual, no time is wasted setting up the characters: Melanie is immediately a wealthy, entitled brat and pathological liar; Mitch a crafty, patronising charmer. Pursuing Mitch up the coast from San Francisco to his weekend hometown retreat, Melanie bristles up against his ex-lover Annie (Suzanne Pleshette) - whose blunt, earthy demeanour contrasts dramatically with Melanie's soft-focus hauteur - and his mother Lydia (Jessica Tandy), whose superficial resemblance to Melanie belies a wary suspicion. The scenes between these characters heave with unspoken feelings: the snappy dialogue is expositional, but looks, pauses, reactions and line deliveries simultaneously tell a whole other story. It's among the finest marriages of writing, directing and acting in the Hitchcanon, and it's easy to get swept up in the human drama.

But just when you forget you're watching a horror film, all flapping hell breaks loose. Hitchcock lets rip with a series of feathered assaults on characters and audience alike, which - while dated in places to modern, cynical eyes - contain some of his most calculated and effective exploitations of the possibilities of cinema. The largest in scale and most obvious of these is the impression of thousands of birds attacking Bodega Bay's residents, achieved via a mixture of live, animated and mechanical creatures, revolutionary optical processes and stunning matte work. But there are smaller moments where Hitchcock uses imaginative framing, contrasting movement and rhythmic editing to devastating effect.

Take Lydia's discovery of Dan Fawcett, a farmer deprived of his life (and eyeballs) by one mercifully offscreen incursion. Lydia's slow, silent investigation of the Fawcett home culminates in three subjective shots of the sightless corpse, each one closer to his scooped-out sockets and five frames shorter than the last, yanking us inescapably towards the horror. That cold, mathematical approach to evoking an emotional response is repeated throughout. As Melanie sits outside the school, oblivious to the aptly-named murder of crows massing on the jungle gym behind her, Hitchcock alternates increasingly tighter shots of her nervously smoking with shots of the birds gathering. The final shot of Melanie is almost 30 seconds long: an unbearable amount of time for Hitch to withhold our view of the crows. When she, and we, finally see what's happened while we've been looking elsewhere, the effect is spine-tingling.

Similar business occurs during the gas station scene. Watch carefully as a recently-incinerated man inadvertently ignites a trail of gasoline that leads back to the pumps. Cutting between shots of Melanie and her point of view, Hitchcock juxtaposes the right-to-left panning shots of the fire trail with static images of Melanie looking left-to-right. Each shot in this seven-shot sequence is two frames shorter than the last (reducing from 20 frames to just eight), accelerating towards the inevitable explosion, which gives way to an incredible, almost 30-second long aerial shot of the flaming carnage. Hitch allows us that breather to take in the devastation before gulls descend on the town in the full flight of fury and more havoc ensues.

The Birds is full of bravura moments like this. What it's entirely devoid of, however, is any kind of explanation for the birds' unprecedented animosity. Plenty of suggestions are floated during the film, and even more have been proposed in critical analysis of it, but Hitchcock and Hunter choose ambiguity over answers. Nature's revenge upon mankind is a popular theory, with plenty of supporting evidence: Melanie represents the intrusion of the urban into the rural with her noisy sports car roaring through the countryside; the first attack on the Brenner house sees the birds force the humans out of their home as if giving them a taste of their own medicine; in the diner, an ornithologist's lament for displaced birdlife is interrupted by a waitress yelling for southern fried chicken.

There's also a strong argument for the film's events as a reaction to Melanie and Mitch's love affair - the closer the two get, the more extreme the attacks become. And when the distressed mother in the diner yells at Melanie, blaming her, she delivers her tirade straight into camera - at us. We're the ones demanding the horror and paying for it to happen. Are we, as she says, evil? Pushed for an explanation, Hitchcock suggested Melanie represents complacency. We take for granted our freedoms and lifestyle, with little thought for what might happen if it were all suddenly upended; in that sense the bird attack resembles a pandemic that appears from nowhere and drags on interminably, forcing us to accept a new normality.

Truth is, the film is all the better for never offering a neatly-wrapped solution. More interesting is what the rest of the film is about: the terror of loneliness, isolation and abandonment lurking behind all the characters' facades. That's a far more relatable fear, and arguably where the true horror of *The Birds* lies. If you must have answers though, perhaps Evan Hunter's explanation for birds attacking humans is the most satisfying: "Because Mr. Hitchcock told them to."

MARNIE

1964, colour
Based on the novel by Winston Graham
Universal
US

The Birds' *Tippi Hedren returns as the titular light-fingered larcenist, but her penchant for easily-crackable safes is merely the tip of her iceberg of problems. Sean Connery sets out to catch a thief in this morbidly fascinating, but eternally problematic, entry in the Hitchcanon.*

Nothing in Hitchcock divides audiences and critics like *Marnie*. Hitchologist Robin Wood called it "one of Hitchcock's richest, most fully achieved and mature masterpieces", while *The Guardian* journalist Bidisha Mamata passionately condemned it for its "full-on misogyny, rampant woman-blaming and outright abuser apologism." It's possible to appreciate both viewpoints: at best *Marnie* is a beautiful, surreal examination of complex, fascinating characters (in front of *and* behind the camera); at worst it's an overly talky, humourless slog with a morally repugnant ideology. Either way, it remains one of the most intriguing case studies of Hitchcock's stylistic flourishes and thematic preoccupations, and represents his final dalliance with knotty psychosexual concepts.

Marnie's very first shot should give you some idea of what to expect. It's a close-up of a handbag full of stolen cash, but this particular handbag is more than a mere prop. Its carefully-chosen design lends it a visual connotation that must have delighted both the smutty child and the Freudian fanboy within Hitchcock, and to him it would have almost certainly signified feminine mystery: a key theme for the following two hours.

The bag, and the mystery, belong to Marnie Edgar (Tippi Hedren), although we soon discover the loot was pinched by one of her many fake identities, Marion Holland. Notably, this isn't the first time the theft of a large amount of money from an office by a woman named Marion has kickstarted a Hitchcock plot, and it's not the only callback to his previous pictures. Marnie's aversion to the colour red recalls Gregory Peck's reaction to seeing wavy lines on white material in *Spellbound*, and similarly holds the key to a repressed memory at the heart of the film's psychological riddle. The long tracking move from a wide shot to a dramatically significant close-up, so effectively deployed in *Young And Innocent* and *Notorious*, returns here as Hitchcock's camera zeroes in on the face of a man about to unwittingly cause trouble for Marnie. And *Psycho*'s climactic exposition dump is back, this time helpfully accompanied by illustrative flashbacks, but still trying to tidy up Hitchcock's ultimate hot mess in convenient, simplistic fashion.

Marnie's apparent kleptomania and pathological dishonesty appeal to Mark Rutland (Sean Connery), a zoologist who, not coincidentally, has a history of taming wild animals. Mark, wearing arrogant entitlement as comfortably as his tailored suits, is almost as dysfunctional as Marnie, and whether he's the film's hero or another of Hitchcock's smooth, sophisticated villains is the subject of considerable critical debate. The casting of Mark is key to this ambiguity: fresh off the back of two films playing James Bond, Connery ports over that character's capacity for brutality but leaves the charm behind. Mark genuinely wants to 'cure' Marnie's crippling inability to enjoy a physical relationship with men (which the film overwhelmingly presents as a problem to be solved), but whether it's for her benefit or to satisfy his own ego and libido is questionable.

Mark's own brand of amateur therapy finds its most unsavoury expression in the scene where, having blackmailed Marnie into marriage and grown frustrated by her sexual antipathy towards him, he appears to force himself on her during their honeymoon on a cruise ship. Whether Mark rapes Marnie, and whether the film - and therefore Hitchcock - condones his behaviour is still furiously debated, but it's worth noting that many of the critical arguments in Mark's defence are much more linguistically convoluted than those against. Yet the woman credited with *Marnie*'s script, Jay Presson Allen, described it as "just a trying marital situation. I did not define it as rape [...] you forgive [Mark]." Obviously it would be too much to expect Hitchcock to clear things up: in a possible attempt to pre-emptively absolve himself of responsibility, he refers to the episode in the film's trailer, claiming with inappropriate drollery that "I'm not certain I understand this scene."

In the course of describing its troublesome content, the scene generates some unique visual shorthand. As the camera pans away from the unhappy couple to a view of the ocean through a porthole, the familiar cliché of crashing waves signifying unbridled passion is absent. Instead, the eerie stillness of a dead calm sea speaks quiet volumes. And the ship itself becomes a grim motif: the vessel where Marnie's ordeal takes place has a counterpart docked in a harbour at the end of the street where she grew up. Given what we eventually discover about her past, the ship that looms over her childhood home signifies the incident that clouds her entire life. When we finally see that formative traumatic event, Hitchcock introduces it with a variation on the contrazoom shot he made famous in *Vertigo*. Here, it performs a different function: a visual representation of the past being pulled forcibly into the present.

Hitchcock's visual style in *Marnie* is almost as controversial as the rest of the film. Several shots are gratingly artificial-looking due to obvious rear projection or poor matte work. And this isn't just from a modern perspective; contemporary audiences and critics also pulled the film up on its unconvincing optical effects. But Hitch had been using such processes since his silent days, so why don't they work here? Some Hitchologists surmise that he lost interest in the film after falling out with Tippi Hedren mid-shoot, while others claim the foregrounded artifice is intentional: a deliberate effort to visualise Marnie's disconnect from the world.

At least one scene in particular is a classic episode in Hitchcockian suspense: Marnie robbing the Rutland safe on one side of a wide shot, while on the other - separated by a wall and unseen by Marnie, but visible to us - a cleaner goes about her business, sure to discover the crime any minute. It's one of the film's few moments of fun (Hitch even caps the scene with a punchline), but it also works to manipulate audience identification. We *want* Marnie to get away with it, just like we wanted Marion's car to sink into the swamp in *Psycho* when it got stuck halfway in. Hitchcock's ability to make us sympathise with his criminals is one of his most mischievous skills, but who the *real* criminal is in *Marnie* is still one of its many hot topics. You suspect Hitchcock wouldn't have it any other way.

TORN CURTAIN

1966, colour
Story by Alfred Hitchcock and Brian Moore
Universal
US

SPOILER WARNING

Hoping to make "a more realistic Bond movie" and inspired by the Burgess and Maclean defection scandal, Hitchcock dreamed up a story from Mrs Maclean's point of view. Julie Andrews plays the defector's fiancée; Paul Newman is the spy who loved her.

All was not peachy in Hitchworld as *Torn Curtain* went into production. Hitchcock's nine-time editor George Tomasini had suffered a fatal heart attack shortly after completing *Marnie*, and Robert Burks - cinematographer for 12 of Hitchcock's previous 13 films - pulled out of the new picture, citing nervous exhaustion. And although *Psycho* had generated unprecedented box office business five years earlier, *The Birds* and *Marnie* brought decreasing returns to Universal's coffers. The studio, fearing Hitch was fast becoming yesterday's news, insisted that for *Torn Curtain* he cast red-hot, budget-draining stars Julie Andrews - whose window of availability was short and imminent - and Paul Newman, who drove Hitchcock up the wall with his method acting and unsolicited feedback on characterisation, dialogue and even the title.

To compound matters, Universal also told Hitchcock to ditch Bernard Herrmann as composer, and to aim for a score more relevant to late-1960s audiences' tastes. The days of Hitchcock running his own show with minimal studio interference appeared to be over. Hitch vouched for Herrmann, but when the composer refused to write a modern score he was forced to depart the project, never to speak to Hitchcock again. Left without three of the key collaborators of his most successful period, the director found himself some distance from his comfort zone.

Unsurprisingly, then, *Torn Curtain* is not Hitchcock's finest hour. Newman and Andrews stand, sit and walk where they're told to, and deliver the lines they're given, but rarely has Hitch's legendary ambivalence towards actors been so evident. The film suffers from extraneous and overlong scenes, and its utilitarian production design, flat lighting and dreary colour palette are enough to put your eyes into a coma. It's a deliberate attempt to convey the functional aesthetic of the Eastern Bloc setting, but a soup of murky greys and browns hardly stimulates the senses like *To Catch A Thief*'s riot of colours, or the symbolically charged reds and greens of *Vertigo*.

And yet, Hitch couldn't help injecting enough Hitchcockery into *Torn Curtain* to make it impossible to dismiss. As a Cold War thriller, it's a nostalgic throwback to the wartime spy adventures of Hitchcock's late British and early American career - right down to the MacGuffin hidden inside a character's head (*The 39 Steps*, *The Lady Vanishes*, *Foreign Correspondent*) and the last-act dramatic business in a theatre (*The 39 Steps*, *The Man Who Knew Too Much*).

Newman plays Michael Armstrong, a scientist from the 'U.S. Interspace Committee' attending a conference of like-minded boffins in Copenhagen with his fiancée and assistant Sarah Sherman (Andrews). Hitchcock sets up their situation and relationship in characteristically efficient style (delegates' name tags wittily negate reams of exposition), before aligning us with Sarah's subjective point of view as she discovers Armstrong is defecting to the East. The first act is characterised by the mystery of Armstrong's intentions, and Sarah's slow approach to discovery finds a visual expression in a press conference, when a series of increasingly tighter shots of Armstrong bring us, through Sarah's eyes, closer to him.

The second act shifts perspective to Armstrong, starting with a remarkable dialogue- and music-free sequence in which he's stalked by the suspicious Gromek, an East German heavy (and easily the film's most fun character). The pursuit takes them through a deserted museum where the soundtrack is provided entirely by the rhythm of the men's echoing footsteps: Armstrong's light and quick; Gromek's heavy and deliberate. The chase ends badly for Gromek, who finds himself the star of one of Hitchcock's most memorable murders - a deliberately protracted lesson on how arduous it is to kill a person when restricted to everyday household items like a saucepan, an insubstantial kitchen knife, a shovel and an oven. The absence of music on the soundtrack here is motivated by Armstrong's need to kill Gromek quietly to avoid discovery, but simultaneously heightens the grim realism Hitchcock was aiming for.

The reveal of Armstrong's long-game plan (his faked defection is a cover to extract vital information from a communist scientist), complicated by a ticking-clock element and the inconvenience of Sarah's dogged loyalty, generates genuine suspense. But the scene when Armstrong finally tells Sarah the truth is a mixed success: Hitchcock slyly shows the conversation in a time-saving silent long-shot (as in *North By Northwest*, we don't need to hear what's spoken), but stages it on an obviously studio-bound, suspiciously verdant hillock that appears to be attached to the top of a building in the middle of Leipzig city centre.

Once Armstrong completes his mission, the third act depicts their exfiltration to the West: a comically convoluted escape which forms Hitchcock's tensest bus ride since 1936's *Sabotage*. The script throws every imaginable obstacle at the fleeing couple, the last of which - an ancient woman with a ludicrous amount of baggage - elicits the film's biggest laughs. Hitch handles the suspense as masterfully as ever here, but fumbles the ball with a subsequent tension-deflating episode featuring an unnecessary character whose interruption of our heroes' quest is less suspenseful than just plain annoying.

A final Hitchcockian flourish occurs in the climactic ballet sequence, where Armstrong realises the ballerina on stage knows and could betray him. Avoiding the cliché of something like a crash zoom, Hitch employs an expressionist technique more likely to be found in the films of his French new wave groupies: as he cuts between shots of Armstrong and shots of the ballerina furiously pirouetting, each shot of her ends with a striking but almost subliminal freeze-frame. The effect is unsettling, and a reminder that there's life in the old dog yet.

The film ends as it began, with the couple taking refuge under the covers (as opposed to undercover, where they've spent much of the film). Likewise, Hitch had also reached for a comfort blanket with *Torn Curtain*, its familiar thematic territory softening the blow of his departed crew members. It wasn't indisputable proof that he could survive without them in an unforgiving cinematic landscape that was about to reinvent itself with The New Hollywood, but those proponents of the *auteur* theory that advanced Hitchcock's status as the overarching creative force in his films would find plenty of ammunition for their argument here.

TOPAZ

1969, colour
Based on the novel by Leon Uris
Universal
US

Pack your passport for Hitchcock's most globetrotting film: we're off to Paris via Moscow, Copenhagen, Washington DC, New York and Havana. It's a long, bumpy ride, and it's almost worth it just for the admirably accurate final line of dialogue: "Anyway, that's the end of Topaz."

Hitchcock's second Cold War story in a row is his most overtly political feature. While his late 1930s and early '40s thrillers used geopolitics merely as convenient ignition for a blast of preposterous spy-based shenanigans, *Topaz* is specifically and inextricably concerned with the East/West power struggle that led to the 1962 Cuban Missile Crisis. This uncharacteristic plot dependence on real-life statecraft must have come as a surprise to many - not least Hitchcock himself, who just a few years earlier confidently told François Truffaut that "the public doesn't care for films on politics [...] most of the pictures dealing with the politics of the Iron Curtain are failures." But with the dizzy heights of *Psycho* almost a decade behind him, and no other viable projects on the horizon, Hitch had little choice when Universal pushed him to adapt Leon Uris' complex Cold War novel.

Hitchcock's estimation of the public's appetite for political pictures may have been a self-fulfilling prophecy. The project failed to inspire him, and consequently failed to inspire audiences. Shooting with an unfinished script, insufficient prep time and no bankable Hollywood stars, Hitchcock delivered an overcomplicated, overlong and old-fashioned clunker. Even the usually deferential Truffaut was disappointed, saying the film suffered from "too many locations, too many conversations, too many characters."

The farcical production of *Topaz*'s final scene gives a fair indication of the film's troubles. Test audiences were baffled by the climax: a daft pistols-at-dawn duel between the hero and the villain that seemed to belong to a film set two centuries earlier. And so another, more pragmatic ending was hastily shot, in which the bad guy - a Soviet mole in the French government - escapes to Russia. But there were fears that *that* version might upset France.

A third ending, implying the traitor's suicide, was then sloppily cobbled together from existing footage, because by this point it was too late for reshoots. Which ending you saw depended largely on when and where you watched the film, but the most widely available version of *Topaz* now carries the second (and most satisfying) of those endings, plus around 20 minutes of footage excised by Universal at the time of release.

The bloated running time of over 140 minutes makes *Topaz* Hitchcock's longest film, and there's a not unreasonable argument that Universal may have had a point. If any of Hitch's final films miss the guiding hand of his long-time editor George Tomasini, it's this one.

Of course it's not all bad - Hitchcock never is, unless you're watching *Juno And The Paycock*. *Topaz* opens with a Russian official attempting an escape from the Motherland with his wife and daughter; the ten-minute-long defection sequence, loaded with mounting tension, furtive glances, hold-your-breath moments and minimal dialogue is in the best Hitchcock tradition. Later, an even longer scene of suspense plays out in which our hero Devereaux (Frederick Stafford) tasks sleeper agent Dubois (Roscoe Lee Browne) with stealing sensitive papers from a Cuban revolutionary. Both sequences are meticulously planned, shot and edited for maximum suspense: Hitchcock uses point-of-view, shot/reverse shot cutting and carefully chosen lenses (shots of Dubois from Devereaux's POV are flattened by an extremely long lens) to put us in the thick of the action.

Sadly, though, action is conspicuously absent from the rest of *Topaz*. The director who once characterised dull movies as "photographs of people talking" challenges even the most attentive viewer with copious scenes of gasbaggery. And while Hitch has never been shy of repeating himself, certain gags are wearing thin. Watch the scene where Deveraux briefs Dubois behind a glass door so we can see but not hear them: it's a device we've already seen in *North By Northwest* and *Torn Curtain*, but each copy suffers from generation loss, and there's no wit left by this iteration. It also seems Hitchcock found neither the time nor the space to weave in the themes that energised him: the psychological possibilities afforded by espionage, so effectively mined for films like *Notorious* and *North By Northwest*, escape him here. The conflict of love and duty that powered those films' emotional cores floats around the edges of *Topaz* but never takes hold.

It doesn't help that his cast seem incapable of expressing inner turmoil: Hitch had hoped to mould Frederick Stafford into a new Sean Connery, but found himself stuck with a George Lazenby. The chronically forgettable Stafford isn't entirely to blame though. Devereaux, whose spymaster role frequently involves putting other people in harm's way while he maintains a safe distance and an immaculate haircut, is easily the film's least interesting character.

If there's a single memorable moment from *Topaz*, it's the death scene of Juanita de Cordoba (Karin Dor). Shot by her enraged lover, Juanita slips slowly to the floor in an overhead shot as her dress billows out beneath her like a pool of indigo blood. The scene required the assistance of five offscreen stage hands pulling strands of thread to achieve the effect. It's an oasis of visual poetry in a desert of otherwise bland imagery, but it's also emblematic of that disturbing late Hitchcockian trope: the concentration of his technical virtuosity on stylising scenes of extreme violence towards women.

The most welcome element of *Topaz* is the appearance of Roscoe Lee Browne as Philippe Dubois, the aforementioned sleeper agent. Dubois has the dubious distinction of being the second (and last) significant Black character in the entire Hitchcock canon, quarter of a century after Canada Lee's not entirely unproblematic turn in *Lifeboat*. Browne fares slightly better than Lee: at least Dubois accomplishes and survives his mission without being called a racist name or being assigned negative character traits. He is, however, casually sent to his potential doom by a white man, and his very presence serves to highlight Hitchcock's dearth of characters of colour. The

Dubois scene takes place in Harlem, and more Black actors are employed in that single scene than in every other Hitchcock film combined.

Anyway, that's the end of the Topaz chapter.

FRENZY

1972, colour

Based on the novel *Goodbye Piccadilly, Farewell Leicester Square* by Arthur La Bern

Universal

UK

SPOILER WARNING

Hitchcock's penultimate feature came off the back of three disappointments in a row. But he knew that when the going got tough, the tough delved into their extensive back catalogue, selected the parts that worked best, shuffled them around a bit and gave them a modern twist.

Frenzy is the anti-*Topaz*. Where Hitchcock's previous film blew an eye-watering budget on a planet-spanning plot about impending nuclear armageddon, *Frenzy* goes smaller in every respect. With Universal keen to keep costs down, Hitch settled on a story about a dozen or so characters in a single location, and rather than the defection of a Russian diplomat or the theft of geopolitically sensitive documents, its most suspenseful sequence hinges on a sack of spuds.

But the most obvious shift away from *Frenzy*'s predecessor - indeed, most of its predecessors since Hitchcock left England in 1939 - is its Britishness. *Frenzy* is as British as fish 'n' chips, complaining about the weather and refusing to learn a foreign language. Specifically though, it's a London film: a fact not-too-subtly alluded to by the opening helicopter swoop up the Thames to the iconic Tower Bridge, and - in the event of any remaining geographic uncertainty - the coat of arms of the City of London slapped on the corner of the frame like a sticker on a luggage trunk.

Returning to London enabled Hitchcock to wallow in nostalgia. The action takes place in and around Covent Garden market: a location familiar to him from his childhood, when his dad sourced fruit and veg there for his Leytonstone greengrocer's. A high wide shot takes in the market's awnings, crates, barrows and trucks, romantically freezing it all in time before the market's relocation to Battersea two years later. Taking that nostalgia further, Hitchcock rendered *Frenzy*'s London as closer to the one he left behind than the one he returned to: only two of its settings - the London Hilton and New Scotland Yard - could have been described as 'modern' in 1972. Meanwhile the prologue, in which a serial killer's latest victim washes up on the banks of the Thames and London's bystanders react with casual morbid curiosity, directly references 1926's *The Lodger* ("the first true Hitchcock movie", in the director's own words). At 72 years old, Hitchcock - no doubt painfully aware he didn't have many films left in him - seemed to be yearning for the past.

But of course, he wasn't. Some of the themes may be as well-worn as the locations, but Hitch found new ways to spruce them up. *Frenzy*'s wrongly-accused man on the run is barely likeable here: chippy loser Dick Blaney (Jon Finch) might have modelled his moustache on that of *The 39 Steps*' Richard Hannay, but that's as close as he gets to his cinematic ancestor's charm. The police are still borderline incompetent, but now humanised in the sympathetic form of Chief Inspector Oxford (Alec McCowen), whose nightly combat with his wife's culinary experimentation is an amusing narrative cover under which Hitchcock and writer Anthony Shaffer smuggle in oodles of potentially dry exposition. And while the ruins of Blaney's marriage are a classic example of Hitch's apparent scepticism regarding long-term romantic partnerships, there's a touching side to Chief Inspector and Mrs Oxford. Hitchologists have noted the Oxfords' similarity to Alfred and Alma Hitchcock in the wife's roles as cook and supportive ear to her husband's professional quandaries, but as a couple who've put up with each other for years and work together to problem-solve (again, just like Alfred and Alma), the Oxfords almost offer a refreshingly positive view of Hitchcockian marriage.

What's also noticeably new is a vulgarity Hitchcock had longed to put on screen. Working in Hollywood throughout its strictest periods of censorship had stifled his ample capacity for lewdness, but by the 1970s anything went. In *Frenzy* this manifests as earthy working class banter (almost everyone casually calls someone a 'bastard' at some point) and a grubby sense of unwashed hands groping harassed barmaids just out of every frame. Graphic nudity was also now not just accepted but expected, and Hitchcock gleefully obliged (as long as the nude bodies were female, of course).

This new permissiveness also gave him an excuse to portray explicit sexual violence. Nobody who's seen *Frenzy* can forget the scene in which the real killer, Bob Rusk (Barry Foster), rapes and strangles Brenda Blaney (Barbara Leigh-Hunt). It's

Hitchcock's most deeply unpleasant, uncomfortable sequence: longer and more lingering than the implied rape in *Marnie* and less stylised than Marion's murder in *Psycho*. Its explicitness, heightened by Hitchcock shooting the sweaty, grunting Rusk and the desperate, pleading Brenda almost entirely in close-up throughout, contributes weight to the argument that he wasn't afraid to resort to an innate misogyny in order to shock.

Having shown that murder in nauseating detail, Hitchcock lets the audience off with a relatively less harrowing portrayal of the next killing. It's an extraordinary use of camerawork and sound manipulation: as Blaney's girlfriend Babs (Anna Massey) exits a noisy pub, her face fills the frame, and for a moment there's an impressionistic silence. Rusk's voice is heard asking if she has a place to stay, and the camera reveals him behind her, appearing from nowhere like a true predator. The sounds of the street return and the pair go to Rusk's first floor flat. We know what's going to happen, but this time Hitchcock doesn't force us to see or hear it (although having demonstrated Rusk's methods, Hitch trusts our imagination to do the job for him). Once Babs and Rusk enter the flat, the camera pulls slowly, silently, almost shamefully back along the corridor, down the stairs and into the street (a passing extra semi-successfully hides the cut from the studio interior to the location exterior) where the roar of late afternoon Covent Garden fades up. It's technically striking and powerful, and the style serves Hitchcock's implication that such horrors are an everyday occurrence.

Frenzy proved Hitchcock could still work his magic: the scene in the potato truck with Rusk struggling to recover his tie pin from Babs's uncooperative corpse, for example, is a riot of dark comedy, and Hitch revels in making us feel the villain's anguish - although that's not to say we don't enjoy it when the dead body gives him a firm kick in the chops. And there's an impression of effortlessness in the film's execution that's been missing since *Psycho*. *Frenzy* would be the last in a long series of comebacks for Hitchcock, and is perhaps best seen as the final chapter of his life's work. All that was left was the epilogue.

FAMILY PLOT

1976, colour

Based on the novel *The Rainbird Pattern* by Victor Canning

Universal

US

In his final filmmaking one-eighty, Hitchcock turns his back on the horrors of Frenzy's *London back alleys, and heads back to California for a gentle comedy with surprisingly little violence. In this one, only one poor bugger plummets to his fiery death in a mangled, exploding car.*

Almost four years elapsed between the releases of *Frenzy* and *Family Plot*: the longest time audiences had to wait for a new Hitchcock film in the 50 years he'd been directing. Hitch's declining health was the main cause of the delay, but his own enthusiasm for what would be his final picture (not that he, or anyone else, knew it at the time) was also on the wane. It's hardly surprising, then, that *Family Plot* is exactly the film you'd expect from a director who was losing his touch but who was also virtually incapable of making a bad movie. On its own terms, Hitchcock's swansong is a perfectly adequate comic thriller, but as far as its legacy is concerned, it's less 'crowning finale to an unparalleled career' than it is 'tricky pub quiz answer'.

Barbara Harris plays Blanche Tyler, a phoney psychic who relies on the surprisingly sharp detective skills of her cab-driving lover George (Bruce Dern) to convince elderly ladies she's communicating with their dearly departed. When one particularly knobbly old client offers Blanche ten grand to track down her dead sister's missing son, Blanche and George find themselves embroiled in an increasingly life-threatening affair. Meanwhile, on the more well-heeled side of the tracks, uptown jeweller Arthur Adamson (William Devane) and girlfriend Fran (Karen Black) are carrying out a series of high-profile kidnappings, ransoming their victims for gigantic diamonds. Blanche and George deduce Adamson is the long-lost nephew, but Adamson assumes they're onto him for his crimes of abduction, and the two plot threads become inextricably tangled. Criss, as they say, cross.

The mechanics of the plot's construction were the primary point of interest for Hitchcock. The intertwining of characters' fates via a catalogue of coincidences and mistaken assumptions tickled him and writer Ernest Lehman, as it had with their previous collaboration on *North By Northwest*. But while these machinations are undeniably fun to watch play out, Hitch and Lehman struggled to conjure up whatever magic they'd worked before. Where Cary Grant's comically unfortunate predicament was laid out in less time than it took him to down his Gibson martini, *Family Plot* spends almost a quarter of its running time setting up its characters - an uncharacteristically languid first act for Hitchcock, and as sure a sign as any that he wasn't firing on all cylinders.

That's not to say there's no fun to be had in the setup. The four leads are all charming, and Devane in particular is lip-smackingly villainous, at any point seconds away from twirling his magnificent moustache. And Hitch crafts an elegant, effortless segue from one couple's introduction to the others' when George almost runs over a mysterious woman in black, who we later discover is the nefarious Fran. But the near-accident (which would have ended the film right there, had George been any slower on the brakes) is merely an excuse for a slick handover of storylines. From the sweaty interior of George's cab, Hitchcock cuts to a long, ambitious crane shot that establishes Fran as a much smoother operator. Diamonds, helicopters, guns and FBI agents are early signifiers of her (and Adamson's) existence on the flipside of Blanche and George's burgers 'n' beer lifestyle.

A louder echo of *North By Northwest* can be heard in *Family Plot*'s chaotic centrepiece: another hairy journey along a coastal road, in a runaway car driven by a man at least three sheets to the wind. Oddly though, Hitch opts for no music under the scene this time, making it feel long and repetitive compared to its frantically-scored predecessor. But as before, Hitchcock keeps his camera almost entirely in the car, cutting from shots of the frazzled occupants to views of the road and various oncoming vehicles ahead. Hitch claimed he did this to increase audience identification, to make viewers feel like they were in the vehicle. No doubt that was a useful end result, but it's no coincidence that avoiding exterior shots of a car barrelling along a cliffside highway would have saved a significant chunk of budget.

That potent idea of audience identification is pretty much absent for the rest of the film. With no avatar to guide us through the plot, we watch through the eyes of an omniscient bystander. It's a perfectly legitimate way to tell a story, but Hitchcock's best work more often than not took the opposite approach. In fact his trademark stylistic showmanship is thin on the ground throughout *Family Plot*: camerawork and editing are, for the most part, unimaginative and functional. His keen eye for visual storytelling eludes him, and the film is excessively talky. Only a couple of brief sequences stand out: the abduction of a priest, which takes place (without dialogue) as a beautifully-assembled montage of wide shots and close-ups; and an unusually-staged pursuit through a cemetery. Filming from above in wide shot, Hitch assumes the role of manipulative overseer as George tails a nervous lead along a maze-like path that must eventually, like the plot itself, bring the two parties together. Ultimately though, none of this is enough to remind you you're watching a film by someone who spent most of his career pushing at the boundaries of what cinema could be. The picture just isn't very cinematic; it feels more like a feature-length episode of *Moonlighting*.

There is at least one Hitchcockian trope that provides a neat, if unintentional, function. *Family Plot* doesn't make as much use of a staircase as some of Hitch's more iconic films do, but the final shot of his final feature is set on one, just as the first shot of his first feature, 1926's *The Pleasure Garden*, was. It's a comforting symmetry for Hitchologists, enhanced by Barbara Harris breaking the fourth wall and winking at the audience. Just as Hitchcock himself had been doing for half a century.

THE END

Family Plot's box office was decent, but it's undeniably a lower-tier Hitchcock, as much of his late, post-*The Birds* period had been. *Frenzy* had been a welcome (if gruesome) throwback to former glories and *Marnie* gained significant critical traction over time, but *Torn Curtain* and *Topaz* were (and arguably still are) tired, old-fashioned films in a time of audacious cinematic experimentalism. Hitchcock's final pictures coincided with the arrival of The New Hollywood: a movement that eschewed the clean narratives of the Golden Age, embraced realism and imperfection over glossy locations and flawless stars, and attempted to process the seismic socio-political issues of the time in ways that Hitchcock had made a point of avoiding since the end of World War II. Meanwhile in Europe, the critics who'd kickstarted a critical re-evaluation of Hitchcock had picked up their own cameras, and were just as maverick as their young

American counterparts. In comparison, Hitch was like their slightly embarrassing grandad.

He tried to get further projects off the ground, and there's every chance he could have moved with the times: the abandoned *Kaleidoscope* was a direct response to Michelangelo Antonioni's *Blow-Up* (1966), which had delivered a semi-Hitchcockian plot with a bohemian, nonconformist ambiguity. *The Short Night*, on the other hand, was an unfinished project that might just have done a *Frenzy* in recalling old-school Hitchcockery (though it could equally have been a corny old clunker; the published script reads very much like the work in progress it is). But Hitch was kidding himself. Lumbering towards 80 and in increasingly bad health, he had neither the strength nor stamina to oversee any more movies. Four years after *Family Plot*'s release, on April 29th 1980, Alfred Hitchcock died of kidney failure. Roll credits; fade to black.

But death rarely marks the end of the story in Hitchcock (quite the opposite, in fact) and, like *The Trouble With Harry*'s deceased Mr Worp, Hitch refused to go away. His *Psycho*-induced infamy had led critics and film students alike to investigate his back catalogue, and his work began to stir in many of them a passion to manipulate the fundamental tools of filmmaking to create their own equally unforgettable stories.

In a delicious irony, The New Hollywood movement, which had so ruthlessly left Hitchcock spluttering in its dust, eventually gave rise to a gang of cineliterate upstarts who applied their movie-geek knowledge of his methods to their own individual styles. The 'Movie Brats' were born: writer/directors who would dominate box offices and critical discourse well into the 21st century, drawing inspiration from countless sources but repeatedly paying homage to Hitchcock. Examples of their debts to Hitch would fill another book, but to cite a handful, Steven Spielberg's *Jaws* (1975) took Hitchcock's nail-biting suspense to almost unbearable lengths while borrowing *The Birds*' man-vs-nature thrills and *Vertigo*'s unsettling contrazoom shot; Martin Scorsese's *Taxi Driver* (1976) was influenced by *The Wrong Man*'s sense of guilt and paranoia and employed a haunting Bernard Herrmann score; Brian De Palma seemed virtually possessed by the spirit of Hitchcock for almost all his films from 1972's *Sisters* onwards. Meanwhile Francis Ford Coppola would repeatedly refer to Hitchcock while making *The Godfather* (1972), not least in the almost intolerably suspenseful scene in which Michael Corleone murders a rival gangster and a crooked cop.

These directors were honest and open regarding their influences, and they in turn passed the Hitchcock torch on to future generations of filmmakers. Again, there are too many to mention here, but you can sense Hitch's ghost lurking in the corners of John Carpenter, Pedro Amoldóvar, David Lynch, Park Chanwook, David Fincher, M Night Shyamalan, François Ozon, Guillermo del Toro, Edgar Wright and Jordan Peele (female directors, perhaps keen to tell the kind of stories Hitchcock's dominance helped suppress, seem less inclined towards obvious homage). Wes Craven's *Scream* (1996) couldn't have killed off its biggest star, Drew Barrymore, in the prologue without *Psycho*'s Janet Leigh leading the way; Wes Anderson's *The Grand Budapest Hotel* (2014) slips in a gloriously deferential appropriation of an entire scene from *Torn Curtain*; John Krasinski's *A Quiet Place* (2018) is fuelled by a bold use of sound, of which Hitchcock would definitely have approved.

But it's not just Hitchcock's filmmaking that echoes throughout cinema history. *Psycho* revolutionised movie marketing and the way people went to the cinema: before 1960, people thought nothing of bimbling into a film half way through, watching the end, then staying for the next show to catch up on what they'd missed. Hitch forbade such disrespectful behaviour with

Psycho, whose specific and prolific marketing insisted nobody could enter the auditorium once the film had started. Before long, the revolutionary idea of getting to the pictures early and watching the film from start to finish - in that order - became standard practice.

Hitchcock had also managed to cultivate a public persona, becoming the first director who was a household name. His cameos, his little sketches at the top and tail of his TV shows, his personal appearances in the trailers for his later films and his extremely self-aware branding, which included the self-designed logo of his own profile, all fed into the cult of Hitchcock. No other director before him had done such a hard sell of their own name and image. Thanks to him, and the critics who boosted his reputation (and his ego), ordinary cinemagoers - not just film nerds - began to take an interest in who was at the helm of the pictures they most enjoyed.

So Hitchcock lives on in the filmmakers he influenced, the way we approach cinema as entertainment, the way films are sold to us and the way we understand their construction. But crucially, he lives on through his astonishing filmography: 52 films you can fairly easily watch whenever you like, plus one that - fingers crossed - may turn up one day soon. Those movies are a film school in themselves. To repeat Dr Catherine Wheatley's quote from the very beginning of this book: "Hitchcock's work is the best for learning and teaching what film can be, and what it can do." It can also show what film *shouldn't* be (minority-averse; a bit misogynistic; *Juno And The Paycock*). But for true film fans, there are fewer pleasures as great as the study of the work of Alfred Hitchcock. And that's **Hitchology**.

ONE MORE THING

If you've finished **Hitchology**, thank you. If you haven't, you're reading it in the wrong order. Either way, please let me and, more importantly, the rest of the world know what you think of it. This book is a passion project, and depends on word of mouth like *Vertigo* depends on you not asking why Gavin Elster went to such ridiculously convoluted lengths to get rid of his wife.

So wherever you bought **Hitchology**, please leave a review, as long or as short as you like. In fact, leave a review in places you didn't buy it. If you have a Goodreads account, please leave a review there too. Mention it on social media. If you think your local bookshop or library should stock it, please tell them so. And if you want to chat about Hitchcock, I'm on various forms of social media at @MrNeilAlcock. I hope that between you, me and Hitch, we can prolong the suspense.

MR. HITCHCOCK

ACKNOWLEDGEMENTS

Thanks to Mum and Dad for a million things, but on this occasion for taking it in their stride when I decided to do A-Level Film Studies at South Cheshire College, and then to continue on this almost certainly futureless path by studying film at Staffordshire University. I very much appreciate you letting me do my own, ridiculous thing.

Thanks to Bryn Youds, lecturer at the aforementioned South Cheshire College, for introducing me to the wonderful world of Alfred Hitchcock. This is largely your fault.

Thanks to those who gave me feedback on **Hitchology** and encouragement along the way: Nick de Semlyen, Ali Gray, Stuart Richards, Stephanie Roberts, Luke Whiston and Ed Williamson. Extra special thanks in this department to Matt Looker, who not only read the words but also forced himself to watch the films so the words made more sense.

Thanks to Christopher Laverty, the first of my friends to write a book, making me think it might be something even I could do. We miss you.

Thanks to readers of The Incredible Suit, a very silly blog where I practised writing about films for several years. I'm still practising, but on paper now.

Finally, thanks to Wendy, my very own Alma. I am infinitely grateful for your unconditional support, for patiently listening and helping me work things out, for believing in me, and for a steady supply of tea and fourses (like elevenses, but at four). I love you more than Hitch loved steak.

BIBLIOGRAPHY

BOOKS

Ackroyd, Peter. *Alfred Hitchcock*. Chatto & Windus, 2015.

Anobile, Richard J (ed). *Alfred Hitchcock's Psycho*. Picador, 1974.

Aulier, Dan. *Hitchcock's Secret Notebooks*. Bloomsbury, 1999.

Barr, Charles. *English Hitchcock*. Cameron & Hollis, 1999.

Barr, Charles. *Vertigo*. BFI, 2002.

Beach, Christopher. *A Hidden History Of Film Style: Cinematographers, directors, and the collaborative process*. University of California Press, 2015.

Bell, James (ed). *39 Steps to the Genius Of Hitchcock: A BFI Compendium*. BFI, 2012.

Bennett, John Charles (ed). *Hitchcock's Partner In Suspense: The Life Of Screenwriter Charles Bennett.* University Press of Kentucky, 2014.

Bloch, Robert. *Psycho.* Simon & Schuster, 1959

Bordwell, David & Thompson, Kristin. *Film Art* (4th edn). McGraw-Hill, 1993.

Bouzereau, Laurent & Hitchcock O'Connell, Pat. *Alma Hitchcock: The Woman Behind the Man.* Berkley, 2003.

Buchan, John. *The Thirty-Nine Steps.* William Blackwood and Sons, 1915.

Condon, Paul & Sangster, Jim. *The Complete Hitchcock.* Virgin, 1999.

Du Maurier, Daphne. *The Birds.* Penguin, 1952.

Duncan, Paul (ed). *Alfred Hitchcock: The Complete Films.* Taschen, 2019.

Freeman, David. *The Last Days of Alfred Hitchcock.* Pavilion, 1985.

Giblin, Gary. *Alfred Hitchcock's London: A Reference Guide to Locations.* Midnight Marquee Press, Inc, 2009.

Glancy, Mark. *Cary Grant: The Making Of A Hollywood Legend.* Oxford University Press, 2020.

Goldman, William. *Adventures In The Screen Trade.* Grand Central, 1983.

Jacobs, Steven. *The Wrong House: The Architecture of Alfred Hitchcock.* 010, 2007.

Kerzoncuf, Alain & Barr, Charles. *Hitchcock Lost and Found: The Forgotten Films.* University Press of Kentucky, 2015.

Krohn, Bill. *Hitchcock at Work.* Phaidon Press, 2000.

Laverty, Christopher. *Fashion In Film.* Laurence King, 2016.

Leff, Leonard J. *Hitchcock and Selznick: The Rich and Strange Collaboration of Alfred Hitchcock and David O. Selznick in Hollywood.* Weidenfeld and Nicolson, 1988.

McGilligan, Patrick. *Alfred Hitchcock: A Life in Darkness and Light.* Wiley, 2003.

Modleski, Tania. *The Women Who Knew Too Much: Hitchcock and Feminist Theory.* Methuen, 1988.

O'Hara, Helen. *Women vs Hollywood: The fall and rise of women in film.* Little, Brown and Company, 2021.

Paglia, Camille. *The Birds.* BFI, 1998.

Pomerance, Murray. *Marnie.* BFI, 2014.

Pomerance, Murray. *The Man Who Knew Too Much.* BFI, 2016.

Rebello, Stephen. *Alfred Hitchcock and the Making of Psycho.* St. Martin's Press, 1998.

Rohmer, Eric & Chabrol, Claude. *Hitchcock: The First Forty-four Films.* Roundhouse, 1977.

Russell Taylor, John. *Hitch.* Faber & Faber, 1978.

Ryall, Tom. *Blackmail.* BFI, 1993.

Spoto, Donald. *The Dark Side of Genius: The Life Of Alfred Hitchcock.* Collins, 1983.

Sullivan, Jack. *Hitchcock's Music.* Yale University Press, 2006.

Thomson, David. *The Moment Of Psycho: How Alfred Hitchcock Taught America to Love Murder.* Basic Books, 2009.

Truffaut, François. *Hitchcock.* Simon & Schuster, 1983.

Walker, Michael. *Hitchcock's Motifs.* Amsterdam University Press, 2005.

Weis, Elisabeth. *The Silent Scream: Alfred Hitchcock's Sound Track.* Fairleigh Dickinson University Press, 1982.

White, Patricia. *Rebecca*. BFI, 2021.

Wood, Michael. *Alfred Hitchcock: The Man Who Knew Too Much*. Amazon, 2015.

Wood, Robin. *Hitchcock's Films Revisited*. Columbia University Press, 1989.

ARTICLES, ESSAYS AND PAPERS

Allen, Jeanne Thomas. *The representation of violence to women: Hitchcock's Frenzy*. Film Quarterly. 38 (3), pp. 30-38. 1985.

Eaton, Michael. *The man who wasn't there: A profile of silent film screenwriter Eliot Stannard*. Sight & Sound. 5 (12). 2005.

Krohn, Bill. *Shelling the Lifeboat*. Eureka! Masters Of Cinema Lifeboat Blu-ray booklet, pp. 7-18. 2012.

Mulvey, Laura. *Visual Pleasure and Narrative Cinema*. Screen. 16 (3), pp. 6-18. 1975.

ONLINE

Frost, Adam & Vasiliev, Zhenia. *The 39 Stats: Charting Hitchcock's Obsessions*. 2013. https://static.guim.co.uk/sys-images/Guardian/Pix/pictures/2013/8/12/1376319176691/hitch_1024px.jpg [Accessed 2020-2022].

Hutchinson, Pamela. *Silent London (various pages)*. 2010-2022. http://silentlondon.co.uk/ [Accessed 2020-2022].

Mamata, Bidisha. *What's wrong with Hitchcock's women*. 2010. http://www.theguardian.com/film/2010/oct/21/alfred-hitchcock-women-psycho-the-birds-bidisha [Accessed August 2022].

Morris, Nathalie. *Alma Reville*. 2016. https://wfpp.columbia.edu/pioneer/alma-reville/ [Accessed 2022].

Reid, Brenton. *Brenton Film (various pages)*. 2015-2022. http://www.brentonfilm.com/ [Accessed 2020-2022].

Unknown author. *The Alfred Hitchcock Wiki (various pages)*. https://the.hitchcock.zone/wiki/Main_Page [Accessed 2020-2022].

Unknown author. *BFI Screenonline (various pages)*. http://www.screenonline.org.uk/ [Accessed 2020-2022].

DOCUMENTARIES

78/52. dir Alexandre O. Philippe. France, USA and UK, 2017. Sensorshot Productions, Exhibit A Pictures, Screen Division, Milkhaus and ARTE.

Alfred Hitchcock: The Early Years (1925-1934). dir Noël Simsolo. France, 2004. StudioCanal & Point du Jour.

Alfred Hitchcock's Lifeboat: The Theater Of War. dir Peter Ventrella. USA, 2005. Rolling Thunder Productions.

All About The Birds. dir Laurent Bouzereau. USA, 2000. Universal Studios Home Video.

Alma: The Master's Muse. dir Gary Leva. USA, 2008. Leva FilmWorks.

Aquarius: Alfred The Great. dir Derek Bailey. UK, 1972. London Weekend Television.

The Art Of Film: Vintage Hitchcock. 1978. Janus Films & Perspective Films.

Becoming Cary Grant. dir Mark Kidel. France, 2017. Yuzu Productions, ARTE.

Before The Fact: Suspicious Hitchcock. dir Laurent Bouzereau. USA, 2004. Blue Collar Productions, Warner Home Video.

Bernard Herrmann: Hitchcock's Maestro. dir Gary Leva. USA, 2008. Leva FilmWorks.

Beyond Doubt: The Making Of Hitchcock's Favourite Film. dir Laurent Bouzereau. USA, 2000. Universal Studios Home Video.

The Birds: Hitchcock's Monster Movie. dir Gary Leva. USA, 2012. Leva FilmWorks and Universal Studios.

Cary Grant: A Class Apart. dir Robert Trachtenberg. USA, 2004. Turner Classic Movies, Turner Entertainment, Mosaic Films, Eagle Rock Entertainment.

Cinema: Alfred Hitchcock. UK, 1966. ITV Productions.

Cinema: Alfred Hitchcock. UK, 1969. ITV Productions.

Destination Hitchcock: The Making Of North By Northwest. dir Peter Fitzgerald. USA, 2000. Fitzfilm, Turner Classic Movies, Turner Entertainment and Warner Home Video.

Edith Head: Dressing the Master's Movies. dir Gary Leva. USA, 2008. Leva FilmWorks.

Guilt Trip: Hitchcock and The Wrong Man. dir Laurent Bouzereau. USA, 2004. Blue Collar Productions and Warner Home Video.

Hitchcock And Dial M. dir Laurent Bouzereau. USA, 2004. Blue Collar Productions and Turner Entertainment Co.

Hitchcock And Stage Fright. dir Laurent Bouzereau. USA, 2004. Blue Collar Productions and Turner Entertainment Co.

Hitchcock, Selznick and the End of Hollywood. dir Michael Epstein. USA, 1999. Thirteen, Eagle Rock Entertainment and American Masters Pictures.

Hitchcock: The Early Years. dir David Lemon. UK, 2000. Carlton International Media.

Hitchcock's Confession: A Look At I Confess. dir Laurent Bouzereau. USA, 2004. Blue Collar Productions and Warner Home Video.

In the Master's Shadow: Hitchcock's Legacy. dir Gary Leva. USA, 2008. Leva FilmWorks.

The Making Of Psycho. dir Laurent Bouzereau. USA, 1997. Universal Studios Home Video.

The Making Of The Man Who Knew Too Much. dir Laurent Bouzereau. USA, 2000. Universal Pictures.

The Making of To Catch A Thief. dir Laurent Bouzereau. USA, 2002. Paramount Pictures.

North By Northwest: One For The Ages. dir Gary Leva. USA, 2009. Leva FilmWorks and Warner Home Video.

Obsessed With Vertigo: New Life For Hitchcock's Masterpiece. dir Harrison Engle. USA, 1997. Signal Hill Entertainment and AMC Studios.

On Location: Sabotage. dir Steve Rehman. UK, 2000. Kulture Vulture Productions & Carlton Cinema.

On Location: The 39 Steps. dir Steve Rehman. UK, 2000. Kulture Vulture Productions & Carlton Cinema.

Plotting Family Plot. dir Laurent Bouzereau. USA, 2001. Universal Studios Home Entertainment.

Psycho Path. dir D-J. USA, 2000. Madman Films, ViaVision and Universal Pictures.

Rear Window Ethics. dir Laurent Bouzereau. USA, 2001. Universal Studios Home Video.

Rope Unleashed. dir Laurent Bouzereau. USA, 2001. Universal Pictures and Kappa Studios.

Saboteur: A Closer Look. dir Laurent Bouzereau. USA, 2000. Universal Studios Home Video.

Shipwrecked In A Studio: The Making Of Alfred Hitchcock's Jamaica Inn. USA, 2015. Cohen Media Group, LLC.

The Story of Frenzy. dir Laurent Bouzereau. USA, 2001. Universal Studios Home Video.

Strangers On A Train: A Hitchcock Classic. dir Laurent Bouzereau. USA, 2004. Warner Home Video.

Topaz: An Appreciation by Leonard Maltin. dir Laurent Bouzereau. USA, 2001. Universal Studios Home Video.

Torn Curtain Rising dir Laurent Bouzereau. USA, 2001. Universal Studios Home Video.

The Trouble With Harry Isn't Over. dir Laurent Bouzereau. USA, 2001. Universal Studios Home Entertainment.

The Trouble With Marnie. dir Laurent Bouzereau. USA, 2000. Universal Pictures.

Writing and Casting To Catch A Thief. dir Laurent Bouzereau. USA, 2002. Paramount Pictures.

DVD / BLU-RAY COMMENTARIES

The 39 Steps: Marian Keane

Jamaica Inn: Jeremy Arnold

Strangers On A Train: Peter Bogdanovich, Joseph Stefano, Andrew Wilson, Joe Alves, Peter Benchley, Tere Carrubba, Whitfield Cook, Katie Fiala, Richard Franklin, Alfred Hitchcock, Patricia Hitchcock O'Connell, Kasey Rogers, Richard Schickel, Mary Stone

Rear Window: John Fawell

To Catch A Thief: Dr. Drew Casper

Vertigo: William Friedkin

North By Northwest: Ernest Lehman

Psycho: Stephen Rebello

Milton Keynes UK
Ingram Content Group UK Ltd.
UKHW031044020824
1130UKWH00003B/35

9 781739 522200